OPRAH WINFREY

Recent Titles in Greenwood Biographies

OPRAH WINFREY

A Biography

Second Edition

Helen S. Garson

GREENWOOD BIOGRAPHIES

 GREENWOOD

AN IMPRINT OF ABC-CLIO, LLC
Santa Barbara, California • Denver, Colorado • Oxford, England

Library of Congress Cataloging-in-Publication Data

Garson, Helen S.
  Oprah Winfrey : a biography / Helen S. Garson. — 2nd ed.
    p. cm. — (Greenwood biographies)
  Includes bibliographical references and index.
  ISBN 978-0-313-35832-6 (hard copy : alk. paper) — ISBN 978-0-313-35833-3 (ebook) 1. Winfrey, Oprah. 2. Television personalities—United States—Biography. 3. Actors—United States—Biography. I. Title.
  PN1992.4.W56G37   2011
  791.4502'8092—dc22
  [B]   2011002272

ISBN: 978-0-313-35832-6
EISBN: 978-0-313-35833-3

15 14 13 12 11   1 2 3 4 5

This book is also available on the World Wide Web as an eBook.
Visit www.abc-clio.com for details.

Greenwood
An Imprint of ABC-CLIO, LLC

ABC-CLIO, LLC
130 Cremona Drive, P.O. Box 1911
Santa Barbara, California 93116-1911

This book is printed on acid-free paper ∞

Manufactured in the United States of America

For My Beloved Husband,
Neil, Once Again

CONTENTS

SERIES FOREWORD

In response to high school and public library needs, Greenwood developed this distinguished series of full-length biographies specifically for student use. Prepared by field experts and professionals, these engaging biographies are tailored for high school students who need challenging yet accessible biographies. Ideal for secondary school assignments, the length, format, and subject areas are designed to meet educators' requirements and students' interests.

Greenwood offers an extensive selection of biographies spanning all curriculum-related subject areas, including social studies, the sciences, literature and the arts, history and politics, as well as popular culture, covering public figures and famous personalities from all time periods and backgrounds, both historic and contemporary, who have made an impact on U.S. and world culture. Greenwood biographies were chosen based on comprehensive feedback from librarians and educators. Consideration was given to both curriculum relevance and inherent interest. The result is an intriguing mix of the well known and the unexpected, the saints and sinners from long-ago history and contemporary pop culture. Readers will find a wide array of subject choices from fascinating crime figures like Al Capone to inspiring pioneers like Margaret

Mead, from the greatest minds of our time like Stephen Hawking to the most amazing success stories of our day like J. K. Rowling.

While the emphasis is on fact, not glorification, the books are meant to be fun to read. Each volume provides in-depth information about the subject's life from birth through childhood, the teen years, and adulthood. A thorough account relates family background and education, traces personal and professional influences, and explores struggles, accomplishments, and contributions. A timeline highlights the most significant life events against a historical perspective. Bibliographies supplement the reference value of each volume.

INTRODUCTION

Oprah Gail Winfrey has been a world-famous television star for more than 25 years, so well known that people refer to her as Oprah, with the assurance of no misunderstanding. Her programs are shown in many parts of Europe, Asia, and Africa, although her career began in the United States, her country of birth. She has been both an actress and producer almost as many years as her television program has run. Adding to her fame and fortune, 16 years after reaching the pinnacle of television stardom, in conjunction with the Hearst Company, she launched O, The Oprah Magazine in 2000. Even though she closed The Oprah Winfrey Show at the end of 2010, publication of the magazine continued.

Born January 29, 1954, the illegitimate child of mother Vernita Lee and father Vernon Winfrey, in the small town of Kosciusko, Mississippi, until she reached the age of six she lived on the farm of grandparents Hattie Mae and Earless Lee. Vernita, who never married, had settled in Milwaukee, Wisconsin, where she gave birth to another daughter, Patricia, and later to a son, Jeffrey. Although the reasons are unclear, Vernita decided to have Oprah move to Wisconsin to live with her and the other children. It was an arrangement fraught with problems from poverty to indifferent supervision that led to Oprah becoming an angry, hostile, promiscuous teen, completely out of control and subjected to the sexual advances of relatives and her mother's male visitors. In 1968, a pregnant teenage Oprah was sent to live with her father, Vernon, and his wife, Velma, in Nashville, Tennessee. Shortly after the birth and death of her baby boy, Oprah's world changed completely.

The Winfreys had no children together, so Oprah became the focus of their home life. It was a religious, organized existence in which Oprah was expected to follow strict rules, earn the highest grades, attend church regularly, and set the example of a model student. She joined a number of clubs in East Nashville High School, including both a drama club and forensics club; was admitted to the honor society and student council; and served as a representative at a White House conference. All of these activities obviously were forerunners of her later successes in radio and television. Oprah was developing the personality that brought her the vote for the most popular girl in her senior class.

During her last years in high school, an active Oprah won a number of awards and contests. Upon graduation, she went to Tennessee State University. She had been awarded a scholarship and she accepted it, despite the fact that she would have preferred a school with a more mixed student body. She remained at Tennessee State until her senior year but left before graduation; several years later—after she had become famous—the university awarded her a degree. Her decision to work rather than stay in college came when she was offered a job as a reporter and co-anchor for an evening news program in Baltimore. During her time in Baltimore, she met Gayle King, who became and remains her closest friend.

After two years working on the evening news show, Oprah was transferred to a morning program, *People Are Talking*. After several years with that show, she accepted an offer to host the Chicago program *AM Chicago*. Chicago became her home, a city where she found her niche. There she met two men who have been very influential in her life: Stedman Graham, her longtime significant other, and Quincy Jones, who recognized her potential and gave her a leading role in his movie *The Color Purple*, bringing her an Academy Award nomination and starting her on the path to national and international recognition. Not long after that triumph, in 1986, Oprah's television program was renamed *The Oprah Winfrey Show*, making her the first African American woman to have a nationally syndicated program. She also formed her own company that later became Harpo Productions, a company that still belongs to her, and bought an elegant penthouse condominium on Chicago's lakefront.

Following her success in *The Color Purple*, she played a role in a movie based on another famous novel, *Native Son*, and a year after that had a cameo role in the movie *Throw Momma from the Train*. Moviemaking of various kinds became a part of her work, something she continues to this day. Through the years, she has continued to appear in and produce films, including *Waiting to Exhale*, a work based on a very popular novel.

By 1988, having gained ownership and control of Harpo, Oprah became the first black woman to own both a studio and production company. With increased income, she was able to buy a farm and other homes. Even as she continued to expand her interests in various types of films, series, and documentaries, she initiated the National Child Protection Act, which President Clinton signed in 1993. In 1996, she made news by running in the 25-mile Marine Marathon. Additionally, she helped her chef in the writing of *In the Kitchen with Rosie*, as well as doing a small part of Bob Greene's exercise book, *Make the Connection*. Another chef, Art Smith, gained fame and fortune through his association with Oprah, appearing on her show, writing a cookbook, participating in charities, and opening restaurants in prime locations, including one in Washington, DC, during the period when then-candidate Barack Obama was running for president. Because of his connection to Oprah, when Smith and his partner were married in 2010, the event was covered by multiple newspapers.

Over two decades, Oprah was given one award after another for her many achievements, including the prestigious Peabody Award. Another great success came with the introduction on her show of what became the most famous book club in the United States. There were, however, some roadblocks in her career along the way, one of which was a suit brought by the Independent Cattlemen's Association of Texas, which claimed that on her show she had been disparaging beef products, production, and distribution. It was necessary for Oprah to move her daily show to Texas for a short time while fighting the case. While there, she met Dr. Phil McGraw, who became one of her advisers and joined her television program after the cattlemen lost the case. McGraw became a star when Oprah sponsored a new show for him, and he continues with his own program. Oprah has proved to have another skill—that of star maker, with her support of chef Rachel Ray's program as well as the exceedingly popular medical guru Dr. Oz. After joining the *Oprah Winfrey Show* in 2005, where he remained for five years, Mehmet Oz became host of his own immediately successful show.

Briefly, Oprah had a foray in politics, something she has always avoided in the past. The nomination of a black presidential candidate in 2007 brought her into the activities of a democratic partisan as she campaigned vigorously for Barack Obama. Every involvement of hers in the election was reported, bringing strong support and equally strong anger among Oprah's fans. With the conclusion of the campaign and election, which brought an ecstatic and tearful Oprah before the public, she appears to have retired from her role in the political arena.

Ten years earlier, Oprah had created the Angel Network, a charity that flourished until Oprah decided to bring it to an end in 2010 in order to focus on her future shows as well as other charitable activities. Harpo Productions has continued to produce successful movies, while Oprah, with the support of the Hearst Company, created O, *The Oprah Magazine,* first publishing it in the United States, then later an international version followed in South Africa. Two years after the first issue of the magazine appeared, Oprah announced the discontinuation of her very popular book club, because, she claimed, there were no more worthwhile current books to read. However, when a strong reaction among her followers and much public criticism ensued, the club was reborn, but, as her daily television show comes to an end, she suggests the club also, again, will be dropped.

Oprah's interest in South Africa was fanned by Nelson Mandela, who convinced her of the need for schools in his country. His persuasion led to the construction in the beginning of 2003 of the Oprah Winfrey Leadership Academy for Girls. In 2005, the academy was opened to much acclaim as well as dire predictions about failure. The road has not been a smooth one, with scandals reported throughout the media. Lawsuits in Africa and in the United States have been brought; questions have been raised about the validity of her efforts to establish schools abroad. But the difficulties appear to be resolved, and the first graduates have been visiting U.S. colleges and universities to make choices of future education. Oprah has emphasized her determination to continue with this type of philanthropy, even as she winds down her 25-year-old television show and makes plans for the coming years of her different role in television.

ACKNOWLEDGMENTS

My thanks to the following people for their enthusiasm and help in undertaking this book: Aissatou Barry, Ibrahima Sidibe, and, above all, to my clever, patient assistant, Binta Barry, without whose help this work could not have been written.

TIMELINE: EVENTS IN THE LIFE OF OPRAH WINFREY

1954   Oprah Gail Winfrey, the illegitimate child of Vernita Lee and Vernon Winfrey, is born on January 29 in Kosciusko, Mississippi, where she lives until the age of six with grandparents Hattie Mae and Earless Lee.

1960   Oprah goes to live with her mother Vernita and half-sister Patricia in Milwaukee, Wisconsin. Her half-brother Jeffrey Lee is born later.

1962   Oprah spends a brief time with father, Vernon, and stepmother, Velma, in Nashville, Tennessee, and attends East Wharton Elementary School in Nashville.

1963   While living with her mother in Milwaukee, Oprah is raped by a cousin and victimized by other sexual predators.

1968   Oprah receives a scholarship to attend Nicolet High School in Milwaukee. Vernita sends Oprah back to Nashville, where she gives birth to a son who dies shortly afterward. She attends East Nashville High School, where she becomes a member of the drama club, the National Forensics League, the honor society, and the student council and is voted the most popular girl of her senior class. She also serves as representative to a White House conference.

1969   Sometime during the year, Oprah begins to keep a journal, which she still maintains.

1970   While representing Nashville radio station WVOL, Oprah wins the contest for Miss Fire Prevention. She is also selected as the first Miss Black Tennessee.

1971   Oprah graduates from East Nashville High School and wins a scholarship to Tennessee State University. She is hired to read the weekend news at radio station WVOL and, on occasion, reads the weekday news.

1973   After working for a time at radio station WLAC, Oprah goes to its television station WLAC-TV. She leaves college before graduating to accept a job in Baltimore.

1976   At station WJZ-TV in Baltimore, Oprah works as a reporter and co-anchor of an evening news program. There she meets production assistant Gayle King, who becomes and remains her closest friend.

1978   At WJZ-TV, Oprah is taken off the evening program and is made co-host of the morning show *People Are Talking*.

1984   Oprah accepts a job in Chicago as host of *AM Chicago*.

1985   Oprah meets Stedman Graham, who becomes her significant other. She also meets Quincy Jones, who offers her the role of Sofia in *The Color Purple*, for which she is nominated for an Academy Award.

1986   Her program is renamed *The Oprah Winfrey Show*. It has been purchased by King Brothers Corporation and is nationally syndicated.

Oprah becomes the first African American woman to host a talk show that is nationally syndicated.

Oprah forms her own company, which later becomes Harpo Productions.

Oprah appears in the movie *Native Son*, a film based on the Richard Wright novel.

She is given the National Organization for Women Achievement Award.

She purchases a penthouse condominium on Chicago's lakefront.

Oprah is a guest at the marriage of her friend Maria Shriver to Arnold Schwarzenegger in Hyannis, Massachusetts.

1987   More than a decade after leaving Tennessee State University, Oprah is granted a degree in speech and drama and delivers the commencement address.

Oprah produces and makes a cameo appearance in the movie *Throw Momma from the Train*.

1988   Named Broadcaster of the Year by the International Television and Radio Society, Oprah is the youngest person to receive the award.

She begins to produce her shows after gaining ownership and control of the company. Naming her production company Harpo, she purchases the studio facilities, becoming the first black woman to own a studio and production company.

She buys a farm in Indiana. In later years, she purchases other homes, including one in Colorado and one in California.

Her friend and assistant, Billy Rizzo, dies of AIDS, the disease that was to kill her half-brother.

1989   Half-brother Jeffrey Lee dies of AIDS.

With another investor, Oprah opens a restaurant, The Eccentric. Although the restaurant has multiple chefs and menus, it fails and closes in 1995.

1990   Oprah produces and appears in the television series *The Women of Brewster Place*, which is dropped after 10 weeks. She also produces and appears in the documentary film *Listen Up: The Lives of Quincy Jones*.

1992   Oprah makes the documentary *Scared Silent*.

She meets Bob Greene, who becomes her fitness trainer and friend.

Oprah produces and appears as herself in the television show *The Fresh Prince of Bel-Air*.

1993   Oprah appears in the television film *There Are No Children Here*, which she also produces.

President Clinton signs the National Child Protection Act that Oprah had initiated.

1995   Knopf publishes *In the Kitchen with Rosie*, a cookbook written by Oprah's chef with some input from Oprah.

Bob Greene's book *Make the Connection* is published under the names of Bob Greene and Oprah Winfrey.

Oprah runs in and finishes the 25-mile Marine Marathon.

1996   Oprah is given the George Peabody Individual Achievement Award.

She produces the movie *Waiting to Exhale*.

The Independent Cattlemen's Association of Texas brings a suit against Oprah for disparaging beef on one of her shows. The cattlemen later lose the lawsuit.

Oprah meets Dr. Phil McGraw in Texas, and he becomes one of her advisers.

Oprah's Book Club becomes part of the television show.

1997   Oprah creates the Angel Network.

Oprah appears in and, with Harpo, produces the television film *Before Women Had Wings*.

Oprah gives the commencement speech at Wellesley College, from which Stedman Graham's daughter is graduating.

Art Smith becomes Oprah's chef and writes a cookbook.

Newsweek magazine names Oprah the Most Important Person in Books and Media.

TV Guide names her Television Performer of the Year.

1998   Oprah Winfrey Presents produces the television miniseries *The Wedding* starring Halle Berry.

Phil McGraw (Dr. Phil) joins Oprah's television show.

Oprah receives a Lifetime Achievement Daytime Emmy Award.

Oprah stars in and produces the movie *Beloved*.

She is described in *Time* magazine as one of the 20th century's most influential people.

Oprah produces *David and Lisa*, starring Sidney Poitier.

The National Academy of Television Arts and Sciences awards her a Lifetime Achievement Award.

1999   CBS Corporation buys the King Production Company.

Oprah buys a share of the Oxygen Cable Network.

Oprah's company presents the television film *Tuesdays with Morrie*.

The National Book Foundation awards her the 50th Anniversary Gold Medal.

2000 *O, The Oprah Magazine* is launched by Oprah and the Hearst Company in April.

The international edition of the magazine is published at a later time, in South Africa, extending her "Live Your Best Life" message to a larger audience.

2001 Harpo produces the movie *Amy & Isabelle*.

2002 Harpo productions develops a program for Phil McGraw.

Oprah is awarded an honorary doctorate from Princeton University.

Oprah receives the Bob Hope Humanitarian Award.

Oprah and Stedman stay at the home of Nelson Mandela in South Africa.

Mandela convinces Oprah to build a school in South Africa.

Oprah's Book Club is discontinued.

2003 Oprah receives the Marion Anderson Award.

Oprah and others celebrate the 85th birthday of Nelson Mandela.

Oprah's half-sister, Patricia Lee Lloyd, dies of a drug overdose. The Book Club is reborn.

Oprah becomes the first black U.S. billionaire.

Construction begins on the Oprah Winfrey Leadership Academy for Girls (on 22 acres of land) in Henley on Klip, Meyerton, Guateng Province.

Oprah receives the Association of American Publishers Honors Award.

2004 *O At Home*, a quarterly magazine designed to help readers create a home that reflects their personal style, makes its debut.

The United Nations Association of the United States of America awards Oprah the Global Humanitarian Action Award.

The National Association of Broadcasters gives Oprah a Distinguished Service Award.

Time magazine lists her among the 100 Most Influential People in the World.

2005 The Oprah Winfrey Leadership Academy for Girls opens in January in South Africa.

Oprah produces *Their Eyes Were Watching God*, starring Halle Berry.

Oprah, with Quincy Jones, produces the Broadway musical *The Color Purple*.

The National Civil Rights Museum awards her the 2005 National Freedom Award.

The National Association for the Advancement of Colored People adds Oprah to the Hall of Fame.

Time again lists her among the 100 Most Influential People in the World.

The International Academy of Television Arts and Sciences awards her the Emmy Founders Award.

Dr. Mehmet Oz begins the first of five seasons on Oprah's show, prior to having his own program.

2006 Accusations are made against a dormitory matron at the Oprah Winfrey Leadership Academy for Girls. Court action is postponed several times.

Oprah joins the satellite radio XM channel 156 with *Oprah and Friends*.

Oprah produces *Charlotte's Web* and plays the voice role of Gussy the Goose.

Time magazine again lists her among the 100 Most Influential People in the World.

The New York Public Library Award is given to her.

2007 *Time* magazine names Oprah one of the 100 Most Influential People in the 20th century. She is the only person to be listed five years in a row.

Oprah becomes involved in presidential politics for the first time and campaigns for Barack Obama.

Oprah launches a new channel on YouTube.

Oprah produces the movie *For One More Day*.

Oprah produces *The Great Debaters*.

The Elie Wiesel Foundation gives her the Humanitarian Award.

Oprah endorses *The Secret*, a self-help book that becomes a bestseller.

2008 The first Oprah store opens in the West Loop in Chicago.

Oprah creates the Oprah Winfrey Network (OWN) cable network.

Oprah makes a new will, reputedly leaving out Stedman Graham.

Oprah launches a new TV show, *The Big Give*, which is not successful.

Nelson Mandela's 90th birthday is celebrated with a party in London.

2009   Oprah and Eckhart Tolle teach a 10-week course based on his best-selling book *The New Age*.

Large numbers of Evangelical ministers attack Oprah's views as anti-Christian.

Dr. Oz leaves the Oprah program to lead his own show; supported by Harpo, it is successful immediately.

2010   After 25 years, Oprah announces the closing of her show will take place at the end of 2010, leaving Chicago for a new venue and format.

Oprah is one of five people chosen for the Kennedy Center Honors.

Chapter 1

THIS POWERFUL CELEBRITY

For decades, she has been so well known that few people use her last name. It seems unnecessary. Undoubtedly, someday not far into the future, there will be girls named Oprah. A few years ago, actress Meg Ryan thought of naming her baby girl Oprah Winfrey Ryan. However, as of now, the world seems to know of only one Oprah. Furthermore, according to a television news writer, the noun will soon be used as a verb.[1]

Simple references to Oprah do not have to be explained. Her huge fortune makes her the wealthiest celebrity in the United States: with an income of several million dollars per year just from television, she is the highest paid television personality. Talk shows are public favorites, and in the Harris poll for five years in a row, Oprah was chosen as the public's favorite television star. Only in the sixth year did she lose ground, to Ellen DeGeneres, according to that poll. Her yearly viewership average is 7.3 million. Despite numerous rivals, her daily television show has remained on or near the top of daytime programs. Suffice to say, many people polled by the *Guardian* on May 27, 2008, found her personally number one and have called her daytime television's undisputed queen. In another poll, some admirers picked former Senator

Hillary Clinton as their favorite woman, but a Fox News Opinion poll showed Oprah to be more powerful than Clinton.

Another type of poll taken in 2008 at Sacred Heart University found one reason for Oprah's decline in popularity: more than half of the respondents objected to celebrities' involvement with public policy. Because of Oprah's huge following, many polls tracked the effect of her involvement in the presidential race of 2008, and specifically her support of the Obama campaign. This was a first for Oprah, who had attempted to be impartial in previous campaigns. When interviewed at the 2008 Democratic National Convention, Oprah's closest friend, Gayle King, stated that she and Oprah think of politics differently. Oprah generally has little interest in politics, but Gayle is completely immersed in everything political and describes herself as someone who "eat[s], sleep[s] and breathe[s] politics." For Oprah, Obama made the difference. By endorsing her longtime friend, Oprah thought her personal participation was more valuable than money; Obama's popularity went up, but her involvement affected her own ratings adversely.

From the time she first announced her political partisanship, there was a steady drop in the numbers of people who would be likely to vote for an Oprah choice. It wasn't clear what brought on the decline. Some reporters claimed that white women were angry at Obama but not at Oprah; it also has been attributed to women who had great hopes to see a woman (Hillary Clinton) elected. The matter remained controversial until after the election, when suddenly opinions changed and Oprah's involvement in Obama's campaign was seen as a large inducement to vote for the candidate.

A number of political experts question the value of celebrity support.[2] Ross Baker, a political science professor at Rutgers University, has said there are people who "resent being told how to vote." Media expert Ellis Cashmore claims that there is a tendency to suspect entertainers who give us advice of a political, scientific, medical, or religious nature. And Daniel Drezner of Tufts University suggested that celebrities should choose a safer road to impress the public by confining themselves to "charities and other 'do-good' works." He pointed to the changes that took place in opinions toward actor Angelina Jolie when she began to use much time and money for philanthropy.

Democratic presidential hopeful, Senator Barack Obama, D-Ill., his wife Michelle, right, and Oprah Winfrey wave to the crowd at a rally in Manchester, New Hampshire, on December 9, 2007. (AP Photo/Elise Amendola)

Many writers, from professional journalists to bloggers, seemed to take a certain amount of satisfaction in Oprah's drop in the ratings. One headline captured this sentiment with "Oprah's talk show crown slipping." Another, an eye-catching headline on May 29, 2008, in the tabloid *Star Magazine* questioned: "Has Oprah passed her expiration date?" Comedian Roseanne Barr went further in her blog than most liberals in her attack on Oprah (as well as aiming a verbal barrage at a number of other well-known Democrats, whom she accused of wanting to lose the election by nominating Barack Obama). Her most hostile, and somewhat hysterical, language, however, was directed at Oprah. Barr stated, Oprah "always gets her republican friends elected!" Additionally, Barr wrote that Oprah succeeded in splitting the women's vote and destabilizing the entire Democratic Party.[3] Yet only a few years earlier, Roseanne had lavished praise on Oprah.

The friendliest advice Oprah might have followed was given by a *Los Angeles Times* writer after Obama failed to gain more votes than Hillary Clinton in Indiana: "Her [Oprah's] estimated fortune of billions might have enabled her to purchase an entire state, such as Indiana."[4]

Because of Oprah's announced partisanship, an angry group, the Florida Federation of Republican Women, denounced her because she decided not to have the Republican vice presidential candidate, Sarah Palin, on her show. Even though Oprah's spokesperson announced that Oprah didn't want her show to be used as a platform for a candidate, the statement did not soothe the Florida Federation spokesperson, who called upon "Republican sisters" to boycott Oprah's shows. Ironically, in the election, Florida voters chose the Democratic candidate.

Earlier, *Time* magazine, in its May 2008 issue, listed Oprah as one of its 100 most significant people of the year, with Michelle Obama as the author of the accompanying piece. Like other brief biographies of people chosen for the issue, this one is filled with praise for Oprah and her accomplishments. Obama also refers to their long friendship. Two of the editors of the magazine, when questioned about their reasons for picking Oprah, noted her important influence on U.S. culture. A line that appears periodically in tabloids suggests that the two women, Michelle Obama and Oprah, don't like each other, and some hint at antipathy on Oprah's part. After the election, an article in the *National Enquirer* added to the fire by writing that Mrs. Obama was angry at Oprah's assumption that she could enter the White House at will and that she does not believe Oprah had any significant role in Obama's election. No other writers, however, have made such a declaration. In fact, mediatakeout.com has listed on its Web site reputed leaks from various sources that Michelle Obama and Oprah have become very close (although some tabloids keep repeating that they don't like each other), and Gayle King is said to be the person having problems with Mrs. Obama. Oprah makes her own decisions about friendships and allegiances. King has become more and more visible in Oprah's world, and the differences between them seem the product of a publicist's activities. Reporters generally use whatever information they think will capture readers' attention, even publishing the fact that the name of President Obama's school in Hawaii was Punahoe, that his sister's name is Maya Soetoro-NG, and her husband is Konrad NG.

Frank Rich, in a *New York Times* Sunday Opinion, wrote a column titled "Latter-Day Republicans vs. the Church of Oprah," in which he labeled Oprah's endorsement of Obama a "faith-based political show," an "Oprahpalooza." Although Rich agrees that Oprah is a "megacelebrity," he pointed out that "selling presidents is not the same as pushing *Anna Karenina*." Despite her effect on "the cultural market," he noted that a *Times*–CBS News poll found a tiny number—1 percent—of voters would follow Oprah's choice of candidates. People in various professions usually disagree on the value of endorsements. Calling the political alliance between Obama and Oprah an ecumenical movement, Rich stated, "It preaches a bit of heaven on earth in the form of a unified, live-and-let-live democracy." Rich quoted a laudatory description of Oprah from Billy Graham's evangelical journal, *Christianity Today*: She is "an icon of church-free spirituality," and her beliefs "cannot simply be dismissed as superficial civil religion or so much New Age psychobabble." In contrast, a group of evangelical Christians, labeling Oprah "the queen of the new age gurus," places her among those "who are sucking millions of people into false doctrines."[5]

Rich also derided some pundits' uncomplimentary views of people who might have been inclined to vote for Oprah's choice. He painted such savants as negative conservatives hostile to Obama's large white constituency. For them, Rich wrote, all those Obama voters are a "Chardonnay-sipping, NPR-addicted bicoastal hipster crowd." On the contrary, he pointed out, Oprah's television audience is as many as 80 percent white, blue-collar people; half are estimated to have yearly incomes under $40,000, and they are mostly women aged 50 or older.

Rich is only one of many journalists who have written about the Oprah–Obama connection. An article titled "Oprah Slips in the Polls," by Anthony Randazzo for *World* on the Web, stated, "Oprah is standing for change with Obama, but thus far the biggest change she's seen is in her approval ratings." Such statistics are considered significant by a number of entertainment reviewers, for whom ratings are bread-and-butter issues.

While some black writers, professional and otherwise, praised Oprah for her support of Obama, there are those who argued that all blacks love Obama, but not all would vote for him. Gender might be a factor in such decisions; some, voicing the feelings of many women, criticized Oprah for failing to stand up for women, particularly for overlooking Hillary Clinton, the wife of the man whom Oprah's closest friends have called "the first black president."

Oprah's form of politics reflects her beliefs. In her book *Reading Oprah,* Cecilia Farr invokes the views of conservative political columnist David Brooks, who tells readers there are varying paths to salvation, as there are "varieties of happiness, distinct moralities and different ways to virtue." Farr's conclusion is the complete opposite of the one expressed by writer Ed Pilkington. Where Pilkington frowns upon Oprah's influence as a false guru, Farr labels her "the perfect guru for [our] democratic age," one who insists we each have our own power and control in making choices.

Few journalists have actually analyzed the reason or reasons for Oprah's declining popularity, a fall that may be only temporary given the fact that almost everything she touches seems to succeed. Tim Bennett, president of Harpo Productions, disagrees with those who claim that the fall in Oprah's ratings is related to her political choices and points to an across-the-board drop in television viewing. All of this analysis, however, may have played a significant role in Oprah's decision to make major changes in her career.

People supposedly in the know—the pundits who state that celebrities don't influence votes—seem to have underestimated Oprah's persuasiveness. Yet, regardless of the polls about Oprah's television ratings, it seems her support of Obama provided an important influence on more than a million voters. Ted Johnson, writing in the August 8, 2008, edition of *Variety,* listed several surveys that saw a positive effect of Oprah's participation, particularly in the study of two graduate students of economics, Craig Garthwaite and Tim More, at the University of Maryland. The two doctoral candidates did a mathematical study of Oprah's role, which resulted in a 58-page report. It was happenstance that led to their work, as they speculated whether Oprah's effect on consumers might also create the same results among voters. They found that more than a million people cast votes for Obama in the primaries as a result of Oprah's endorsement, which Johnson labeled "Oprah Winfrey's million-voter march" (a play on the name of an event of several years earlier.)

Writer Shankar Vedantam, in the *Washington Post*, devoted an entire six-page column to "The Oprah Effect," on geographic areas where she is most popular. Not only did pro-Obama votes spike in those places but so did campaign contributions. In that same Labor Day issue of the *Post*, in "The Reliable Source" (in the Style section), the reporters noted that ticket lines for the Winfrey program featuring medalists from the 2008 Olympics began to form at 6:00 A.M., and by noon the line covered six blocks. Although the program featuring Olympic winners was expected to be a great draw, the reporters speculated that Oprah's "accomplishments will resonate long after the athletes' successes are forgotten." Such views appear to negate statements of naysayers about her influence on the election.

When Obama gained the nomination, Oprah described herself to *Entertainment Today* as "ecstatic," "euphoric," "doing the happy dance," and declared she'd cried her eyelashes off. Joining the huge celebration in Chicago's Grant Park after the election of Senator Obama, Oprah emotionally expressed her joy, calling the outcome of the election "the right thing" for America, something unexpected "in our lifetime." The feeling, she said, is "like hope won."

Multiple reports that previously were doubtful or negative about Oprah's influence in the campaign soon reversed, finding that she had given a huge boost to Obama; famed longtime reporter, David Broder, writing during the campaign in Iowa, told of the enormous crowds never before seen in the history of Iowa caucuses. Other writers said the same and, like Broder, began to call the events "the Oprah-Obama show." After the election, many stories surfaced about Oprah's selection of a dress for the Inauguration Day festivities. Several rumors were floated about Oprah's plan for a post-inaugural celebration, but some reporters disputed the story. As it turned out, Oprah had several events planned. Two were part of her TV show: one for the day before the big event and one for the day after. The Monday program was held at the Opera House of the Kennedy Center, with stars from the entertainment world and an equally impressive audience. A nontelevised affair took place when Oprah hosted a party at the White House the night of the inauguration. The following day, she moved her show briefly to a new Washington restaurant called Art and Soul, owned by her former chef Art Smith. The somewhat informal program was a recap of the historical implications of the election. Among the guests was Doris Kearns Goodwin, the historian who, among her other books, has written about the two presidents—Abraham Lincoln and Lyndon Johnson—whose efforts for civil rights ultimately led to the election of the United States' first black president.

All of Oprah's activities continue to interest the world at large. Not a day passes without our seeing or hearing some reference to Oprah, whether it is important or minuscule. Oprah's rental of a house in Denver for the period of the Democratic National Convention became the subject of many television and newspaper stories. The report about the reputed price of $50,000 for a week's stay was probably what brought out a large number of angry and negative blogs in the Colorado papers that were anti-Oprah, anti-Democrat, and anti-celebrity. Many newspapers, including some in Europe, made much of a publicist's spokesperson's announcement that Oprah would be in Denver's Invesco Field football stadium for the nomination of Barack Obama; they also quoted Gayle King's statements that Oprah would not address the crowds. None of this coverage is particularly surprising; there are almost daily stories, blogs, and reports about Oprah on the Internet. One blogger even elevated her to the status of "THE Oprah."

Harsh attacks against Oprah began once her support for Obama was announced and continued after the Republican convention. Furthermore, many feminists felt betrayed because she'd chosen Obama over Hillary Clinton. During a heated discussion, at one point, Oprah had to remind some people that she was "a free black woman." However, the anger became even more intense when Republicans angrily denounced her for refusing to showcase another woman, the Republican choice of Sarah Palin for vice president. Even Fox network, completely ignoring Oprah's policy of not having any political figure on her show, used its program *Fox and Friends* to denounce Oprah for her decision not to interview Palin before the election. Oprah counter-charged the statement, denying the claim on *The Drudge Report* that there had been a large division among her staff about the Palin matter. It wasn't helpful that her executive producer, who would not comment about the matter, is said to have contributed a large amount of money to the Obama campaign.

Although there may be nothing of consequence in a story, every mention of the star is good business, for it captures many a viewer's eye and interest. An example may be found in the *Washington Post* gossip column "The Reliable Source."[6] Alongside a photo of Oprah riding in a snowmobile driven by Tom Cruise in Telluride, Colorado, is a typically earthy humorous comment of hers: "There's something about being scooched up to his butt that makes you want to sing."

Such stories, reports, and the hundreds of advertisements in all the Oprah publications and shows attest to her influence on followers. Oprah's photos on the cover of any magazine attract shoppers in large numbers, particularly if a current issue is placed strategically near a checkout counter. Products touted by Oprah, no matter how limited their previous sales have been, when advertised on the Internet find a much larger audience than most of Oprah's own publications. Millions of television viewers provide similar types of sales. Anything Oprah eats, drinks, or wears reaps much benefit from the Oprah connection. Green tea, a particular diet, and a special type of brassiere, when touted by Oprah, become instant best-sellers. On one of her shows, Oprah featured Susan Nethero, chief fit stylist and founder of a group of lingerie shops. Members of Oprah's staff, and Oprah herself, were fitted with bras. At the end of the show, Oprah proclaimed she finally got the right size. The featured company gained publicity that has led to the opening of more shops. Sales of products featured on the show, which caters to a mostly female audience, become astronomical.

Thanks to a television appearance on Oprah's television show in 2004 by a second-grade teacher who proclaimed the efficacy of a particular cold remedy, the product became an important item to purchase by the frequent-flying public. Sales skyrocketed from $21.4 million to more than $100 million a year after the teacher's appearance. Shortly thereafter, in the public interest, a class-action lawsuit for deceptive advertising was filed by the Federal Trade Commission's Bureau of Consumer Protection against the company, which claimed that its product protected people from the common cold. Although Oprah and her show fired up customers, in 2008, the Federal Trade Commission fined the company $30 million for "perpetuating misconceptions" about the product. (The company remains in business and continues to advertise.)

Whether a business is large or small, the magic of Oprah's name increases revenues. A company called Spotlight Tribute, which features trading cards, noted that "the Oprah Winfrey trading card is an item that Oprah's fans have made a valued collectible in its group of 72 cards of the World's Biggest Stars."

Even though women around the world are enthralled by her program, men are generally not Oprah watchers. The camera, panning an audience in her television studio, picks up few male faces. Although many men admire her, just as many seem to be in the same group as columnist Daniel Kline, who wrote in the *Swampscott Reporter* (his column appears weekly in 100 papers) that he is unimpressed by Oprah. With a headline "Perhaps Oprah's appeal [is] lost on men," Kline explains his indifference, calling her "a fairly tepid talk show host" who is "unremarkable" and "unfunny," a person who "has no special talent as an interviewer" and engages in "unnecessary fits of hysteria." His remarks suggest she is grossly overpaid, and so is her closest friend, Gayle King, who has become rich simply from "knowing Oprah."

Yet, despite critics such as Kline, Oprah's programs are viewed by Europeans, Asians, and South African women, black and white, in a country where the white population is only 8 percent of the total. An estimate of worldwide viewers is more than 20 million each day. (The stated numbers of people watching the show vary widely. For instance, a writer for the *Shreveport Times* estimates that there are 49 million viewers just in the United States.) Oprah's appeal crosses racial lines, even though the studio audiences for her live television shows in the United States and her nationwide tours are predominantly white. However, reruns of her shows on an Arab satellite channel draw huge numbers of women viewers.

Obviously, Oprah's celebrity, influence, star power, and following do not mesh with the views of all journalists, television critics, and religious figures, whose writings frequently provide ironic or harsh contrast to the flattering language of her followers. Ever since the Internet became popular and widely available, many people have joined in the conversations about Oprah. They are the bloggers who have become participants in online discussions about her; they run the gamut from devoted followers to detractors, although the latter are fewer in number. If there is any hint of disparagement of the star, it will probably appear in a blog or tabloid rather than in a seriously considered article. Yet the bloggers have found that there is little to keep them from venting feelings about every imaginable topic: religion; bloggers' families, including their pets; requests for personal assistance and donations for charities (even from far-off Malaysia); warnings about the coming end of the world as well as the readiness of all to meet their maker. But more common, as might be expected, is exuberant praise for the writer's idol—Oprah. Bloggers exist in many areas of the world, and complimentary statements have come from such unexpected European countries as Portugal and Belgium.

Bloggers may have their own Web sites, or, when invited, attach friendly or unfriendly comments to others' Web sites. The *Chicago Sun-Times* has an Oprah-dedicated blogger, Mark Bieganski, who calls his blog "It's all about Oprah. All the Time." Bieganski is described as someone who "follows the Oprah phenomenon like it's a religion."

Computer expert Phil Wainewright, a commentator and strategist in the software industry, describes the effect of an Oprah program on the Internet as a tsunami "that assails consumer web sites when they get 'Oprah'd.'" As few as eight million viewers in the United States alone could overwhelm Web sites if the providers are not prepared for the onslaught, says Wainwright. That onslaught occurred when Oprah invited viewers to join an online class discussion of a book, *The New Earth*, she had chosen for her club. Sales were also tremendous.

The outpouring of affectionate interest of fans and bloggers in most Oprah activities sharply contrasts with Swampscott reporter Daniel Kline's harsh evaluation. Yet he is considerably milder than the angry and inflammatory blogger's remarks of April 8, 2008, in *Politico's* "Join the Conversation." In one blog, the writer, who calls herself Mayme, quotes some mocking dialogue, she states she heard, between Oprah and her closest friend, Gayle King, on XM satellite radio, during which they laughed at the ways of "white folks." Making fun of white women who treat their help like underlings, Oprah "yells" she wishes her grandmother could see her now, with "WHITE FOLKS WORKING FOR ME." (Caps are from the blog. Also, most readers are aware that many blogs are unreliable, and this particular one seems at odds with Oprah's public persona.)

Then there are the mixed blogs. In one instance, a blog from British Columbia uses offensive language yet continues with kudos for Oprah's opposition to wars. Nonetheless, it is not all the wars of history against which Oprah has spoken out, and Oprah does not take a pacifist's position on every military action. A trip to Israel, she stated, "changed the trajectory" of her life. In a speech during a visit to the United States Holocaust Memorial Museum in Washington, DC, Oprah told the audience about her trip with author Elie Wiesel to Auschwitz, the concentration camp. That and her stay in Israel helped her to understand the impact of Hitler. Both became a path to understanding that a single individual had such immensity of power as to bring about the deaths of six million Jews. These enlightening experiences created a deeper-than-ever awareness of the responsibility and moral obligation each person has "to serve somebody other than ourselves." With each passing year, that view has become stronger. In recognition of her significant international activities, she was awarded the Elie Wiesel Humanitarian Award in May 2007.

Humanitarian issues generally need some form of publicity. When *New York Times* columnist Nicholas Kristof wrote about a little-known physician who had been performing fistula surgery for three decades on young Ethiopian women, Oprah's show brought the subject to the attention of millions of viewers; the program was also shown in the Addis Ababa clinic, and millions of dollars in donations were raised to help the cause. Once her employees had convinced Oprah how important the cause was, she made it her own. She traveled 7,000 miles to the Fistula Hospital to learn firsthand about the work and the doctor who saves the lives of young girls.

Oprah has long held the conviction that every life has a purpose. As *New York Times* writer Alexandra Stanley has said of Oprah, she has "never concealed her messianic sense of purpose." For her, events have led to a life-changing question: what could a "once colored woman" accomplish with a talk show? Stanley calls Oprah "her own version of a United Nations educational and cultural organization: "O"-nesco. In her 2005 *New York Times* article about Oprah's 20 years as a talk show host, Stanley both criticizes and praises Oprah's activities. With her "frilly pulpit," she is "crass" as well as extremely generous; "maudlin" as well as "mesmerizing." Describing the star's 50th birthday party as a "fawning tribute worthy of an Ottoman potentate," Stanley lists the multiple saccharin details that were part of the event. Yet she also writes admiringly of Oprah's worldwide influence and embrace of worthy causes and help to the needy.

Oprah's involvement exists not only in causes but even in small gestures. A brief news report tells of an encounter she had with a woman in Chicago who was trying to enter a polling station to vote, but she was not admitted until Oprah came along to help her. One small gesture took place, but it created a difference in one person's life.

The importance of the smallest gestures is emphasized in an interview for an article titled "Little Things Matter."[7] Telling Jeanne Wolf, the interviewer, of her memories of a fourth-grade teacher who always praised her, Oprah recalls the words of that teacher, who told her she "was just the smartest little girl [the teacher] had ever seen." That memory, a "shiny moment," has led her to attempt to do the same for any little girl she meets. In saying, "I always try to have a shiny moment," Oprah means it to be an expression of her basic philosophy, a "sharing" that is "self-fulfilling" and also provides for others "validation and appreciation." Such small gestures combined with Oprah's humanitarian work have led some admirers to propose she be nominated for the Nobel Peace Prize.

An "aha" moment, the kind she writes about monthly in O, *The Oprah Magazine*, came to Oprah not only through such experiences as her trip to Israel. When she fully understood political power and the force of the media, Oprah decided to expand her activities: to become more involved in education, reach out to more people in need, and help bring about national awareness through a political campaign she could believe in. Although a number of people have maintained that Oprah's political support, like that of other celebrities, did little to change votes, the media has photographed every sighting of her in every town she appeared with a candidate.

Possibly the composition of future live audiences might change since Oprah became actively involved in politics, drawing huge crowds of black voters wherever she spoke. Her political appearances, however, might be just a testing of the water after the multiple contradictory evaluations of her effectiveness. When Oprah arrives in any town, for any reason, the excitement is palpable, be it for one of her Live Your Best Life tours or for rallying voters for a candidate, where there is hope that the thousands who fill the seats will turn into donors, campaign organizers, and other workers, as well as voters for Oprah's choice.

In earlier years, when she was not yet the phenomenon she has become, the press—particularly the tabloid press—fixated on her imperfections, watching her every move and photo, even to the extent of making personal and cruel remarks, such as comparisons of Oprah to famous overweight entertainers of the past: the hefty late singer Sophie Tucker and the late, overly large black actress Hattie McDaniel, who played the simpering maid to Vivian Leigh's Scarlet O'Hara in the film *Gone with the Wind*. Oprah's weight problems were a constant topic from her first days on television; although now they are still spoken of, the belittling language of most writers has changed. In fairness to the press, it should be noted that, formerly, Oprah herself made the topic of her weight central. However, the days of mea culpa are over. She no longer speaks of food binging and lack of exercise as the source of her weight. (In fact, she coolly voices her dislike of exercise, as her trainer Bob Greene also mentions, but admits her love of comfort food.) Oprah, the public, and, recently, writers all spoke of her struggle with weight as a difficult thyroid problem. The January 2009 cover of her magazine featured two Oprahs: one exquisitely thin and one matronly, overweight, and unhappy looking. The topic—and the struggle—go on and on.

New York Times correspondent Ted Pandeva Zagar found Oprah's weight problems linked to astrology; Oprah's birth at 4:30 P.M. on January 29, 1954, is related to her thyroid condition and is caused by a "sun-venus conjunction," he wrote. Pandeva Zagar, "a pioneer in Wellness Astrology," sees her difficulties with variations in weight as a reflection of the "union of the sun to the thyroid planet in the thyroid house."[8] Oprah herself has not blamed the conjunction of the planets for her difficulties. However, in a somewhat abrupt shift in her effort to control her burgeoning figure, at one point she announced she was changing her food habits, and, furthermore, three members of her staff were joining her in the effort.

Assessing the reasons for the ongoing interest and generally greater respect among people who write about her can't be limited to any one explanation. Oprah has become queen of all she surveys, a powerhouse player in every form of media: radio, the Internet, and women's publications—O, The Oprah Magazine; O At Home (now suspended); and The O Magazine Cookbook.

Most importantly for reaching a wider audience, there are television ventures. Even when one of her new shows, The Big Give, was initially disparaged, the public, schools, individuals, businesses, and multiple organizations flooded her company with contributions and offers of assistance. The program was the first prime-time series developed by Oprah's company Harpo Productions. Despite its critics, the show appeared to be an instant success, as, from week to week, the ratings increased. Gifts of every type were made. One of many examples was a large sum of money donated for smoke alarms to a firehouse in Fresno, California. In another example, a contestant from the show was inspired to write a book about his experience; hoping to motivate others, the author, who grew up in Nigeria, describes his and his father's efforts to improve the lives of those in need. Despite poor reviews, *The Big Give* appealed to a large audience. Clearly, no matter what critics wrote about the program, Oprah and company had assessed correctly the U.S. psyche and generosity to those in need.

Still, there were complaints of various kinds. One person filed a copyright infringement lawsuit, claiming *The Big Give* had used a clip from the television showing of *Grease* without his permission and had not paid him a residual fee. After discussions among all the involved parties, Harpo announced a settlement had been reached. Another suit, also a copyright infringement claim, was filed in Boston's U.S. District Court against Oprah, the show, Harpo Productions, and ABC Television by a Massachusetts woman who maintained that the idea for *The Big Give* had been stolen from her. Her plan, describing a reality show titled *The Philanthropist*, was rejected by Oprah's company after some time had passed; yet the focus of the complaint was about the plan Oprah's company had for a series that was "eerily similar" to the concept of *The Philanthropist*. Although the case was dismissed, an appeal was filed, and the appeal has yet to be ruled on. The outcome may never be known because of the tight control of information by Oprah's company.

Meanwhile, however, Oprah reacted to the unfavorable reviews of *The Big Give* and the loss of a third of her audience within a few weeks. She did not renew her contract, although the chairman of ABC claimed he'd urged her to continue. Perhaps Oprah pays more attention to critics than she claims.

In the political field and elsewhere, significant changes have been taking place. There appears to be a growing respect in recent years toward racial differences. Some would call it political correctness, but anything suggesting the racism of only a few years ago is seen as offensive in parts of the United States. Still, social analysts of racial bias in the United States have talked of hidden discriminatory views, but concrete evidence is difficult to pinpoint. Oprah's audience does not appear to consider race in its devotion to her.

The foreign press generally has been and continues to be kinder and gentler than the U.S. press in its assessment of both the star and her work. The words of Indian writer Anita Chicklet of *Zee News* reflect the almost worshipful attitudes of various overseas journalists in dubbing Oprah "the Queen of Hearts" (a phrase reminiscent of the adoration of the late British Princess Diana), a person of substance, and a much-loved role model. U.S. columnists, in contrast, over the years have used language about Oprah that appears patronizing: "Oprify," "Oprahization," "Empress," "Saint Oprah," and the "Czarina of popular culture" in "the Oprahsphere" that is ruled by the "daytime queen of empathy." Perhaps as Oprah has become more involved in significant activities, the critical weather has undergone a change, with more frequent serious statements and fewer flippant articles about her, and when the comments are light, they tend to be more friendly than negative. Along with the growth of Oprah's empire and influence, leading journalists in both the news and entertainment industries have developed an affectionate type of deference toward her.

As Willie Geist pointed out on a "Morning Joe" television program, there is an "eleventh commandment: thou shalt not criticize Oprah." Her status over the years, which has grown far beyond the reaches of the television audience, has become immeasurable. Oprah, *Washington Post* columnist Eugene Robinson wrote, "transcends even the transcendent."

At times it is as though anything hinting about an Oprah connection will be published. Oprah is news to the extent that Google gathers daily items from all over the world for "Oprah Alert," which is available to Internet users who want to follow everything about the media queen. All it takes is the mention of her name to be labeled a story of interest. When a mining disaster occurred in Tasmania in 2006, numerous companies phoned an Australian hospital to offer large sums of money to the survivors to buy the rights to their stories. But the only prominent name noted in the press and the Web site was *The Oprah Winfrey Show*.

No matter the occasion, in recent years, if Oprah's name can be brought in, even the most far-fetched subject for a report appears somewhere. Perhaps this was the strangest, when in 2007, a real estate poll was conducted about the popularity of Oprah versus that of Donald Trump. More baby boomers and seniors picked Oprah rather than Trump as their preferred real estate agent. Of all the areas that Oprah has been involved in, selling real estate isn't one. Nevertheless, the very use of her name has cachet, regardless of whether the event has any relationship to Oprah. Her name, or even something that sounds like it, will make news: thus, the naming of a now four-year-old horse as Oprah Winney of Sanford Characters stables.

Because of her popularity and fame, Oprah's career is frequently compared to that of Mary Kay Ash, the late cosmetics entrepreneur whose business empire continues to thrive even after her death. When Mary Kay died in November 2001, the obituary in the *Washington Post* noted her significance in revealing to women like Oprah an understanding of the methods she had used in gaining success; later, the same methods worked for Oprah, most significantly involving groups in her company's business activities.

Few would debate that Oprah has won her stripes the hard way: national and international celebrity have made her someone to be reckoned with as owner or partner in networks, schools, and businesses. On television and radio, the conservative talk show host Bill O'Reilly, not known for his lavish praise of media stars, has described her as "the most powerful woman in the world," a woman who has "credibility" and "talent." Even her well-known rival, Jerry Springer, who also has a television empire, has stated she is "the best there is or has ever been," a position apparently supported by *Forbes* magazine. *Forbes*, like O'Reilly, has named Oprah the world's most powerful celebrity.

There is no overlooking her vast wealth. For several years, *Forbes* listed Oprah as the highest paid African American in the United States, the world's only black billionaire, and the first black billionaire in world history. Oprah's earnings top those of Tiger Woods, whose wealth is greater than that of any other athlete in the world, and she had, for a time, even more billions than J. K. Rowling, author of the Harry Potter series. (In July 2008, the British paper, *The Guardian*, reported that Rowling's final Harry Potter book, *Harry Potter and the Deathly Hallows*, put Rowling's earnings higher than Oprah's.) However, Oprah remains the highest-earning media personality; reputedly, recently she signed a three-year contract that is said to bring her $55 million from XM satellite radio alone.

In contrast to the mixed assessments of polls and critics, public praise of Oprah is frequently hyperbolic. Many people go through periods of intense loyalty to entertainers in the music, television, and movie industries, and Oprah's fans are among the most dedicated. She is seen as a "parable of the American dream," Alexandra Stanley wrote in the *New York Times*; someone who preaches "self-help" to an accepting audience.

Audiences stand, cheer, and applaud when she enters a room, and not all of the adulation can be ascribed to managerial directions given in advance. Women—there are far fewer men in attendance at her shows or reading her magazines—laugh at her slightest suggestion of humor—some quite earthy—and cry when Oprah's eyes tear up. She is regarded as a woman who helps show others how to live. The worshipful attitude has reached a point where some admirers have seriously suggested that Oprah be nominated as a vice presidential candidate. In support of such sentiments, a television writer has borrowed a term formerly used to describe Bette Midler; the "divine Ms. M" has become "the divine Ms. O."

The now-defunct MS magazine once repeated a fan's accolade, labeling Oprah as the "most accessible and honest" American psychiatrist. Oprah's television role in the daily lives of numerous viewers may or may not fulfill the calling of a doctor, but if one thinks of her many venues available to her followers, in addition to her support of psychologist Dr. Phil's program five days a week and his monthly column in her magazine, O, Oprah's role as psychiatrist to the nation is not untoward. Eva Illouz, in her book *Oprah Winfrey and the Glamour of Misery*, states, "Oprah shows us how to cope . . . by offering a rationalized view of the self, inspired by the language of therapy." *Newsweek* credits her with playing a role in creating "the cult of confession."

On air, Oprah urges children to confide in trusted adults to protect themselves from predators. Oprah sees her role as consummate helper. During the Clinton administration, she played a part in having a bill passed for child protection. Informally, the bill was called the Oprah Bill, but the actual legal document is named the Child Protection Act, which became law in 1992 when President Clinton signed it. Oprah was so committed to seeing success of the law that she provided money to hire attorneys to protect children from sexual predators, and her name is frequently invoked in such matters. Protection of children against predators has been a lifetime interest of hers, resulting from her own bitter experiences as a child. In July 2008, the Associated Press carried a story of a prosecutor, Jill Starishevsky of the Bronx, New York, Child Abuse and Sex Crimes Bureau, who had successfully brought to trial a case against a man who had been constantly raping his stepdaughter from the time she was six years old. The little girl had been watching Oprah's show, in which the message told sexually abused children to inform parents or teachers about the molestation. Three years had passed since the beginning of the abuse, but the child, who had been silent all those years, informed her teacher about it the day after she heard Oprah speak. Although most events of this type rarely make the newspapers, this particular one did, and it stresses the importance of the Oprah effect.

She remains a strong advocate for abused children. On a September 2008 television show, the subject was Internet predators. The aim was to influence Oprah's audience to urge support of a new Senate bill, the Protect Our Children Act, which targets child pornography.

Oprah's national role as healer expanded for a time during the Bush presidency, when the nation was attacked by terrorists. Oprah served in that capacity following the national disaster of September 11, 2001. When the terrorist attacks on New York City and Washington, DC, were the only subjects of the media for days, Oprah, along with other celebrities, was prominently featured as a participant in the healing process, using her daily program to move toward that goal. Oprah appeared with First Lady Laura Bush as they held hands in their shared grief over the thousands of lives lost in the assaults. For weeks after the horrific events, Oprah appeared to be everywhere, taking on, more than ever, the role of therapist to a troubled country.

At that time, Oprah was avowedly apolitical. However, toward the end of the Bush presidency, when Oprah became a partisan in the political process as a supporter for Democratic candidates, she altered her impartial national role of therapist to the country. It is highly unlikely she will be called upon or volunteer to participate in any future events presented by a Republican administration. Her lover of many years, Stedman Graham, has been said to be an Obama supporter, and, although Graham is known as a staunch Republican, Oprah probably will no longer be on the A-list of desired speakers for his party. (She has never participated in such events.) Inasmuch as Oprah and Graham have usually gone in different directions in political matters, it cannot be of any great concern to her. She seems to take a firm stand against those who are angry about her involvement in politics different from their own.

Because of her fame, we expect to find library shelves filled with Oprah biographies of all kinds, but that assumption is incorrect. Although there are biographies, they are not all kinds. A few out-of-print and out-of-date adult books of earlier vintage exist, and there are some children's books as well. These works fall into two main categories: biographies and books of sayings. However, a problem exists with several of those publications, particularly those that are a collection of sayings without specific dates. Some statements that lack dates could lead readers to believe something to be true of the mature Oprah, whereas she, like most of us, surely has altered some of her views over a period of time. Perhaps the best example is Oprah's change of heart about remaining steadfastly outside the political arena.

In several books and articles, careless but not insignificant errors appear. An entry in an encyclopedia erroneously lists the paternal rather than the maternal grandmother as the person with whom Oprah spent her early years. A 1990s biography lists a wrong birth date for Oprah. Another claims Oprah's mother married a man with whom she had a longtime relationship; in fact, she never married. One describes Oprah as short, a description completely at odds with reality, because she is five foot six. Furthermore, tabloids may present a special problem because their sources of information are typically "friends" who are never identified.

Even before opening some of the books about Oprah, readers are confronted with titles that usually contain words similar to the hype of advertisements such as "wonderful" and "remarkable." Although many of the books are excessively benevolent, none is authorized. (At one time, Oprah planned to write her autobiography, but she was persuaded to abandon the project because some of her intimates, including

Stedman Graham, believed it would be a detriment to her career.) Shortly before a well-known tell-all author released an Oprah biography, Bill Zwecker, a columnist for the *Chicago Sun-Times*, suggested the *London Times* was exaggerating in describing that writer as "the poison pen biographer." On the other hand, Josh Schollmeyer, of the magazine *Chicago*, took another view, perhaps more centrist, that the book would not be "a puff piece." Nonetheless, it was always unlikely that Oprah would sanction it, and, when asked, Oprah stated she would have no input. Not long ago, Oprah's father, Vernon decided he'd write a book about his daughter, something he neglected to tell her.

When Oprah took umbrage, gossip columnists reported that she had threatened suit. Her more mild public statement was that they had "talked." Vernon Winfrey's book will not appear. Generally, information about Oprah is selective, and if she does not want something made public, it is carefully controlled when possible. However, the tabloids frequently run stories about her that claim to be true. Nonetheless, the sources generally are not named, though reporters, not on the payroll of the gossip papers, have said that the tabloids have very large and persistent staffs that track stories constantly.

The implication suggests that most of the stories are true. Although it may appear that her life is an open book, because much is personal in nature, it is Oprah herself who determines what she tells readers of her thoughts and life story in her magazines and on radio and television. She grants few interviews.

Oprah brought suit against a man who later became the author of a self-published book, *Ruthless*. She charged that the author, Keifer Bonvillain, had maligned her and attempted extortion. Newspapers exercised much caution in reporting the situation, giving little publicity to the matter or sale of the book. The case was dismissed without much notice, yet the book remains in print. Bonvillain's account seems confused and defensive as he tells his story of being an innocent party who had received the revelations from a former employee of Harpo, Oprah's company. Whatever the truths behind the matter, the book was marketed through Amazon.com. Although the number of purchases has not been publicized, references to the work continue to surface. Still another hostile, self-published book appeared a year later, and it also may be purchased. Titled *Don't Drink the Kool-Aid*, the author

Carrington Steele lambasts Oprah for her religious and spiritual views, something frequently done by bloggers.

Few books critical of Oprah are written by the professional press. Most are scholarly and focus on specific areas of research. One that has covered a larger territory and has been reviewed more widely is Janice Peck's *The Age of Oprah: Cultural Icon for the Neoliberal Press*. One reviewer of Peck's book describes her as "a prosecutor" who regards Oprah as a "symbol of this age of navel gazing narcissism." Peck sees the country as "self-centered" and Oprah's gospel of self-reliance as "pitiless toward the poor." In a lengthy "Black Agenda Radio Interview" hosted by Brace Dixon, Peck agrees that she regards Oprah's message as political, a politics "that puts the personal responsibility for being poor and oppressed exclusively on the poor and oppressed."

Furthermore, Peck maintains that U.S. society has not transcended race, that we cover up and avoid many issues, which is what Oprah has done, with the result that her "majority white following" remains comfortable with her.

Unlike most monthlies, Oprah's magazine, O, rarely prints any fault-finding letters to the editor, an omission that suggests that readers who take the time to write to the editor have nothing critical to say. Although few would question the U.S. public's affection for the entertainer or her impressive social and cultural roles, the constant praise contributes to an adverse effect that is diminishing, at least as far as critics are concerned.

Several scholarly specialized books, each focusing on some aspect of Oprah's work or philosophy, have been published in recent years: one is about Oprah's concepts of religion; another explores her effect on U.S. national culture; and another follows her rise in becoming a cultural icon. Two analyze her book club as well as her selections of books for the club. One writer, Kathleen Rooney, the author of *Reading with Oprah: The Book Club That Changed America*, wrote a lengthy piece for the *Washington Post* in which she explores the stories that followed Oprah's support of Obama.[9] (Rooney also produced a collection of essays, *For You, I Am Trilling These Songs*.)

There have been announcements of several books, among them another unauthorized biography of Oprah, as well as articles, books, and comic strips about her. Comedians find multiple avenues of humor about her and her activities. On a Comedy Central show titled *The Root of All Evil*, comedian Louis Black presented "Oprah versus the Catholic Church." Neither Oprah nor spokespeople for the Church have commented publicly about the presentation.

Over the years, Oprah has declared several times her intention to retire from her daily television program, but until September 2009, she kept changing the date. Despite unconfirmed reports that her show continued to lose viewers, she signed a new contract to extend the date to 2011, including those roles of actress and television producer. However, rumors persisted that Oprah would not renew her contract with CBS after 2011, once she bought into the new network, OWN. In 2009, Oprah tearfully announced the news. Also, she has expanded her publishing empire twice in recent years. Her original venture with her first magazine, *O*, has grown hugely. Although recent statistics show a decline in subscriptions, the largest loss has been in individual purchases at supermarkets. What is happening is considered part of the general economic decline, and *O* remains the most popular women's magazine in the United States. However, not long after the report that her other magazine, the *O At Home* publication, was in trouble, the magazine ceased publication when another backer could not be found to replace Hearst. Still Oprah's wealth permits her to explore new ventures in many fields. Not only has she expanded her business empire, but she also has enlarged her role in educational projects large and small as well as her role as international philanthropist. Whatever her future options, the likelihood is that she will continue to be a major player in multiple areas.

As for her personal life, it is and will undoubtedly remain a topic of interest to readers and writers. For the tabloids and entertainment magazines, she is an industry, with her activities being reported on an almost daily basis. Should she ever retire completely, they would lose a valuable commodity.

NOTES

1. *Arizona Republic*, 12 Nov. 2007.
2. *Philadelphia Enquirer*, 21 May 2008.
3. Eurweb.com, 20 Aug. 2008.

4. "Top of the Ticket," *Los Angeles Times*, Apr. 2008.

5. "The Other O-Factor in Oprah's Gentle Decline," *Guardian* (New York), 27 May 2008.

6. "The Reliable Source," *Washington Post*, 1 May 2008.

7. Jeanne Wolf, "Little Things Matter," *Washington Post*, 16 Dec. 2007.

8. "The Astrology behind Oprah's Thyroid Problem," 21 Apr. 2008.

9. Kathleen Rooney, "The Five Myths about Oprah, Obama," *Washington Post*, 14 Sept. 2008.

Chapter 2

A ONCE COLORED GIRL

Mississippi, historically one of the poorest states in the nation, has made more racially based political news than most other states in the South. Despite its role as an important focal point of the civil rights movement in the 20th century, it did not move as quickly or as well into acceptance of black and white integration. In Mississippi, there was strong resistance to many of the changes in race relations and laws.

Only a few years ago, political battles were still being fought over issues that had long been settled in other parts of the country. Some leading politicians appeared nostalgic for a preintegration world of separate restaurants, toilets, and seating on trains and buses. In fact, when a Mississippian, a prominent U.S. senator now retired and a member of a lobbyist firm, voiced sentiments unacceptable to many citizens of the modern South, he was considered a hero among his constituents. Journalists have written that the now former senator had associations with ultra conservative groups, racists, and extreme rightists. A great irony is that Barack Obama, a biracial man, became a candidate for president of the United States during that period. In the Mississippi primary, which Obama won, several newspapers described the contest as "racially polarized" and the state as having "a striking racial divide." In the deeply

Republican state, election history reveals that no Democratic candidate for president since Jimmy Carter had won Mississippi.

Mississippi is also the birthplace of Oprah Winfrey, perhaps the most famous black entertainer ever, known throughout the world for her work in television as well as her philanthropic, educational, and social efforts. In the aftermath of Hurricane Katrina in New Orleans, many people hastened to the aid of those who had suffered in the storm, but, where only a few of the volunteers received publicity for their efforts, Oprah's assistance was written about in papers everywhere. Not only did she give $10 million for hurricane relief on the Gulf Coast, but she also gave gifts of stock to volunteers who helped after the disaster. News reports told of her call to celebrity friends to help her bring attention to the desperate plight of those she described as abandoned or mistreated by the government. Angered by what she saw, she used her show, which was broadcast in the devastated city, to apologize in the name of the American people for the suffering and deaths that had taken place.

When she asked viewers to donate money through her Angel Network after the devastation of Hurricanes Katrina and Rita, the appeal raised $15.6 million, and more than 300 new homes were built or restored with the money. The project took place in eight communities in Oprah's home state of Mississippi as well as Texas, Louisiana, and Alabama. Additionally, the Angel Network and First Book's Book Relief program provided new books to thousands of children who had lost their books along with all their other possessions.

Because of Oprah's longtime commitment to improving the lives of children, her foundation established Oprah Winfrey Boys and Girls Clubs, one of which is located in the small Mississippi city of Kosciusko, Oprah's birthplace. And, undoubtedly because of her fame, the magazine *Southern Living* featured an article showing members of the club cooking with Art Smith. Formerly Oprah's chef for 10 years as well as author of a cookbook, Smith is owner of the Chicago restaurant Table 52 and a newer restaurant in Washington, DC, called Art and Soul. He edits an article each month on Oprah's Web site and frequently contributes to her magazine. Smith's latest restaurant is on Capitol Hill, in the Liaison Hotel, where a postinaugural 2008 live television Oprah show was filmed as part of the election week festivities. (Rumors beforehand, resembling those in Colorado, placed Oprah's whereabouts in multiple parts of the city; the most intriguing detail generally is the cost of hotels and amenities for Oprah—in this case, $15,000 per night.)

Staff on *Southern Living* learned about Smith's work with children, which focuses on some of the same interests as the magazine: nutrition and physical well-being. Because of the mutual concerns, photographs of the children appeared in the July 2008 issue of the magazine and in the local paper, the *Star-Herald* of Kosciusko. The pieces, which featured interviews with the children and described their experiences, provided publicity, which made the group feel like celebrities. Chef Art Smith is a philanthropist who gives time and money to help educate children about their health. In his attempt to practice what he preaches, he has been changing his eating habits toward achieving a healthy lifestyle. Like First Lady Michelle Obama, he is committed to reducing what has been called the childhood obesity epidemic in the United States. Oprah, on Smith's 50th birthday, donated $250,000 to his nonprofit charity Common Threads. His undertaking runs 20 after-school programs in various parts of the country, and the chef himself lost 90 pounds following his own teaching about healthy eating.

Mississippi also was the early home of another idol of the entertainment world, music legend Elvis Presley. Elvis was so newsworthy that everything he did seemed to be recorded, and there are people who look at Oprah through a lens similar to Elvis's, though she is very much alive and constantly in the news. Furthermore, Oprah believes she is related to Elvis's daughter, Lisa Marie Presley. Because she has referred to Lisa Marie as "my cousin," a Fox columnist, Roger Friedman, criticized Oprah for her statement, even though a search of her roots and DNA found a link.[1]

Although not well known for its cultural life, Mississippi is the birthplace of three of the United States' great literary figures: William Faulkner, Eudora Welty, and Richard Wright. Both Faulkner and Welty lived most of their lives in the state. Wright, though, went north, following the path of numerous black people who sought what they hoped would be friendlier, more hospitable surroundings. But changes took place, albeit slowly, after World War II, with some segments of the Southern population returning to their home territory. For most of the 20th century, other Southern states—Georgia, Louisiana, Tennessee, Alabama,

and Virginia—provided more fertile ground than Mississippi did for
writers, novelists, and essayist. Oprah often speaks of the books that affected her most in growing up, and, in an issue of her now-defunct *O
At Home* magazine, she reminisced about them. (In 2009, *O At Home*
suspended publication.) Many of her favorites came from the literary
list of Southern writers, traditional and contemporary poets, literary
critics, novelists, playwrights, and essayists.

Of particular interest in the cultural study of these writers is the
great cultural chasm between the races but the many similarities within
each racial group. Black writers inform us of their suffering and oppres-
sion caused by white people in addition to portraying the wretched-
ness and despair of family life. Certainly, white Southern writers also
explore the tragedies of black people and their families as well as their
own dysfunctional family relationships, but different from the writing of
white Southern writers is an additional common, sometimes biographi-
cal, thread running through the work of many black authors: illegiti-
macy, desertion, abandonment, promiscuity, and sexual abuse. When,
in adulthood, Oprah and some of her friends have spoken of these matters, their words reflect the books, poems, and stories that are part of
the United States' literary and cultural heritage. Oprah and various
friends have lived these stories. In many ways, her life reads like one of
those stories, but the outcome of hers is more like a fairy tale.

The work of Southern writers remains an integral part of many cur-
ricula in U.S. universities. The lives of the authors have an ongoing effect on current writers and continue to provoke interest.

The small towns, the wooden churches, the music, and the food all
seem to be part of the blood of most Southerners—evident in their
thinking, their attitudes, and their accents. The South is famous as the
birthplace of several kinds of music, the most familiar being jazz and
country. Mississippi, early in the 20th century, had famed jazz players
about whom books now are being published. But when people speak of
New Orleans, the most renowned Southern area of the musical past,
they evoke reminders of the many musicians, piano players, saxophon-
ists, clarinetists, and drummers who created jazz. Yet, because most of
the musicians were black and lived during the years of segregation in
the South, most of their names have been lost to history. Whether the
musical tradition of New Orleans will be revived in the aftermath of

Katrina is questionable. A large piece of the cultural past would be lost should that happen; according to musicologists, black musical history goes back to the early days of slavery, when a unique kind of music evolved.

The South is not only the birthplace of jazz and country music but also of gospel singing. The sounds of gospel were early forerunners to mountain music and jazz. Country ballads familiar to many Americans are derived from gospel singing. Although both gospel and country music had been sung and played throughout the South, these forms of music tend to be associated with Nashville, Tennessee, the city to which numerous aspiring artists later gravitated. Worldwide, any mention of Nashville conjures up images of certain singers, special types of music, song, and instruments that are the inheritors of mountain culture and gospel music, although those are not the exclusive property of Nashville.

Universally heard in the small towns of the South, gospel music has only a few names tied to it, whereas jazz and country composers and singers are much better known. Nevertheless, gospel music is as much a part of Southern culture as ham and grits, biscuits and gravy, fried chicken, and catfish. Children brought up in the small towns of the Bible Belt seemed almost to inhale gospel music along with the weekly church-going and rituals. The influence is embedded in their lives, even when they leave the region. Oprah—as well as Elvis—is a prime example of that effect. Because of her early conditioning, her preferences in music, years after her moves elsewhere, reflect what she regards as the healing effect of religion and music. Oprah recently learned she is a distant cousin of a famous gospel music singer, Mavis Staples. For Oprah, gospel songs are related to faith and hope and healing, and, when unhappy, perhaps terrible things occur, she tells us she turns to gospel music. One such time came after the tragedies of September 11, 2001.

When we turn away from the instant recognition of famous figures from the musical or literary world—after all, their faces often appear on postage stamps—most of us probably would find it difficult to come up with more than a few names of entertainers associated with the South; it is not usually the area we link with entertainers, other than country, blues, and jazz musicians, despite the fact that a great many composers, musicians, singers, and dancers were born there. Yet, cultural history notes they had to head north or west, where they gained fame and sometimes—but not always—fortune.

For most Americans, entertainment is connected to the glitter of New York, Hollywood, and Las Vegas—not Mississippi. However, Oprah Winfrey, one of the most famous celebrities in the world, was born in a little-known area of Mississippi. With the rather unlikely and unfamiliar name of Kosciusko, the city was named after the Polish general Thaddeus/Tadeusz Kosciusko. Known as the "Hero of Two Worlds," he fought for the independence of the colonies in the American Revolution as well as for the independence of his home country. Much admired for his abilities, he also served with the Continental Congress, which appointed him an engineer with the rank of colonel. Outside of history books and biographies, like many other valorous figures, General Kosciusko has been largely forgotten, except for the naming of the town that honored his role in 18th-century United States. Few people know of his legacy and his historic actions to help liberate the slaves.

Kosciusko is only 70 miles north of the capital city, Jackson, but there is almost no resemblance between the two places. Little distinguishes Kosciusko from other small farming areas of the state, yet during the nation's early years, it was an important segment of the frontier route to Nashville. Although people used the Mississippi River whenever possible to transport goods, that method often was difficult for primitive navigation. The alternative was a land route called the Natchez Trace that connected Natchez, Mississippi, to Nashville. Kosciusko still celebrates that early period of its history with a Natchez Trace festival every April, even though, unlike other cities along the route, it failed to develop in any significant way. Those other cities became famous as well as heavily populated, but that was not the case for Kosciusko.

The city is located in a region of rivers and frequent rain, with hot and humid weather and pines and flowering trees. In the middle of the 20th century, when Oprah was born, there was scarcely more variety of work than there had been a hundred or two hundred years earlier. Small farms provided the major source of income. Although Kosciusko today has a highway called Veterans Memorial Boulevard, which leads into the Natchez Trace Parkway, more than half of Mississippi remains rural. Its 36 percent African American population is larger than that of any other state in the country—a statistic that generated strong interest during the presidential campaign and election of 2008, when the black population was ardently courted.

When we listen to her accent and words and consider her attitudes, we associate few Southern characteristics with Oprah, although she lived in two Southern states, Mississippi and Tennessee. She spent a few damaging childhood and teenage years in Milwaukee, Wisconsin, and in her 20s moved to Maryland, another Southern state. Ultimately, Chicago became her primary home. Psychologists and psychiatrists have stated that the first five years determine much of who and what we are, and if we accept that thesis, we must apply it to Oprah, even though in most ways she does not appear to fit the Southern image. She did attend high school and college in Tennessee, but she claims she felt little association with her early surroundings—although with the passage of time she has become reconciled to the past, speaking more and more frequently of her Mississippi grandmother. Yet she never thought of any Southern town or city longingly as home. Once she left the South of her youth, she has returned only occasionally and never lived there again, although she has relatives in the region.

At the time of Oprah's birth in 1954, what little industry had existed was almost gone; jobs were scarce, and young people—particularly young blacks, who continued to be victims of prejudice and poverty—left if they could, in search of a livelihood. During the time of Oprah's slave ancestors, and during her grandparents' lives, her mother's life, and her own early years, Mississippi was (and remains) close to the bottom of the economic ladder despite its association with some of the great names in U.S. culture.

Unhappy childhood memories have turned many Southern artists to other places, but they either maintained homes in the South or returned frequently to keep the connection. Mississippian writer Welty settled in her childhood home after a short foray in the life of New York. Even novelist Truman Capote, who declared himself a New Yorker because he'd spent only part of his early years in Alabama, frequently felt the pull of Monroeville and New Orleans. Most of his work is Southern to the core, created in large measure by a childhood that Oprah's close friend Maya Angelou and others have described as appalling and tragic. Nevertheless, he often felt the need to revisit the South. And Angelou, who is always identified as a Southerner, lived in many parts of the country and elsewhere but finally settled in North Carolina. In contrast, Oprah, who spent more years in the South than either Capote or Angelou, turned her back on it, saying at various times throughout the years that she knew when she moved to Chicago at 30 that she had found her home.

We must accept her statement, but, when we look carefully at the person she is, we can't help but recognize the Southern roots that are part and parcel of her character and personality: the influence of and love of gospel music; the strong spiritual side of her nature; her deep affection for Southern novels; even her love of Southern food and cooking.

Although Oprah always credits two members of her family—her maternal grandmother, Hattie Mae Lee, and her father, Vernon Winfrey—with the qualities that have led to her success, her memories of childhood and early years are filled with more pain and sadness than joy. At times, she claims to have overcome the effects of the past, yet she speaks so frequently of a particular time in her childhood that it seems to be a still-open wound. Those hardships, reflected in many of her interests and activities, are recognizable to all Oprah watchers, some of whom share similar experiences.

A series of accidents are part of Oprah's heritage; she was born illegitimate, the child of two very young people. Her mother, Vernita Lee, at age 18 claimed that a 20-year-old man named Vernon Winfrey on leave for two weeks from the army had made her pregnant. At times she changed her mind, saying she was uncertain who was responsible. In an interview in a tabloid newspaper, Vernon Winfrey "confessed" he could not have fathered Oprah because he was on army duty at the time. Service people do go on leave, however, and it's been reported again and again that Winfrey was on leave during that period. Vernita recently modified her story once again, insisting that Vernon is the only person who could be Oprah's father. Winfrey was a soldier stationed at Camp Rucker in Alabama. Apparently with typical carelessness, Vernita Lee didn't notify him about the pregnancy until the child was born. Then, she sent a newspaper announcement along with a request that he mail clothes for the newborn baby.

Like the pregnancy, the name that has become a household word, Oprah, was also an accident. The family had chosen the biblical name

Orpah from the book of Ruth. Although the name is recorded on the official birth certificate as Orpah, people tended to transpose the *r* and the *p*. The name Orpah isn't used anywhere else, and the spelling of Oprah's name became the one we know today.

Some time after her baby's birth at home on the farm, Vernita left the infant with her mother, Hattie Mae. Oprah's grandfather, Earless Lee, had little to do with the child. Much is made of the fact that Oprah spent her early years with her grandmother, yet she is only one of a number of famous people who had the same experience, among them former President Bill Clinton, Tipper Gore, and Supreme Court Justice Clarence Thomas. Oprah remained until she was six on the little farm that Grandmother Lee owned in the Mississippi Delta region. Then she went to live with her mother in Milwaukee, Wisconsin. Different stories are told about the reasons for Oprah's move. One version is that Vernita sent for her; another is that her grandmother found her too difficult to look after, and yet another is that Hattie Mae had become ill.

Whatever brought about the child's departure from Mississippi, friends and relatives have talked of Hattie Mae's love for her first grand-child, who was regarded as unique because of her precocity.

Life on the farm was basic. The grandmother boiled clothes on the screened-in back porch, using a large iron pot since the family had no washing machine. Water had to be drawn from a well. The tiny farm-house lacked indoor plumbing, so an outhouse was the substitute for an indoor toilet, and one of Oprah's daily chores was emptying the slop jars each morning. In remembering details from her childhood, Oprah has half humorously and half seriously referred to the use of the Sears catalogue in the outhouse. From early on she also had to help with the cows, pigs, and chickens. Because she had no room of her own, she slept with her grandmother in a feather bed, often lying awake terrified that her grandfather would come in during the night and commit a mur-derous act against both her and her grandmother. An incident did occur one night when Oprah was about four years old. An uncontrol-lable Earless Lee came into the bedroom, and Oprah's grandmother had to rush out into the darkness to scream for help from a neighbor. Al-though the neighbor was old and blind, Oprah remembers him as a res-cuer. In the daytime, Grandfather Lee also was a fearsome presence, threatening the child with his cane or throwing various objects at her.

Much like life on the farm, her grandmother was rigid and harsh, meting out punishment for any infringement of rules, even for happenings over which the girl had little or no control. Whippings were part of Oprah's upbringing, in accordance with the old credo "spare the rod and spoil the child." Strongly religious, Hattie Mae Lee spent most of her free time at the nearby Faith-United Mississippi Baptist Church, where she also took Oprah from her earliest days. Because her grandmother's other preoccupation after religion was reading, even in babyhood Oprah was taught how to read and to memorize passages of the Bible, activities that gained renown for her when she was only a toddler. With the strong discipline at home, only at the local Baptist church was she given the opportunities to express herself. As a result of her ability to recite pieces from the Bible, she was called on to do Easter selections. Oprah still remembers some of the recitations, one of which was "Jesus rose on Easter Day, Hallelujah, Hallelujah, all the angels did proclaim." While fanning themselves against the heat of the season and listening to the toddler's recitations, the women of the church would praise the little girl to her grandmother, calling her a gifted child. Oprah has said that her first Easter speech was probably made at the Kosciusko Baptist church when she was about three and a half. Only a few years later, she was able to recite the entire series of the seven sermons of poet James Weldon Johnson from "The Creation" to "The Judgment."

In recalling her early years, Oprah has reflected that, at various times, she spoke at all the churches in Nashville. When interviewed by evening talk show host Larry King, she told him she'd been a keynote speaker in many different kinds of places from age 13 on. Although once she became famous admirers often pointed to her many years of experience in broadcasting as a part of preparation for film work, her entire life actually prepared her for that. So many elements came together ultimately in her career. Her religious fervor in childhood, however, was a mixed blessing, because the hostility of other youngsters to her talents earned her the nicknames "The Preacher" and "Miss Jesus." A more hurtful name that other children bestowed on her was "the sack girl," because her grandmother made some of her overalls from potato sacks. During the early period that she lived with her mother, Vernita, she became known in Milwaukee as "Little Speaker" because of her pious zeal. Not only did she recite sermons and biblical passages, but,

by age seven, she was declaiming, with full gestures, inspirational poems such as William Ernest Henley's "Invictus" without understanding
a word of any of them.

On the Lee farm, Oprah was lonely, isolated, and friendless. One of
her cousins, Alice Cooper, from the same small town, has told of the
solitude children felt in those days because the farms were so far from
each other that relatives found it difficult to visit back and forth. Oprah
envied children who had easier lives, particularly white children, whose
families owned television sets and washing machines; children who had
store-bought clothing and who could go to movies; and children who
were not punished for every little misdeed, knowing or unknowing.
Even though the whippings she endured were common in her nar-
row world and time, she has observed that white children rarely were
beaten; however, she has remarked, if white girls had to be punished,
they got "spanked," whereas black children got "whupped." Without
indoor plumbing, the wash tub was also used for bathing, which took
place once a week, on Saturdays, in preparation for the Sabbath. Every
garment the family wore was made at home, and shoes were worn exclusively for Sunday churchgoing. The rest of the time, the child went
barefoot. Food consisted of what they grew or raised on the farm, with
Grandmother Hattie Mae selling eggs to earn some cash, as did many
a poor Southern farm woman for decades, if not centuries. Yet, despite
the fact that some writers have called Oprah's life one of extreme or
grinding poverty, because her grandmother owned a farm, she was able
to feed and clothe her family, and they never went hungry. (One of
Oprah's relatives claims that Oprah had exaggerated the matter.)

Visitors to Grandmother Lee's house were adults who expected children to be not only well behaved but silent as well. As a result, Oprah's
sole companions were the pigs she helped take care of. Away from the
little house, she could read, talk, and tell stories to them; her restrictive
grandmother and her friends believed that Oprah talked too much. Although they praised the child's articulateness and cleverness in church
activities, they did not extend that kind of openness to other places. It
is no wonder that, by the time she was six, she looked forward to living
with her mother in Milwaukee.

Her expectations of a different kind of existence were fulfilled, but
not in the ways she anticipated. Only in adulthood did she recognize

how fortunate she had been to live with her grandmother for the first six years of her life; only then could she sort out the love that existed beneath her fear. It took maturity for Oprah to understand that her grandmother had shaped her character, that it was Grandmother Lee who taught her to be strong, to be spiritual, a believer in God. That spiritual quality has never left her, and, during agonizing national times such as the days after September 11, 2001, she shared that spirituality by offering public prayers on her television programs. She developed not only the devotional part of her character from her grandmother but also her ability to reason and gain her sense of self that was shaken but never lost; the knowledge that she had a place in the world; and, with her later success, a feeling of obligation to help others.

Oprah has said she expects to be spiritual in the ways her grandmother was, to be someone who fits into the amen corner. Oprah's mother, Vernita, seems to have lacked the qualities of her own mother that Oprah admires and cherishes. In fact, Oprah's stepmother, Zelma, who died in 1996, enforced the strict rules and discipline that made her resemble Grandmother Lee more than Vernita did.

Vernita had no room in her apartment for another person, so six-year-old Oprah had to sleep in the foyer. Vernita was a poor woman who lived on a combination of welfare money and earnings as a maid who cleaned houses, although she denies it nowadays. In retrospect, she doesn't appear to be someone who could or would take on the burden of raising another child. While Oprah lived on the Mississippi farm, a second illegitimate daughter had been born to Vernita, who also had a third illegitimate child when Oprah was about nine years old. In Vernita's household, Oprah felt unloved and unwanted, a burden and an outcast, inferior to a half-sister she thought prettier because her skin was lighter. In Vernita's home, the younger girl was always praised for her looks, whereas Oprah, the more clever one, was never complimented for her intelligence. The owner of the house in which they lived, a Mrs. Miller, preferred the younger child to Oprah, who was convinced it was because the younger girl was light-skinned.

Even though Oprah credits her grandmother for her spiritual inspiration and introduction to public speaking when she was only a little girl, Vernita told an interviewer that she "likes to think" that she was the person responsible for Oprah's "love of God and . . . talent for public speaking." In the same interview, Vernita Lee's memories of herself when Oprah lived with her bear no resemblance to those of Oprah, nor of the writers who have interviewed the family. The youngest of seven children, after she left her baby with Hattie Mae, Vernita chose Milwaukee over Chicago, where her brothers had settled. In reminiscences about her life, Vernita has spoken of having been a salesperson at a clothing store when her children were young and later a kitchen worker and then a supervisor in a Milwaukee hospital. As she describes her struggles, she tells of taking classes at a local community college, of having to pay $100 per month to rent a three-bedroom apartment, and of a life that involved no partying, no hanging around the streets, but one "mostly of work and going to church." Today, she saves copies of O magazine because she thinks they might someday be important, but she also has been annoyed by people who would refer to her as Oprah's mother.[2]

From an early age, like many African Americans, Oprah has been conscious of color—not only in terms of race but of what differences in color mean in people's lives. When she was a small girl, she envied white children for what she perceived as their easier and more pampered existence. It also seemed to her that white children were more beautiful than she was; she envied not just skin color but also noses, lips, and hair. Oprah's longings were neither unique nor limited to blacks. Mexican American writer and television critic Richard Rodriguez has written of "wanting to be white: that is to the extent of wanting to be colorless," of wanting to have the feeling of "complete freedom of movement." Being white in America for Rodriguez, for Oprah, and for other minorities of color meant being free of color. In time, Rodriguez writes, he achieved self-assurance.[3] The same is true of Oprah, who believes today that all things are possible.

As Oprah grew up, her color awareness was not limited to observations about whites. She became conscious, particularly in the all-black college she attended, of subtle and unsubtle patterns among those who had varying shades of blackness. She has said she picked one black college over another, even though she didn't want to be at a school with a student population composed entirely of black students. Never one to accept the idea of black power—particularly the uncompromising form practiced in the 1970s, when militancy was common—she felt out of

place in an atmosphere that was frequently hostile. But aside from the
political aspects, the color issue troubled her deeply. The cultural history
of race in the United States has revealed that favoritism of many kinds
had always been shown to the lighter-skinned person of color. During
the time of slavery, light-skinned men and women were more likely to
become house servants with easier lives than those with darker skin,
who were put to work as field hands. As a dark-skinned African American who had some experience of prejudice once she left Mississippi,
Oprah has been outspoken on many occasions in her views of racial
snobbery that exists even among blacks.

When she got into college, Oprah felt cynical, if not bitter, about the
kinds of color discrimination practiced not only on the outside but also
within the black community. It was a type of racism she claims she
never experienced as a little girl in Kosciusko, which somehow avoided
the problems of most Southern communities—at least until the 1960s,
when segregationists fought against the new laws that had been passed.
However, during Oprah's girlhood in Milwaukee and Nashville, she
learned of color issues she'd not confronted before. Long after her college years were behind her, she continued to speak of blacks as being
"fudge brownies," the color she identifies with herself; "gingerbreads,"
black people who have the eye coloring and features of whites; and the
group many regard as the most desirable in color, the "vanilla creams,"
or black people who can pass as whites.

Oprah's undeniable interest in black history in the last two decades
has taken many forms in books, movies, and artifacts. Her preferred
books tend to focus on racial issues: slavery; segregation, both overt
and covert; violence against blacks—rape, lynching, and other forms of
murder; injustice and the legal system; and discrimination in all its varieties. Many of the novels she has chosen to read over the years are either by black writers (often women) such as Zora Neale Hurston, Alice
Walker, and Toni Morrison, for example, or they are about black characters, and some of the books have been made into films. Oprah's reading and acting interests meshed when Quincy Jones asked her in 1985
to take the role of Sofia in a movie about African Americans, Alice
Walker's *The Color Purple*, which became a controversial but financial
and popular success. The picture brought her renown, but she had no
role in the production. That would change within a few years with

Oprah's fame and wealth and the opportunities they brought. She was able to produce and act in films of her choice, and she brought shows to the stage, such as the 2005 coproduction with Jones of a musical based on *The Color Purple*. The show won or was nominated for many awards, including a Tony and a Grammy and awards from organizations such as the Outer Critics Circle, the Drama League, and Theater World.

Not all critics had universally praised the book and the play. In his review of the show, writer Richard Corliss noted that there had been something of a simplistic message: "Men bad; Women good." The play, he writes, emphasizes that point with a statement of Sofia's friend Celie: "God just another man." But he finds a different message in the second act: God is really a woman, "decent [and] caring . . . who ministers to the least of the world's children." In effect, says Carliss, that woman is Oprah.[4]

In a lengthy review, *New York Times* writer Ben Brantley found the play sumptuous as well as less harrowing and bleak than the book. His generally positive evaluation of the show drops, however, when he speaks of the too-rapid progression of the play, comparing it to the type of "inspirational fiction" written by Barbara Taylor Bradford and Danielle Steel.[5]

One novel that had haunted Oprah for a long time after reading it, Toni Morrison's *Beloved,* was a work Oprah felt she had to turn into a film because of its historic corrections about ancestry and its humanizing of slavery: living flesh-and-blood people whose days were uncertain and agonizing. Oprah played a major role in the movie, having prepared fully to capture the feelings of an 18th-century slave. Dressing as a field hand in a replica of the clothing and wearing a blindfold, she walked down a country lane to a plantation house. At another time, in order to grasp the sensations of runaway slaves, she walked through wooded areas as they did in attempts to escape. The film, which took 10 years to make, was released in 1998. However, despite Oprah's dedication to the story; her acting, money, and publicity; and famed director Jonathan Demme, it was a significant failure at the box office and was rejected by black audiences and critics, who found it too long and complex. Turning novels into films is an enterprise that fails frequently. Even with the outpouring of praise for Oprah's performance and Disney's enormous efforts to market the picture, nothing could save it. The

financial return of approximately $22.5 million was about a third of the
cost of production. The loss was more than monetary to a disheartened
Oprah, who had a tremendous emotional commitment to the work and
its author. So strong are her ties to *Beloved* that at the top of a marble stair-
case in her studios hangs a huge painting of herself from the film. In
2008, Morrison wrote another book, *A Mercy*, which was an Oprah's
Book Club selection.

Because of the interest that had been stirred by *The Color Purple*,
Oprah had high expectations for her later films, several of which preceded *Beloved*. A year after her triumph in *The Color Purple*, she followed it with another African American movie, *Native Son*. However,
that picture, based on the acclaimed autobiography of Richard Wright,
turned out to be a loser both with critics and audiences. Rita Kempley,
formerly with the *Washington Post*, reflected the critiques of others,
calling the film "morally medicinal," talky, and "preachy"; a work that
is weighed down by "a sense of its own nobility." Despite the flop, the
acting bug never left Oprah, and she has continued to perform in and
finance movies for television and theater, and she has experienced both
success and failure.

The next work she produced and starred in was a 1989–1990 television series, *The Women of Brewster Place*. The series was dropped when
a poll showed audience disinterest. Portrayal of black men was and is
a sensitive topic. Although few women viewers considered the work
judgmental, the National Association for the Advancement of Colored People called the program's portrayal of black men antagonistic.
Whereas white writers were critical of the garrulousness of the characters, some African American columnists found the programs offensive,
reflecting views reminiscent of those that had been voiced with the
showing of Oprah's first movie. Dorothy Gilliam, who was then a staff
writer for the *Washington Post*, damned the series as "one of the most
stereotype-ridden polemics against black men," and she angrily found
the hackneyed portraits of the women comparable to the thinking of
extreme racists.[6]

Nevertheless, when the movie *Waiting to Exhale* was released in January 1996, Gilliam liked it so much she saw it twice. However, Gregory
Kane, writing for Baltimore's *Sun Sentinel*, found it as offensive as Gilliam
had the Brewster Place series. His hostile column depicted Oprah as

the "I used cocaine but the man made me do it" host on her program featuring a group of women stars from the movie, and in bristling language speaks of her and her guests as "cackl[ing] about how black men do black women wrong in relationships."[7]

Nothing was controversial in *Listen Up: The Lives of Quincy Jones*, a movie about Oprah's dear friend, another film she produced in 1997. Jones is one of the most famous musical figures in the United States. In addition to being a trumpeter, he has done almost everything in the musical world one might think of. He is a composer, conductor, arranger, and record producer. Nominated for a huge number of Grammy Awards, he has received 27 of them, including the Grammy Legend Award. One of his most famous productions was the charity song "We Are the World," which he also conducted. Among the most notable forms of recognition, he was awarded the prestigious French Legion of Honor Medal; inducted into the California Hall of Fame, and awarded honorary doctorate degrees from Princeton University and Washington University. His is a career of firsts, often in the category of "first African American. . . ." He is the founder of the Quincy Jones Listen Up Foundation, a charity that introduces young people to music, other forms of culture, and technology. There is also a building program through which 100 homes were built in South Africa and an intercultural exchange program between underprivileged girls and boys from South Africa and Los Angeles. With support from the World Bank, some United Nations agencies, and others, in 2004, Jones established a project, We Are the Future, to help poor children in troubled areas. An endowed chair for African American music in Harvard University's African and African American studies made Jones professor of African American music. Like his friend Oprah, Jones is someone who uses his celebrity to help children. Before Oprah began a search for her roots with Henry Louis Gates, friend to both Oprah and Jones, Jones led the way. A search of Jones's roots revealed that he is related to both George Washington and Senator John McCain (but Jones supported Hillary Clinton in the 2008 primaries).

Although the movie *Before Women Had Wings*—which Oprah's Harpo Productions made for the ABC network in 1997—was one of her more successful film ventures, some movie critics found it to be too much of a tearjerker. (Similar criticism has been leveled about the choices for her highly successful book club.) A year later, as one of Harpo Productions, she made a four-hour miniseries called *The Wedding*, starring Halle Berry, who later would win an Oscar at the 2002 Academy Awards.

Dorothy West, who died in 1998, was the author of the novel *The Wedding,* a work inspired by the wedding of her niece, Abigail McGrath. McGrath lives in the house next door to the one West had owned, and she has humorous reminiscences of her aunt. Apparently, West felt a kinship to Oprah, because she had her number on speed dial and didn't hesitate to use it, as she did one day to complain to Oprah that someone had parked illegally in front of her house. Unfortunately, we don't know what Oprah's response was.

Although there is a street named Dorothy West Avenue in Oak Bluffs (also known as the Highlands) on Martha's Vineyard (Massachusetts), West's cottage is on Myrtle Street. In West's youth, the poet Langston Hughes referred to her as "the Kid," because she was the youngest member of the Harlem Renaissance, a famous group of writers. West was also the last survivor of the group. In the 1930s, during the presidency of Franklin Roosevelt, she had worked for the Works Progress Administration Federal Writers' Project. After the 1948 publication of her first book, *The Living Is Easy,* almost 40 years passed before she wrote a second one. *The Wedding* was edited by Jackie Kennedy in 1995 when West was 88. Despite the fact that West wrote only two books, she has played such an important role in literary history that her house has been dedicated as a site on the African American Heritage Trail of Martha's Vineyard.

Another much-loved book of Oprah's, *Their Eyes Were Watching God,* was made into a film in 2005. Even though the author, Zora Neale Hurston, died when Oprah was just six, for her and others, the book became part of the must-read novels of contemporary literature. Only after Hurston's death did national recognition come to her work. Turning the book into a movie became an important project when Oprah sought more public awareness of Hurston, who had died in poverty, almost forgotten. Like many of Oprah's choices of more recent novels, it focuses on a woman who rebels against societal rules to live the life she chooses. Once again, Oprah selected Halle Berry to play the lead.

Oprah's most popular television movie, also under the label Oprah Winfrey Presents, was made in 1999 from Mitch Albom's phenomenally successful book *Tuesdays with Morrie*. The film drew 22.5 million viewers, unmatched in numbers by any other television show for the entire week. The leading television critic for the *Washington Post*, Tom Shales, who doesn't offer praise lightly, describes Oprah as someone who "doesn't mess around . . . is no slouch at presenting" or "at anything [else]" she undertakes. Furthermore, as others have done, he jokes that she is "not even a slouch at slouching."

Another first for Oprah was her role in an animated film titled *The Princess and the Frog*, a cartoon from Pixar Studios and Walt Disney. Although she isn't seen, she is the voice of the character Eudora, the mother of the main character, Princess Tiana.

Oprah's absorption in the historic life of slaves has led her, like a number of other famous and well-to-do African Americans, such as writer and professor Henry Louis Gates, Jr., to collecting artifacts of their past. Her purchases of bills of sale from the days of slave auctions made the news about the time that Oprah's production failure of *Beloved* was reported. Clearly, Oprah has not been the first person to discuss the favored treatment of light- and lighter-skinned Americans. History and literature have recorded the situation. Essays, plays, novels, and poetry have documented the stories of lives shattered by the issues of race. William Faulkner's *Absalom, Absalom!*, perhaps the greatest American novel to record the tragedies of race in the poetic, moving, and terrifying description of the destruction of a dynasty, creates a symbolic way to understand the tragedy of a nation.

Another work about that same period was written in 2008 by historian and Harvard University president Drew Gilpin Faust. *This Republic of Suffering*, a comprehensive account of the Civil War, includes explicit descriptions of the harsh treatment of black soldiers who fought on both the Union and Confederate sides. Even in death, they were treated as lesser beings, in unmarked graves, unworthy of care or recognition. Other historians have described the work as "wise, informed, [and] troubling," a book that goes beyond statistics, revealing "what it was to live amid such loss and pain."

Oprah's interest in the life of slaves and her search for her own roots in the writings from the troubled era of earlier centuries have become part of her persona. Secretary of state in the Bush administration, Condoleezza Rice, wrote a brief essay about Oprah for *Time* magazine in 2007 in which she identifies Oprah's life as the story of America: the Southern girl who lived in poverty, whose childhood years were spent in a home that had neither electricity nor running water; a girl who later used her education, her work, and her fortune to better the lives of many people in her own country and abroad.

Oprah, in matters of family, color, and other issues, came to understand and forgive much that embittered her in earlier years. Time helped to distance her from bitterness toward Vernita, whom she saw as an angry, hostile parent, a woman with no love to spare for Oprah. The problems Vernita faced as a single mother bringing up three illegitimate children on a minimal income, in tiny quarters, seem overwhelming to any onlooker. Yet she took much pride in her appearance, and even during the periods when the family was on welfare, she saw to it that the children, like herself, were nicely dressed. Although some black women were able to improve their lives before the civil rights movement of the 1960s, Vernita, with no training or education, could expect nothing more or better than she had, and survival was a constant struggle.

Oprah's success as an entertainer and her generosity years later improved Vernita's life. The less-favored child has given money to her siblings and her mother and has given homes to her mother, sister, and father. Vernita Lee has come a long way since her days as a domestic worker. She now lives in a luxury high-rise apartment, paid for by her daughter. Oprah's father, by far the better parent, asked for almost nothing. Oprah has recounted in interviews that her half-sister, Patricia Lloyd, was never satisfied by anything Oprah gave her and that she betrayed Oprah's intimate secrets to the newspapers and contradicted much that Oprah had previously said. It took several years for Oprah to forgive her. They were never close, and Oprah has said that she feels little affection or obligation to any other family member except her father, Vernon Winfrey. Yet she continued to give money to the family. After failed attempts to get Jeffrey, her brother, to change his life and take responsibility for his actions, Oprah refused to help him financially—although without his knowing it, she provided extra money for him through Vernita. Filled with envy and bitterness, he accused her of ignoring him while helping an associate of hers, Billy Rizzo, who was dying from AIDS, the same illness from which Jeffrey died at age 29

in January 1989. Like Jeffrey, Patricia had a drug addiction, and her cocaine habit killed her at the age of 43 in February 2003.

Some of Oprah's anger toward family members after she'd achieved
fame and fortune resulted from the expectations of relatives and their
friends that she would help them monetarily, combined with the fact
that they, like her sister and brother, did nothing to help themselves.
Relatives still expect or ask for gifts of various kinds. One relative, however, praises her aunt Oprah for setting an example.

The woman, a niece of Oprah's who lives in Milwaukee, was interviewed by a reporter about the business she and her husband run and
the volunteer work they do for the program Discovering Our Destiny.
The function of the group is to teach leadership skills to African American girls. In talking about herself and her famous aunt, Alisha Hayes
tells a story of earlier years when she'd asked Oprah for a new car; after
her aunt refused, the young woman accepted the idea that she would
have to provide it for herself. Oprah has repeatedly stressed the importance of self-help and responsibility, and, although she has said little
about her siblings' lack of initiative for changing their lives, she has
little pity for such weakness. Oprah has been generous to her nieces in
many ways. To give them strong educational and social backgrounds,
she sent them to prestigious (and predominantly white) schools.

Some biographers have claimed that Oprah holds back nothing
about her life, but writer Barbara Grizzutti Harrison notes that Oprah
does skirt issues having to do with her family. Even though the press reports whatever news there is about her parents, Oprah is reticent about
their doings.[8]

The ghetto world of her mother offered few examples of betterment.
Although Vernita had started out as a boarder and eventually had a two-
bedroom apartment, her three children shared one of the bedrooms.
Thus, the living conditions were much worse for Oprah than they had
been on Grandmother Lee's farm. Vernita's hopes for marriages brought
disappointments in her personal life that were and are not uncommon,
something Oprah learned to understand but which were beyond her
comprehension when she was a child. Men came and went, even though
Vernita had a relationship for several years with the man who fathered
her son. She wanted and expected her children to follow rules about
sexual behavior, yet she was no exemplar of what she advocated.

Experience in the larger world brought the mature Oprah into contact with many poor young black women whose lives resemble Vernita's. If Oprah had remained with her mother, the direction of her own life might well have been similar to Vernita's. For a time, it seemed as though her future would be as bleak as that of many young ghetto black girls and women. Oprah's huge success and wealth opened doors for Vernita that she never could have achieved on her own.

Vernita has moved into a different world as a result of her daughter's help. Her elegant apartment overlooks a lake in Milwaukee. Because of Oprah's fame and fortune, Vernita's life resembles that of many a rich person. Merchants report that she is a woman with numerous social engagements and a full calendar. She is on a preferred-client lists in some shops and gets special treatment such as private showings, early notices of events and sales in certain high-end shops, and delivery service. However, Vernita has run up debts that have led to embarrassing newspaper accounts of lawsuits. One elegant shop that sells designer clothing sued her for nonpayment of a large bill. Lee first told the managers she didn't believe she owed any money, then blamed them for advancing her credit, and later brought suit against the company. The stories continued to run. An account in the entertainment section of the Milwaukee *Journal Sentinel* in September 2008 led a story with the heading, "Oprah's mom is accused of being a deadbeat." After many months of that type of publicity, Oprah settled her mother's debt. Although Oprah continues to support her mother and is concerned about her welfare, their relationship is far from close.

When Oprah was eight and had reached the end of her first term in the Milwaukee schools, Vernita, who was struggling financially, sent her to her father and stepmother in Nashville, to an environment completely opposite from the one Oprah had been living in. Her father, an industrious, hardworking man with a regular income, owned (and still does own) a barber shop and a small adjacent grocery store. The grocery store was where Oprah first had a job, though it was a job she has said she despised. An upstanding person, Vernon Winfrey later in life became a member of the city council. By any measurement, he could provide a better milieu than Vernita could for their daughter. The Winfreys, Zelma and Vernon, at that time, had a home in an established black, middle-class community, totally different from the poor, rundown

Milwaukee area where Vernita lived. Today, Vernon and his second wife, Barbara, own a home in a beautiful Nashville suburb. Because Vernon and Zelma had no children of their own, they wanted to raise Oprah themselves. Strongly religious, Vernon Winfrey was a deacon and was very active in his church, Faith United, and he saw to it, as Grandmother Lee had, that Oprah attended all services and youth-oriented activities. The Winfrey home was rigorously run, a place where learning for a child was central, and Zelma, known as a strict disciplinarian, required Oprah to read a certain number of books on a regular basis, write, learn math, and develop a strong vocabulary.

After Zelma died, Vernon remained a widower for several years until he met the woman who became his second wife. Barbara Winfrey was a 59-year-old retired educator, the oldest child in a family of eight, as well as the first of the family to graduate from college. Her life story is the kind of achievement that Oprah believes is possible for girls who aim high. Born to a father who had only a third-grade education but who brought books home and a mother who left school after the eighth grade yet tried to discourage her daughter from pursuing an education, Barbara was determined to find a way to go to school. She did cafeteria work, washed dishes, and served food "so she could get lunch every day." In college she was a waitress, a cashier, a unit clerk in a hospital, and the first black secretary for an insurance company.

Barbara Winfrey has degrees in business education, a master of science degree in psychology, a master of arts degree in education, and a doctorate in administration. As poor as she was, it took 10 years of determination for her to earn her first degree. When she received her second master's degree, she began to teach at an inner-city school in Tennessee; her last 6 of more than 31 working years were spent as an administrator in a high school. She retired on the sixth anniversary of her marriage to Oprah's father, whom she had met because of his generosity to her students—that is, troubled teens. Much impressed by his work as local council member and his community involvement, Barbara was the person who lobbied to have Vernon Winfrey Avenue named in his honor. Even though Barbara is retired, Vernon Winfrey has no plans to do so himself. Nonetheless, his wife says that he is now willing to take "advantage of the opportunities that his daughter" has given him, that his life is no longer exclusively the barber shop. However, she also plans to get involved in some way in furthering education for others. In 2007, it was reported that the Winfreys were working on having a retail and residential development built not far from Vernon's barber shop in Nashville.

When Oprah first went to live with Vernon and Zelma, they sent her to East Wharton Elementary School in Nashville. Encouraged by a fourth-grade teacher named Mrs. Duncan, whom she still remembers with deep affection, the child flourished. Over the years, Oprah has spoken of how Duncan inspired her so much that for a time she wanted to become a teacher also. In middle age, Oprah achieved that particular ambition, teaching a graduate credit course called The Dynamics of Leadership with her boyfriend, Stedman Graham, at Northwestern University's J.L. Kellogg School of Management. In 2001, an undergraduate course about Oprah was offered. Its description in the catalogue refers to its subject matter as "Oprah the Tycoon." This was a graduate history course of one semester offered at the Urbana-Champaign campus of the University of Illinois.

The memory of her early teacher always had a favored place in Oprah's heart. Because of Duncan, Oprah has said that she believes strongly in the influence of teachers on the lives of children. No doubt, people like Duncan were an unconscious part of Oprah's decision in later years to play an active role in providing schools for poor but clever girls. However, despite Duncan's affection for Oprah, the other children in her class were hostile, much as the children had been when she lived with her grandmother because she preached to them. They disliked her and thought she was crazy. Nevertheless, influenced by strong faith and the moral atmosphere of Vernon Winfrey's home, Oprah decided she'd become a missionary when she grew up, and she even collected money for the poor of Costa Rica. Although she did not become a missionary, the desire to help others became part of her ethical fiber.

All of the future promise of the Winfrey household seemed to dissipate for Oprah when she was nine; in the summer of 1963, Oprah's mother, expecting to be married and hoping to have a real family life, insisted on her return to Wisconsin. Vernon Winfrey wasn't happy about having his daughter go back to the environment of Vernita's household. Oprah experienced regression in the overcrowded, unsupervised, undisciplined life she'd led before, only worse. She soon became the frequent object of sexual abuse. After being raped by a cousin at an uncle's house when she was nine, over the next five years she experienced molestation that she has described as unending and persistent until she went to live again in her father's home. She was abused by numerous men, among them other relatives and her mother's boyfriends. When she was first raped by her cousin, she says, she didn't understand what had happened, particularly when the cousin convinced her not to tell by bribing her with an ice cream cone and a trip to the local zoo.

Although she kept the violations a "big, looming, dark secret" for more than 12 years, Oprah has said that she always believed that her mother knew about them and had failed to protect her. Also, like many rape victims and abused children, she blamed herself for the terrible things that had happened to her, and she maintained her silence. She has said she thought of herself as a bad girl, and only when she reached her 30s and 40s did she give up the belief that the sexual abuses had been her fault. When, at the age of 24, she finally told her mother and other members of the family about the abuse, nobody would accept what she said. Her father also strongly denied her statement that a brother of his had been one of the perpetrators.

Her mother's refusal to discuss the matter was so traumatic that Oprah never brought it up again with her. Nevertheless, the matter of her abuse became a public confession years later for Oprah on her television program when a woman, Trudy Chase, who appeared on the show, spoke of the suffering she had experienced as a child as a result of sexual abuse. The identification for Oprah was so intense that all her efforts at concealment over the years slipped away in the shared moments of suffering with her guest. But she says that it has taken her a very long time to understand the anger and rebellion that came about from the destructive assaults she suffered. She needed and wanted affection that she couldn't get at home from her mother and siblings, and her feelings made her vulnerable to sexual predators. This pattern would repeat itself even after many years, something other women in similar circumstances have endured.

Almost three decades after the abuse first occurred, when Oprah had become an internationally famous entertainer on television and in film, she chose to use her celebrity as a means of speaking out against the terrors of child abuse and the secrecy that surrounds it. In 1992, she introduced a documentary titled *Scared Silent*, describing her harsh child-hood experiences of rape and molestation by male relatives, among them an uncle, and family friends. Urging both children and adults to watch the documentary, to talk about the issues, and to seek help, she appeared on a number of morning television programs, including the *Today Show*, *This Morning*, and *Good Morning America*. Abuse, she stressed, on those programs and elsewhere, is not limited to any one class, race, or economic level.

Her concern for other problems in the lives of children was expanded professionally the following year, 1993, in several ways. Her distress about the tragic results to children from the availability of handguns became the source of several child alert programs. *There Are No Children Here* is a combination fiction and documentary, referred to as "a true-life drama." In the picture, Oprah plays a black everywoman. Although the film specifically focuses on blacks, when Oprah uses the term *everywoman* to define herself, in life, as she presents her talk show and speaks with interviewees, she does not limit her scope to one race or color. She says that she believes a great many of her experiences to be the same as those of *every woman*. In the film, her role is that of an African American mother attempting, in the midst of dire poverty and social ills, to raise her family and keep them together. The family, in addition to the central figure of the mother, consists of a grandmother played by Oprah's friend Maya Angelou, an undependable husband/father, and three sons: one already lost to the prison system, one "in the undecided column," and the youngest, for whom there is still hope. The setting was the Henry Horner public housing project in Chicago, a place that had caught Oprah's attention for a long period of time as she drove past it on her way to work.

Talking about her experience of filming the project, Oprah said that she gained knowledge and insight into not only people's needs but also the longings and dreams for their lives that everyone harbors; she came to understand that everyone goes through some basic human circumstances. Living in a housing project doesn't alter such emotions as joy, sorrow, and disappointment. But poverty and deprivation can shape existence. Over the years, as her income grew, she attempted to help children with financial assistance and motivation. Her philosophy of personal responsibility and self-help, as well as her belief in the vital role of education, is played out in practical ways again and again in all kinds of situations: in talks, interviews, on her television show, and in *O, The Oprah Magazine*, which she started in 2000 with the partnership of the Hearst Corporation, she emphasizes the possibility of change. She once wanted to keep most experiences private, but now she appears more open—although some interviewers have said that she is carefully selective. But Oprah herself asserts that sharing the truth with others is freeing and uplifting. No one should allow the past to define him or her, and she points to her own life as validation of that view.

Her early years taught her much of this philosophy, even though she could not have had any idea of the direction her life would take. In a lengthy interview she gave to *Newsweek* reporter Lynette Clemetson, she insists that the efforts and rewards of her life were never calculated.[9] But she has also said that all the different experiences of her childhood and youth have given her greater understanding of the problems others must deal with. When she lived with her mother for the second time, despite finding herself in more and more emotional and physical trouble, she did very well at the Lincoln Middle School, located in the poor inner city of Milwaukee. Clever and talented, a good student as well as an ardent reader even then, Oprah was able, with help from a teacher, to change to Nicolet, a newly integrated Milwaukee high school. Because she lived 20 miles from the school, she had to take three buses to get there, often riding with her mother and the other maids on their way to work.

Each trip brought a change of landscape, taking her from the dilapidated, rundown area that was her home to a neighborhood of houses surrounded by greenery, lawns, trees, and flowers. It was an entrance into another world, and she was an outsider, a penniless black child, spending days with rich white children who often invited her to their homes after school. She longed for everything these girls had: normal families, elegant clothing, spending money, pets. In their houses, the children would introduce her to their black maids as if all black people should know each other, and they made the same assumption about Oprah's supposed familiarity with black entertainers. For Oprah, these memories linger. With a certain wry humor on her television show, she points out that some white people imagine many untrue things about blacks.

The year that Oprah attended Nicolet High is also a time that will long be remembered in history. In 1968, both Martin Luther King, Jr., and Robert Kennedy were assassinated. From the period of Oprah's birth through the decade of the 1960s, upheaval was prevalent. The year she was born, 1954, the U.S. Supreme Court ruled that segregation in public schools was unconstitutional, although Mississippi did not integrate its public schools until 1964. Violence was part of life in Mississippi, an extremism that "entered the national awareness in the summer of 1955," the year after Oprah's birth. That summer in Mississippi, white men murdered a 14-year-old black boy named Emmett Till, who allegedly had whistled at a white woman.

Till's murder became civil rights legend, along with the refusal by Rosa Parks, a poor seamstress in Montgomery, Alabama, to give up her seat on a bus to a white person. (In an article about the last of the Pullman porters, Jennifer Lee, a writer for the *New York Times*, told of an action generally not noted in stories about Parks: it was a Pullman porter, E. D. Nixon, who'd chosen Parks to take the steps for what became the Montgomery bus boycott. Nixon also recruited the young minister, Martin Luther King, Jr., as the leader of the protest.[10] Parks's behavior landed her in jail, an act that brought about the Montgomery boycott of bus transportation and led to more legal changes.) Parks's name has long been associated with the Supreme Court's ruling against segregation in transportation. At the time of the incident, however, she was fined for violating the law. A protest followed, when black people in Montgomery boycotted buses for more than a year. Dr. Martin Luther King, Jr., then, a 26-year-old new pastor at a church in Montgomery, later wrote in one of his books that the arrest of Parks was the "precipitating factor" in the protest that followed her arrest.[11]

Historians note that Parks's actions made her a founding symbol of the civil rights movement. Though Parks had been a very private woman, she became active in helping to bring about change even to the end of her life. Memorably, Reverend Jesse Jackson said of her: "She sat down in order that we might stand up. . . . her imprisonment opened the doors for our long journey to freedom."[12] Throughout the years, many people paid homage to Parks, as did Oprah when she included the frail, elderly woman as an honored guest at a screening of *Beloved,* held at Marianne Williamson's Unity Church.

Oprah Winfrey takes the stage to speak during the groundbreaking ceremony for the Martin Luther King, Jr., Memorial on the National Mall in Washington, DC, on November 13, 2006. Former President Bill Clinton applauds in the background. (AP Photo/Lawrence Jackson)

Parks was not the first black woman who attempted to alter U.S. laws and bring about civil rights. But her fame has grown over the years. A forerunner of Parks was Ida B. Wells, born a slave in 1862, in Oprah's home state of Mississippi. Like the later Parks, Wells refused to be segregated. While aboard a train, she was told to exchange her seat in a women's railroad car for a seat in a car set aside for black people. When she would not comply, she was removed from the train. Wells brought and won a suit against the railroad, but the decision was later reversed by the Supreme Court of Tennessee. Her win was surprising even in the post–Civil War South, but the reversal was not. Undaunted by defeat, Wells spent much of her life trying, usually unsuccessfully, to improve the lot of black people. After becoming a part owner and writer for a Memphis newspaper, she was determined to leave the South after the newspaper office was destroyed by white men in retaliation for her anti-lynching columns. Alienated from the South but not from the cause of civil rights, she moved to Chicago, where she founded the first African American civic group for women and became the first president of the Negro Fellowship League and chairman of the Equal Rights League of Chicago. Her greatest and most lasting accomplishment came in 1909, when she helped found the oldest and probably the best-known national civil rights organization in the United States—the one that eventually became the National Association for the Advancement of Colored people. It took almost a century for a biography of Wells to be written, but in the 21st century Paula J. Giddings wrote about her in *Ida: A Sword Against Lions; Ida B. Wells and the Campaign against Lynching.*

Oprah is captivated by the history and powerful heritage left by a few black women. Former PBS reporter Charlayne Hunter-Gault was the first African American woman—along with Hamilton Holmes, also an African American student—to be admitted to the University of Georgia. The year was 1961: 40 years later, the academic building where the two registered was renamed after both of them, and, in 2005, the Myers Hall, in which that first African American woman student had been housed, had a memorial dedicated to her. Hunter-Gault today is the CNN bureau chief for South Africa. The year Oprah reached the age of six (1962) and moved from Mississippi to Milwaukee was the historic time that another black student, James Meredith, also from Kosciusko (as was Oprah), had to be enrolled by force at the University of Mississippi in Oxford.

Of course, Oprah holds no individual knowledge of any of the political events that happened during the early years of her childhood or half a century before her birth, and she was only a small child when the first civil rights bills for blacks since Reconstruction in the 19th century were passed. For a number of years, unrest was prevalent with sit-ins, riots, civil rights marches, and even murders that led to the frequent calling up of federal troops. This period of momentous changes occurred during Oprah's adolescence, and she was more concerned with her familiar world than the political situation around her.

It isn't surprising that Oprah, who was not even a teenager in the 1960s, had no concern about politics in her home state and elsewhere. In adulthood, she has stated that she is neither someone to carry a banner with a message or declaration nor dress like a woman from Africa. She has her own original concept of ways to change society, change that is central to her belief in individual responsibility. For many years, Oprah maintained a neutral stance about politics. Her one and only foray into the political arena has been for the Democrat candidate for president, Barack Obama.

Oprah's early home, Mississippi, has a history of electing Democratic governors and Republican senators. Every governor since 1874, except for two, has been a Democrat, but state senators have been Republicans: The first black mayor of Fayette since Reconstruction, Charles Evers, was elected in 1969.

Oprah has attempted to remain neutral about politics on her television show. She has interviewed Democratic and Republican presidents and their first ladies and has appeared with them on occasions that involved matters of national interest. One exception to her usual stance came when she invited her friends Maria Shriver and Arnold Schwarzenegger, then a candidate for governor in California, to join her on a television program. Her long and close friendship with Shriver obviously had more to do with her assistance to the campaign than a desire to see a Republican elected as governor of California.

Nevertheless, she continues to be independent enough to turn down requests to appear with heads of state. In 2002, she refused an invitation from President George W. Bush to join a group of officials on a trip to tour Afghanistan schools; Oprah responded that she was too much involved with earlier commitments. That unguarded statement provided media with the chance for some Oprah bashing by people who regarded her response as a political snub of the administration. Even though she is very much a feminist without labeling herself as such, she did not choose to support the first woman candidate for the presidency, Hillary Clinton. Her views and actions supported the person she believed could more readily bring about changes in the United States.

Throughout her adult years, Oprah's concern has not been for political movements but for the rights of all women everywhere, as well as other individuals whose lives she celebrates. Furthermore, apart from politics, she has shown a lifelong desire to help those in need and those who are overlooked or discriminated against. Part of her outlook mirrors activist Jesse Jackson's: excellence is the best barrier to both sexism and racism. Responsibility for our lives belongs to each of us; furthermore, both Jackson and Oprah have said that the path to freedom is through education. Above all else, education alters everything, and Oprah is passionate about that. With heartfelt admiration for Oprah, Jackson has spoken of the enormity of her contribution in transforming the social structure, an observation echoed hyperbolically in a *Vanity Fair* magazine article characterizing her influence as greater than almost anyone on the planet except for the Pope. Other publications describe her as one of the 20th century's most influential people.

Jesse Jackson describes Oprah in the same way she depicts her cherished friend Quincy Jones—as a person who lights up the dark places. Year after year, in addition to categorizing her as a prominent figure, polls have listed her as one of the most admired women in the United States, along with first ladies, a former first lady and senator (Hillary Rodham Clinton), and a former British prime minister (Margaret Thatcher). Oprah's style of participation in the lives of the underprivileged and African Americans, however, in the main does not resemble Jackson's. While Oprah's beneficence may be directed primarily toward blacks, it isn't closed to others. After all, most of her television audience at home and abroad, much of her staff, and many of her friends are white. Thus, when Jackson, in March 1996, protested the Academy Awards because of the lack of black nominees—only 1 black person among 166 nominees—it isn't surprising that Oprah, Whoopi Goldberg, and Quincy Jones criticized his action: Jones, incidentally, was the producer of that awards show.

Oprah's belief in individual accountability is much more pronounced in her advocacy for broader, societal changes, though the exceptions are her calls for stricter gun laws, punishment for those who commit sex crimes against children, and the need for education. This emphasis on the individual has at various times led to critics calling her conservative and capitalistic. However, her great commitment to the life-transforming value of education is neither conservative nor capitalistic, although her hands-on individualistic approach might be considered one or both. Her personal principles became evident in, for example, the 10 ongoing scholarships she established in her father's name at her alma mater, Tennessee State University, soon after she became a television star. She continues to give major sums of money to colleges and universities, large and small. She has helped to raise money for scholarships and to help with matching gifts, in recognition of the importance of her own spiritual and educational beginnings. Her extremely generous gifts of millions to the black Morehouse College makes her the school's top donor. She has been very liberal in her donations to many other schools and colleges. Some people have criticized her choices and actions in giving money to foreign countries, because she hasn't limited her educational concerns to the United States. She plays an active philanthropic role in providing funds for international schools. In fact, when she is asked about her plans for the time after she leaves her show, she mentions, among other activities, her wish to become more involved with education in Africa, something she has been doing in recent years. In building schools for girls, she has spoken of her desire to be a constructive force in the lives of those who need it. However, despite regarding herself as a nurturer, she has said again and again— most recently on one of her television shows in October 2008—that she never felt the desire for motherhood. When asked, as she frequently is, whether she ever wanted to be a mother, she answers in the negative, making the point that she never had a role model for motherhood in Vernita.

However, when she established her academy for girls in South Africa, she considered herself their mother. An admiring world forgets or doesn't know the damaged, rebellious girl she was, light years away from the exquisitely coiffed and dressed woman she became. At 14, Oprah's personal problems caught up with her. One sexual episode followed another, including an instance with her father's brother, Trent— another abusive situation she never spoke about until years later, and even then her father found the knowledge almost impossible to accept. Today, she tells girls and women that they must not keep such things to themselves, that the burden of sexual assault cannot be tolerated. She teaches that, in order to become responsible for one's own life, one has to tell the truth about an abusive situation again and again until someone listens. This lesson results from something she did not do as a child herself.

Oprah kept secret from her mother the frequent, ongoing attacks by men who came and went in their home. Vernita, finding it impossible to control her daughter, tried various avenues unsuccessfully, including an attempt to place the girl in a home for wayward children. Finally, Vernon agreed to take Oprah back to live with him and Zelma. Neither he nor Vernita knew at the time that the teenage girl was pregnant, because, like her mother 14 years earlier, she was extremely successful at concealing her condition. Only when she was in her seventh month did she tell her father the truth. Today she recognizes him as an honorable man, the person who saved her life—that is, the one who saw to it that she became more than an unwed mother. Without the influence of Vernon Winfrey throughout her adolescent years, she could not have achieved her later success. Oprah recalls his strength as he considered the choices that existed in her situation and then reached the decision to allow her to have the baby. However, two weeks after the premature birth, the infant boy died. What the 14-year-old Oprah's feelings were at the time may not be precisely what the middle-aged woman describes as an "opportunity" rather than a loss; the opportunity was a choice for her future. Yet there is no question that the path she would have had to take would bear no resemblance to the one she had been on. She freely admits she has no idea of what her life might have been or what sort of mother she would have become. There are many examples of teenagers whose futures have been defined by the boundaries of motherhood, and in 1968 a pregnant black girl of 14 would have had few prospects and little hope. Freed of the oppressions of life in Vernita's home and of teenage motherhood, Oprah began to show signs of promise, although surely nobody in those days could have predicted her later accomplishments. She has said that she remembers telling her father when she was still a youngster that one day she'd be famous. After moving in with the Winfreys once more, she had to follow their strict rules. Vernon Winfrey was uncompromising about grades, demanding she earn As. Cs, he told his daughter, were not acceptable for one who has the capacity to excel. Further, he didn't agree that she should be rewarded for achievements, even with an ice cream cone, because he simply expected her to be the best. Zelma, his wife, also required Oprah to do all the things necessary to become an outstanding student.

Surprisingly, reports that Vernon was writing a "shocking" book about Oprah's childhood, in which he described her as "disobedient" and "out of hand," seem completely at odds with Oprah's recollections, but it is likely that the sources of the stories probably conflated her earlier years at home with Vernita.

When she was about 15, Oprah began to keep a journal, and she has continued to write in it ever since then. Now when she rereads its entries from her teen years, she sees page after page filled with typical kinds of entries: problems with boys; trivial complaints about her father's dos and don'ts—the same complaints as those of most teenage girls. Nonetheless, after entering Nashville's East High School, she became very active; soon she was chosen as vice president of her class and president of the student council, drama club, and National Forensics League. Voted most popular girl in her senior year, at the same time she also was chosen for membership in the National Forensic League. In 1971, during the Nixon administration, when two students from each state and from foreign countries were chosen to attend a White House Conference on Youth, Oprah was one of Tennessee's representatives. Shortly after that, she was interviewed at a small Nashville radio station, WVOL, an event that led to her later career. The station, white-owned but black-operated and with a primarily black audience, wanted somebody to represent it in the contest of Miss Fire Prevention. Oprah was recommended by John Heidelberg, who, all these years later, still recalls how much he was impressed by both her articulateness and ease before a camera. He was the person who had interviewed her when she searched for supporters for a March of Dimes Walkathon. The Miss Fire Prevention competition was a beauty contest in which every girl except Oprah was white, and she has said, with characteristic humor, that all of the girls were redheads. Relaxed, because she was certain she had no chance at winning, but proud and delighted with her new evening gown, she answered the two test questions with her characteristic light-heartedness. First asked what she'd do with the money if she won, she told the judges she'd be a "spending fool." And when asked about her wishes for a future career, she chose something out of the ordinary for that time. She said she wanted to be a journalist in the broadcasting industry. Other contestants had given expected, typical answers, so Oprah won, becoming the first black girl to be named Miss Fire Prevention. Following her unanticipated success, she became the first Miss Black Nashville in a pageant; later, in another pageant, she was named Miss Black Tennessee; and following that, she won a trip to Hollywood, where she participated in, though she didn't win, a Miss Black America Contest. Those were only the beginning of honors that were to come her way throughout the decades.

In 1971, after graduating from high school, she went on to Tennessee State University with a scholarship from an Elks lodge where she had won a contest. She majored in speech and language arts, although she was uncertain about her future plans. Yet, a career path was opening up. The interview she'd had during her senior year in high school after she

was chosen as Miss Fire Prevention led to a job reading the news on radio station WVOL. The station, and particularly John Heidelberg, remembered Oprah's outgoing personality from that interview; just for
fun, she had read some news copy while she was at the station. She
had made a favorable impression with her voice and poise, and when
the station needed someone to read the news, they offered the job to
Oprah. Naive and somewhat unworldly, she knew little about media.
Of course, reading the news would pave the way to a future career and
international fame. She was going to turn down Heidelberg's offer, fearful the job might interfere with school work, but her father encouraged
her to take it. Although he hadn't been too enthusiastic about her
choice of a major, he was pleased by the opportunities that were coming her way. Reading the weekend news, and, later, making occasional
broadcasts during the week, she worked her way up from no pay to $100
a week, a large sum of money at the time.

Later, while in college, she was offered a more prestigious opportunity
with a larger radio station, WLAC, and, not long after that, at the age
of 19, she moved to its television channel, WLAC-TV, where she became a reporter and co-anchorperson, the first woman as well as the
first black person to hold that position. Though still reluctant about
accepting such an offer, she was persuaded to do so by William Cox, a
professor who oversaw her major courses. He pointed out that the job
was in the area of work for which she had been preparing. Furthermore,
her father, who supervised almost everything she did, agreed with Cox.
In later years, when questioned whether she'd seen herself as a token for
the job, she has made light of it; yet at another time, she also said pointedly that she was a paid token. Oprah has never shown any regrets,
surely not publicly, about accepting opportunities of that sort. The
1970s were a changing period in the United States, when doors previously closed to women and people of color were slowly opening as a
result of civil rights laws.

Oprah's world was expanding, not only with a job but also through
opportunities to do some acting in college and sing with Sweet Honey
in the Rock, an all-women's a capella group in Nashville. The group
describes itself as singing of "struggle, perseverance, and triumph," celebrating life "deeply rooted in the African American experience." Naturally, Oprah was attracted to the group, and it was quite popular with

audiences—in fact, three decades later, the group still sings in many parts of the South. But after a time, the restrictions of life at home—with her stern father's rules, which included a curfew, as well as the difficulties of meshing college studies and work—led to a life-altering decision. She left college without her degree and moved on to another job in the media, becoming a reporter and co-anchor of evening news at a Baltimore, Maryland, station. Although some books state that Oprah graduated from college in 1976, the fact is that she did not, and the situation is cloudy. One version is that she received an honorary degree years later. Another is that Tennessee State University awarded her a bachelor of arts degree in 1987. Still another is that she was asked by the university in 1987 to give the commencement address, but she refused to do it until she had finished her courses for credit and obtained her degree.

Whatever the actual facts are, she does have a degree from Tennessee State. Furthermore, Princeton University in 2002 awarded an honorary doctorate of fine arts to Oprah. At the same ceremony, another talk show host, Terry Gross, of the National Public Radio show *Fresh Air*, was granted an honorary doctor of humanities degree. Since that time, Oprah has received many more honorary degrees.

Not long after, another recognition came to Oprah when she received the sixth Marian Anderson Award. Recipients generally donate the prize of $100,000 to a favorite charity. Many who remember the opera star's soul-stirring contralto voice forget that she lived in a period when segregation kept her from many of the venues open to famous singers today. After a board's scandalous recall of an invitation to her to sing at Constitution Hall, Anderson was invited to the White House, where she became the first black singer to perform there. Because Anderson, a native of Philadelphia, broke through one of the most important barriers in Jim Crowism, her home state pays homage to her memory, for that and other significant actions. Every year the award is given to mark the importance of the arts; recipients are those who have used their talents to help better society. Although most people would probably agree that Oprah fits in that category, there are some who question the choice. An unidentified writer in *Philebrity: Philly Media, Gossip, Nightlife & Politics* puts her in a group of "those who have arguably done more harm than good, culturally speaking: *Oprah Winfrey*, anyone?" (emphasis in

Oprah Winfrey cheers with the crowd at the commencement ceremony for Howard University, a historically black college in Washington, DC, on May 12, 2007. The media mogul was awarded with an honorary doctor of humanities, prompting tears from Winfrey, before delivering a speech to the audience. (AP Photo/Jacquelyn Martin)

original). The harshness of the columnist's criticism seems to find her irredeemable. (For good measure the writer includes the names of a few other stars whose work he or she doesn't like. Among them is Oprah's close friend, Maya Angelou, whom he calls "quite possibly the worst published poet of the 20th century . . . a Living God to all who serve in Oprah's Kingdom of Lowered Expectations.")

As much as Oprah is a target for all kinds of criticism (much of it humorous and even when she is using her celebrity for admirable causes), she is also, of course, the subject of much adulation. When Philadelphia Mayor John Street, in speaking of the 2003 choice of Oprah for the Marian Anderson Award, took note of Oprah's work in many social programs as well as her generosity to schools at home and in South Africa, he also pointed to the importance of her television shows that focus on individual self-help. Oprah, said the mayor, serves as "a national mentor." Following the mayor's announcement, the next speaker was Pamela Crowley, chair of the award's board of directors and vice president for a Philadelphia bank. She called attention to the similarities in Oprah's and Marian Anderson's characters; both women, she emphasized, achieved their place in the world through their own abilities and efforts. Several years earlier, Oprah had received the Horatio Alger Award from the association that annually honors those who have triumphed over adversity with their considerable achievements. Almost everyone who mentions Oprah speaks with awe of her astonishing rise from annihilating poverty to her place on the world's stage.

Many experiences in Oprah's younger years were similar to those of other black women of her age. She recalls an event when she was chosen to participate in a black college contest in Chicago. Housed in a rundown motel in a high-crime area on the South Side, the young college participants were outraged by the conditions they found. However, in what was to become typical of the future star, Oprah disregarded the adverse circumstances, becoming one of the winners in the contest with her reading of a passage from Ntozake Shange's *For Colored Girls Who Have Contemplated Suicide When the Rainbow Is Enuf*, a play assigned in many English classes throughout the country.

Could anyone knowing her early life have imagined the heights to which she would rise: recipient of the most notable honor in broadcasting, the George Foster Peabody Individual Achievement Award and the first person to be given the Bob Hope Humanitarian Award? Decades earlier, when Oprah left Nashville to try her wings elsewhere, she was 22, young and unsophisticated in various ways, only at the beginning of the road that would eventually take her to stardom. Going from relatively small Nashville to Baltimore, the 10th-largest city in the country, was not an easy transition for a young woman. It took years for her to become the equal of the assured, self-confident person she praises in Maya Angelou's poem "Phenomenal Woman"; years to learn the secret of being herself—neither cute nor slim as a model but someone both cool and fiery, filled with the joy of life and being a woman. Starting out, she didn't do well in her new job as the anchor of the six o'clock evening news on Baltimore's station, WJZ-TV, the largest station in the city. She was ill at ease, and her unworldly background led to embarrassing gaffes. It became apparent very quickly that Oprah wasn't meant to be a newswoman. Her strength then, as now, was her rapport with people, not her ability to cover the news. Far too emotional to be a reporter, she would get carried away and react to the human aspects of all situations. Although she freely admits her lack of qualifications for journalism, years later—in 2000—she joined the ranks of magazine owners and writers when her highly successful magazine was launched.

When her career was in its infancy, though, both her reportorial mode and her appearance troubled the producers. In an attempt to alter her looks, they sent her to New York for a makeover. A special hair treatment and permanent caused most of her hair to fall out, with the result that she lost her job as well as her hair. It is a great irony that now she is regarded as one of the most elegant women in the entertainment industry. In Baltimore, however, she was not seen as a potential star. She was demoted from her evening anchor position, but a new station manager who liked Oprah's style found a slot for her with co-host Richard Sher on a morning program called *People Are Talking*. Even though the show was quite popular, Oprah didn't particularly like working with another host. Nonetheless, because she enjoyed doing a talk show, something she always has described as being as natural as breathing, she stayed with the job for several years.

Surprisingly, with the large black population of Baltimore and comfortable numbers of viewers in that city, the program had a smaller viewing audience there than it did in 12 other cities. Her program did, however, have a higher rating in Baltimore than the leading national talk show, *Donahue*, a statistic that was to help her find another job. Restless and unhappy in her personal life and tired of what she'd been doing for six years, she began to look elsewhere for work. With the help of a resume expert and an ambitious producer friend, in 1984, at the age of 30, Oprah relocated to Chicago, a city that has the third largest television market in the country and which she has referred to as a "more polished New York." She remained in Chicago for more than 25 years before moving to California.

When she first became a talk show host, the show she took over was low in the ratings. Nervous about the competition she faced, she voiced her feelings to station manager Dennis Swanson, whose response was to be herself since there was no way she could be Phil Donahue. Within months, the program she hosted, AM *Chicago,* was the most popular talk show on the air. With a starting salary of $225,000, she considered herself unbelievably rich.

Only two years after her move to Chicago, her show was syndicated, and, in a sense, a star was born—the star of *The Oprah Winfrey Show.* When the show went national in 1986, 32-year-old Oprah celebrated Thanksgiving with Vernon and Zelma Winfrey; the three of them took a triumphal trip back to Mississippi, where they revisited family and friends and old haunts from Oprah's childhood. Today, Grandmother Lee's house is gone, but the street alongside the property is known as Oprah Winfrey Road. In Kosciusko, Oprah's celebrity is as great as—or perhaps greater than—it is in other parts of the country. Nashville, somewhat later, also paid tribute to Oprah and her father's role in her life by naming the street on which Vernon Winfrey's Beauty and Barber shop is located Vernon Winfrey Avenue, an action in which his wife Barbara had a role.

The year following that vacation, in 1987, Oprah received an Emmy Award for daytime television, the first of more than 30 that would follow over the years. She eventually received a lifetime award, after which she no longer was a competitor for the Emmy. The syndication of her show was the most significant step to stardom, because it made her a national—and soon thereafter an international—figure.

Renaming the program *The Oprah Winfrey Show* was the act of the King Brothers Corporation, a company owned by two well-known distributors who had purchased the show in September 1986. Frequently referred to as "the boys," the King brothers, Roger and Michael, were white, middle-aged men, part of a family of six brothers who had inherited a struggling syndicate business from their father, Charlie King. Because Roger and Michael were super salesmen, they were able to turn the marginal business into a multimillion-dollar company that, in turn, made huge amounts of money for the television programs they represented. They became the powerhouse dealers of television programs. Although most of their clients were very successful game shows, Oprah was the star in their crown, with a show that brought in many millions for the Kings as well as for Oprah.

They soon saw to it that the program was on 137 stations nationwide. Roger, who is now deceased, was known as a high flyer and big spender and the more daring and flamboyant of the brothers. He predicted accurately that syndication would make Oprah rich. However, Oprah has said that the phenomenal success of the program came about from it being on the air at the same time throughout the country. Although the program is shown during the daytime, she considers it to be, as do some critics, a prime-time show. Always giving credit to the Kings for the major role they've played in her career, she has said that without them she wouldn't have achieved her enormous following. Roger King had been a CBS and King World Productions executive when he died of a stroke in December 2007 at the age of 63. King World Productions had merged with CBS in 2000, but Oprah owns and controls her show through Harpo. With Roger King's death, Oprah not only praised his influence on the television industry but also paid tribute to his role in her career.

Despite his extraordinary financial acumen, Roger King was a rather surprising person to have business dealings with Oprah. Yet, without the Kings, Oprah might never have achieved the exposure she has on television nor the vast sums of money she's earned. The Kings, as part of their business style, were known to woo clients with gifts and trips and lavish spending. Oprah, like the other entertainers with whom the Kings dealt, has been the recipient of some of their largesse. When does someone like Oprah become "a once colored girl"? It seems to be a natural occurrence as the woman becomes comfortable with herself and her career, as described by Patrice Gaines, former reporter for the *Washington Post* and author of *Laughing in the Dark*. Gaines was interviewed on Oprah's show about her book, whose subtitle was *From Colored Girl to Woman of Color*.

As Oprah gained fame and fortune, she developed an interest in the lives of slaves, and with that came her decision to learn about her own African heritage. She became one of the increasing numbers of black Americans to seek information about family origins. Fortunately, modern technology has provided tools to retrace much, though not all, of the history of African forebears. A modern pioneer in that research, Henry Louis Gates, Jr., for several years has promoted the heritage search for black Americans, and, through such searches, many have been learning about their African ancestry. Oprah, who wanted to trace her own roots, turned to Gates for guidance. Chairman of African and African American Studies at Harvard University, Gates is also director of

the W.E.B. Du Bois Institute of Afro-American Research. He has been
working on tracing the roots of popular celebrities, including Quincy
Jones (a close friend of Oprah's), Whoopi Goldberg, Chris Tucker, and
Oprah Winfrey. Working with him to unravel the past have been a minister, an astronaut, a neurosurgeon, and other professionals. Through
census and estate records of slaveholders, land deeds, newspapers, maps,
oral histories, inscriptions on tombstones, and now DNA technology,
the Gates group has been able to establish family trees for a considerable number of people.

The search for Oprah's roots revealed information going back to her
matrilineal ancestors in Africa, who were of the Kpelle tribe of Liberia,
on the west African coast, which also includes Guinea, Guinea-Bissau,
Sierra Leone, and the Ivory Coast. Members of the Kpelles also live in
Guinea, as well as neighboring Guerze, which is a part of the Republic
of Guinea. The Kpelle language, which is broadcast in Liberia, is part
of the southwestern branch of Mande, Niger-Congo. A further search of
Oprah's maternal ancestors revealed that her great-grandmother,
Amanda Winters, had been actively involved in education, and Oprah
was understandably delighted. Her DNA test suggests her background
is 89 percent sub-Saharan African, 8 percent Native American, and 3
percent East Asian.

More details were found about the paternal side of the family. Oprah's
great-great American grandfather, Constantine Winfrey, in the early
part of the 19th century, had been a slave for a white family called
Winfrey. Freed by his owner after the Civil War, he negotiated for some
adjacent land held by the former slaveholder. In time, Constantine
Winfrey learned to read and write and increased his holdings to 80 acres
through sales of his farm products. Concerned about the education
of black children, he had the entire building housing the Spring Hill
Colored School moved onto his land. Oprah now has the deed to the
property.

In a reminder of the harsh and troubled period in which her ancestors lived, Oprah was shown two ancient cemeteries: one, a manicured,
well-maintained site where the white Winfrey family was buried and the
other, overgrown and neglected, sunken grave sites of the blacks where
names on tombstones are indecipherable, the conditions the same as
those described in Drew Faust's *This Republic of Suffering*.

Not all black scholars—in fact, not all black Americans—are interested in pursuing the course set by Gates. Charles Johnson of the University of Washington (Seattle), who holds the title of Wilson and Pollack Professor of Excellence, stands at the opposite end of the spectrum from Gates. In the *American Scholar*,[13] Johnson has written "The End of the Black American Narrative" in which he faults Gates for scholarship based on "beliefs and prejudices" as well as distortion of facts. Believing that three decades of affirmative action have "led to the creation of a true black middle class" and that it is time to move beyond the past, he lists the professions in which black Americans have risen to the top of the ladder and mentions Oprah, "the most prominent talk show host." Objecting to the views of prominent deniers such as Louis Farrakhan, who claims that "successful people like Oprah Winfrey . . . give black Americans a false impression of progress," and Reverend Jeremiah Wright for his "paranoid and irresponsible statements" (Johnson calls them "rants"), he notes that the future is here and that all of us should follow the famous statement of Martin Luther King, Jr.: Judge people not by the color of their skin but by the content of their character.

A cover story by Matt Blai in the August 10, 2008, edition of the *New York Times Magazine* asks, "Is Obama the End of Black Politics?" Although it is not about roots but politics, Blai's article leads to an affirmative answer, one that appears to support the position of Johnson— that this generation does not see everything as revolving around race. Thus, roots, one might argue, while important, are not central nor even primary. In Blai's view, here is a reordering of black politics, a new black politics far different from the politics of the fathers. A pollster, Cornell Belcher, whom Blai interviewed, stated that the two worlds are different; the younger generation sees it not through the history of their fathers but "through post–civil rights eyes." An example of these differences, Blai points out, may be understood by the exchanges that took place between the Reverend Jesse Jackson and his son, Jesse Jackson, Jr., a young congressman from Illinois. Jackson, Jr., reminded his father of his "most famous words," which were to "Keep hope alive." Blai sees the differences between father and son as "a basic generational divide" about the meaning of black leadership. Changes over the years, Blai writes, have brought about a "newly emerging class of black politicians."

In her youth, Oprah was inspired by several people, and meeting and talking with them helped her to get her first talk show. When Oprah took on her Chicago program, Phil Donahue was the leader in the talk show business and people spoke of him as the owner of daytime television. He'd had a 29-year run, 26 of those in syndication, the longest continuous syndicated talk show in the history of television. But Oprah toppled him. Despite having learned what to do by watching tapes of his shows (in addition to those of Barbara Walters) and of being grateful to him for paving the way, Oprah's was a different kind of approach. Donahue, who is just as gracious about Oprah as she is about him, praises her ability to connect with her audience, pointing with admiration to the speed with which she gained huge markets: what took him a decade to do she accomplished in a single year, he tells interviewers, comparing her ascent to a skyrocket. Where Donahue was intense, Oprah was easy. Audiences and guests responded to her style, forming a loyal following that continues into the 21st century.

Within a few years of her move to Chicago, the illegitimate daughter of Vernita Lee and Vernon Winfrey became a millionaire and, according to various reports, among the richest entertainers in the world; additionally, *Forbes* magazine listed her as being one of the wealthiest people in the United States and began to tabulate her wealth, which soon exceeded that of producer Steven Spielberg (who had given her the first of her movie roles) and Bill Cosby, comedian, television actor, and venerated friend of Oprah. Years later, when *Forbes* ranked the 100 richest people in the world, Oprah made the list as the first black U.S. billionaire. Her fortune continues to grow as she expands her undertakings, and journalists continue to speak of Oprah's enormous wealth.

By 1986, Oprah had earned enough money to buy what most Chicagoans dream of—a penthouse condominium on the lakefront with a view from the 57th floor of the lake and the city. The apartment has everything anyone could desire: crystal chandeliers—even in the walk-in closets that house elegant designer clothing by Valentino, Ungaro, and Krizia. As "a luxury queen," she enjoys spending on anything and everything that catches her eye, like expensive imported clothing. She gives generously to people who work with her—once giving UGG boots to 200 people on her staff—and gives large amounts of money to friends and staff members. Gossip columnists write of the "fabulous office amenities" available to people who work for Harpo: a café and a workout facility known as Club Harpo, which includes a spa—all of which led one reporter to proclaim, "We wanna work with Oprah!!!!!!" Most of her staff seems dedicated. Oprah is known to be careful about schedules, conscious of attending planned meetings, and she has told journalists that her success with employees comes from her consideration for them: no yelling or mistreatment and no talking down to people.

The amenities at work are echoed in her Chicago apartment, which holds a wine cellar; a marble tub with spigots made to resemble gold dolphins; a tub in which Oprah, known for her love of bubble baths, can soak. After the bath, Oprah, who modestly calls herself "a home-body," has a huge selection of elegant pajamas—dozens and dozens, she says—from which to choose. Her enjoyment of luxury also runs to pricey BMW cars.

Today she owns several homes: a 160-acre farm with a 40-acre meadow designed by Washington landscape architect James van Sweden; a $2 million house in Rolling Prairie, Indiana; a home in Hawaii; another in Colorado; and an estate in California, which is often shown in photos. Oprah, who loves dogs and owns several (including the much-publicized but now deceased Sophie and Gracie), has a heated house for them. When the 13-year-old cocker spaniel, Sophie, died of kidney failure, it was reported that Oprah had a breakdown during the taping of her show after she'd seen a memorial video of the dog. Sophie was her "once-in-a-lifetime" dog. In May 2008, an exhibit in Manhattan was dedicated to the memory of Sophie and Gracie, Oprah's golden Labrador, who died at the age of two after choking on a ball. The sculpture, created by Daniel Edwards and described by columnist Debra Tone as "controversial," shows the two dogs joined together at the hip, sharing a common tail, on top of Oprah's golden-maned head. Codirector John Leo, of the Leo Kesting Gallery, explains that the sculpture is intended to show "how the dogs' deaths may be weighing heavily" on Oprah. A third dog, Solomon, died in October 2008. He, too, was a cocker spaniel and died, as did Sophie, of kidney disease. Oprah's boyfriend, Stedman Graham, had given Solomon to Oprah as a Christmas present in 1994. In memory of Sophie, Oprah donated a room to the animal shelter that Sophie had come from.

A few months after the death and memorial display of the dogs, a billboard purchased by the Main Line Animal Rescue appeared four blocks from Oprah's Harpo studio. It read "OPRAH—please do a show on puppy mills; the dogs need you!" Puppy mills are large facilities that have pure breeds of dogs; they are thought of as breeding machines with interest only in profit from the sale of the animals housed in small cages. The females are bred to have numerous litters until they can breed no more. Usually the litters are sold to pet stores or advertised on the Internet. The mills are not like reputable dog breeders, who are concerned with the health and quality of the animals they raise. Oprah and her staff decided to follow the suggestion of the rescue organization: producers of the Oprah show, along with people from the shelter, through the use of hidden cameras, began an investigation of puppy mills and pet shops. Lisa Ling, the investigative reporter for the show, was in charge of the enterprise. Ling, who began working as a reporter and anchor as a teenager, is also a special correspondent for the show, and she has reported stories from Asia, Africa, the Middle East, and the United States. Her subjects range from bride burning to gang rapes, to child trafficking, to armed resistance in an African country, and a massacre at a Virginia university.

Not long after the Oprah show began to expose the activities of the mills, some pet stores began to lose business; various humane societies became involved in reporting violations of laws; some puppy mills were closed; licenses of numerous breeders were revoked; some breeders retired; large numbers of dogs were rescued from mills; and, in some states, laws were passed that require mills to enlarge the cages of dogs and provide veterinary care for the animals. In December 2008, People for the Ethical Treatment of Animals named Oprah as Person of the Year.

So enamored is Oprah with animals that, according to one news report, she recommends Bow-Lingual, a wireless device that is attached to a dog's collar to register everything the animal does. Furthermore, it has been reported that Sophie, Oprah's much-loved, deceased dog, had her name on the deed of a penthouse in New York. Apparently, Sophie was a real estate investor as well, inasmuch as her name also appeared as owner of a company and financier of house purchases. The Sophie house, worth $7 million, became the property of Gayle King when the deed was transferred to her. Thus far, the name of the company still appears to be Sophie.

In the midst of the devastating fire that spread through southern California in November 2008, Oprah, who was not at her newest home in Montecito at that time, said that her first concern was for her dogs. Next to that worry, her concern was the safe removal of the ashes of Sophie.

Oprah's love of dogs led to a further purchase and loss. In March 2009, another blonde cocker spaniel named Sadie became part of the Winfrey household. Graham helped in the selection, and Oprah, who referred to Sadie as her "new baby," adopted her at 10 weeks, in addition to Ivan, one of Sadie's litter mates. Both dogs soon came down with a deadly canine virus. Ivan died, and Sadie was reported to be struggling for life. (Newspapers confused the names, so for a time it was unclear which dog had died.) Apparently, the shelter, PAWS, from which the animals had been purchased, was affected by the virus. Chicago newspapers printed several stories about the shelter, as well as information about the highly contagious disease that affects young dogs before they have been fully vaccinated. A spokesperson for PAWS issued a statement of condolence to Oprah, citing the shelter's excellent record in controlling the disease and offering advice to prospective owners of young puppies.

During a show in March 2009, on which Sadie and her veterinarian, Dr. Newman, were the focus, Sadie's illness was described in detail, and her diet was discussed as well. Oprah's love of dogs seems never ending. For her 56th birthday, she gave herself two new puppies: 14-week-old sibling Springer spaniels, Sunny and Lauren, bought from the same shelter, PAWS, from which she had adopted her beloved cocker spaniel, Sadie, a year earlier. Introduced to Oprah's studio audience as her "new babies," they were dressed in crystal pink collars in celebration of Oprah's birthday.

In addition to her dogs, Oprah keeps thoroughbred horses on her farm. An additional feature is a helicopter pad. Another famed architect, Bruce Gregg, designed the villa for her 85-acre ranch outside of Telluride, a Colorado ski area. During the 1990s, Oprah owned a condominium on Fisher Island in Florida. The apartment of 1,828 square feet, with two bedrooms and two baths, cost $660,000 when Oprah purchased it in 1996, but the resale asking price was $2.09 million. Both the size and price of that abode differed considerably from Oprah's more recent homes. Today, she owns a 42-acre, $50 million estate with a 23,000-square-foot mansion in Montecito, California. (Rumor has it that Oprah paid for the home with a personal check.) She has named the estate the Promised Land. Her magazine, *O At Home,* featured some of the areas of the estate, including its gorgeous gardens and private retreat. Although Oprah is selective about many details of her private life, parts of the California estate were the focus of photos and narratives about her rose garden and teahouse in the August 2008 issue of *O At Home.* The teahouse has an arched door framed by wisteria, and the gravel path near it is bordered by roses. There is also an English garden planted with a large variety of annuals and perennials just beyond another arched door, and a semicircle of lavender is at the end of the teahouse garden. A cobblestone path lined with thousands of white hydrangeas fittingly is named Halleluh Lane. Planted as "a living, blooming homage to her grandmother," the path runs through the property. Multiple types of gardens, not only flowers, have been cultivated around the estate, which Oprah considers "a gift." A vegetable garden has artichokes, peppers, and heirloom tomatoes, and a grassy meadow is close to an avocado orchard. All of these projects are the work of a famous gardener, Dan Bifano.

In addition to these property holdings, she owns several beachfront lots on the island of Maui in Hawaii, and not long ago newspapers reported that Oprah had purchased some property on Hana, a somewhat remote area of East Maui. (The road to Hana, long, winding, and challenging, follows the spectacular coastline. Tourists often buy T-shirts proclaiming their daring in driving the road to Hana.) To get from one home to another and to other places easily, Oprah bought a jet plane. Every detail about her life makes the news; thus, it is no surprise to see many, many newspapers writing that Oprah was house hunting in the Washington, DC, area in time for the Obama inaugural events. Some printed photos of stunning, multimillion-dollar houses that Oprah supposedly looked at. Despite the denials of intent by Oprah's staff, the story was widely circulated. So too were reports that Oprah was planning a fabulous party after the inauguration. Almost daily rumors about her supposed plans found their way into papers and magazines. Among them, the most concrete was the decision to produce her television show during the celebrations from the Kennedy Center in Washington.

Oprah's growing wealth permitted her to make an even more important purchase a number of years ago. At the same time she joined the ranks of the most famous broadcasters—Walter Cronkite, David Brinkley, Barbara Walters, Ted Koppel, and others—as Broadcaster of the Year, she acquired ownership and control of *The Oprah Winfrey Show* from the Chicago ABC television affiliate WLS and formed the company Harpo. (She will not allow the company to go public.) To house her new business she bought an old building that had been a hockey rink. Taking great pleasure in the renovation, she turned it into multiple offices and production areas and added a spa and a gym where she works out. She personally selected almost everything, from the large—carpets and tile—to the small—doorknobs and doodads that went into remodeling. Many years ago, the land on which the studio now sits was a "makeshift morgue," a cold storage warehouse, briefly used for the victims of a capsized steamer, *SS Eastland*. The facility covers 88,000 square feet.

Students are sometimes given tours of the studios, but not as frequently as in the past. The terrorist attacks of 9/11 made the staff more security conscious. Special tour guides show the visitors around, and young people learn about internships offered to juniors and seniors in college.

Oprah is the first black woman to have her own studio and production company. Only two other American women have achieved that, and both were white: Mary Pickford and Lucille Ball. She is chair and chief executive officer of the Harpo Entertainment Group that operates her show; develops various types of films, prime-time television specials, children's specials, and home videos. By 2002, Harpo, Inc. was estimated by *Fortune* magazine to be worth $575 million, with Oprah as owner of 90 percent of the stock. In 2007 alone, the company grossed $345 million. Estimates of the company's wealth vary. However, it has grown from the original five persons to a multimedia organization of 430 employees. In recognition of Oprah's leadership role in U.S. business, *Black Enterprise* chose Harpo for its 2008 Black Enterprise 100s Company of the Year.

A former entertainment lawyer, Jeff Jacobs, helped her originally set up the company and became president of Harpo a few years later as well as owner of 10 percent of its stock. Tim Bennett, a former television station executive who served as the chief operating officer of the company, has succeeded Jacobs as Harpo's president. With the huge growth of the company, it became necessary to have more administrators, in addition to Bennett. A newly created position of executive vice president was given to Eric Logan, whose job is to oversee various divisions within Harpo; he had been executive vice president for programming and broadcast operations for XM Satellite Radio before joining Harpo. In 2009, although it touted its 24-hour daily programming, Sirius XM Satellite, the company that featured Oprah, Martha Stewart, and Howard Stern, had to file for bankruptcy. Numerous subscribers to Sirius became unhappy with its failure to provide the promised programs. It is now operational again, though in the first quarter of 2009 it was reported that Sirius had lost 400,000 subscribers. It is not surprising that Logan was added to the company, where his work includes Harpo Radio, Harpo Print, Harpo Music, and Harpo Retail.

A large percentage of Harpo employees are women who are involved in the television, radio, or various publishing aspects of the firm; some personnel are employed in more than a single endeavor. Harpo not only produces Oprah's show but also has the responsibility for creating the television programs of prime time, syndication, and cable. *Dr. Phil*, *The Rachel Ray Show*, and *The Dr. Oz Show* are part of Harpo Productions. The company also is responsible for Oprah's Web site.

Harpo Print includes all the Oprah publications. Further, Harpo Films produces feature films and telefilms; Harpo Radio previously produced what seemed a certain winner, *Oprah and Friends*, and a show titled *Soul Series* on Sirius XM Satellite Radio. The programs of the company, which has a number of studios throughout the country, were available only through subscription and were commercial free, with a large number of choices for listeners, including a program hosted by Oprah's friend Gayle King. A daily national self-help radio show hosted by Shmuley Boteach, who writes for the *Jerusalem Post*, also appeared on *Oprah and Friends*. However, on March 4, 2009, the station's name was changed to Oprah Radio. The station announced it would run 24 hours daily, a somewhat misleading statement, inasmuch as the programs soon became reruns of earlier shows. The plans were to feature familiar Oprah picks, such as her close friends Gayle King and poet

Maya Angelou; designer Nate Berkus, who has been featured in Oprah's magazines and television shows; Dr. Mehmet Oz, the medical advisor who became a favorite on her television show and soon had his own program; Bob Greene, the fitness trainer and author of how-to exercise books; sex therapist Laura Berman, a popular and outspoken guest on Oprah's television show (said to be hosting the program *Better in Bed*) and author of *The Book of Love*; financial expert Jean Chatsky; and other guests from multiple fields. *O, The Oprah Magazine* was to have a role in the new program on occasion, and spiritual discussions, poetry, and home matters would be among the subjects. The announced goal of the revised program is a familiar one to Oprah watchers, which is to live your best life. When little of this materialized, angry subscribers and bloggers informed the public of what they considered a betrayal of their trust, and that seems to account for the huge drop in subscriptions.

Harpo Retail manages The Oprah Store and Web site. Periodically, Oprah's own clothing is sold at the store, and the money from those sales is donated to Oprah's charitable causes. Another store, a "microsalon," is opening at a different location, Water Tower Place, on Michigan Avenue, across from the Harpo Studios. Some of the items sold will be the same as those in the first, larger shop, but some new products will be added—memorabilia, collectibles, and pieces of South African crafts and jewelry.

The Harpo Company, Inc., along with Discovery Communication had planned to launch the new Oprah Winfrey Network—OWN—in 2009, under a 50–50 partnership agreement between OWN and Discovery. That is, Oprah has 50 percent of the stock in the joint venture with the company that would be replacing the Discovery Health Network. (Subscription fees from cable and satellite TV providers are expected to rise once Oprah moves over from broadcast networks after 2011.) However, despite all the hoopla about the relationship of Oprah and Discovery Communications, the early agreement hit several snags. After a lengthy period of negotiation over the plans for presentation, the decision was made to postpone the launch. Problems had developed in finding and keeping executives for the new channel. However, the content of the new network replacing the Discovery Health Channel was arrived at. There will be three themes: Best Life All Stars,

Experiences, and Inspiration. Currently, it isn't known how much of a presence Oprah will have on the programs.

It took a year to hire as chief executive Christina Norman, who had been with MTV. However, shortly after that hire, the programming head, Robin Schwartz, left. She had been named president in 2008 but resigned. Two other programmers, Maria Grasso and Nina Wass, subsequently resigned. Under Norman, Allan Singer was appointed as vice president of distribution and strategy. Lisa Erspamer, who had worked at Harpo for 15 years, came into the new organization as chief creative officer. (The *Los Angeles Times*, in reporting the story, wrote that Erspamer had worked "directly for the demanding Winfrey" previously, and the story emphasized the word *demanding* by pointing out that several other people had worked only briefly for the new enterprise before leaving.) Rod Aissa as well as Michele Dix, holding senior vice president titles, will be working on prime-time matters, and a third senior vice president, Drew Tappon, will be working on daytime programs. All of them have had a number of years of experience with various other networks. At the beginning of 2009, Harpo announced its plan to work with HBO on original film projects in a three-year arrangement to make movies, documentaries, and television series. Not surprisingly, given all the publicity about the coming venture and Oprah's star power, the paper trade named Oprah the most powerful woman of 2008 in the world of entertainment.

Oprah's desire to give back to others something of what had been given to her led to her creation of another kind of network. She launched the Angel Network in 1998 to encourage philanthropy and volunteerism by people who have the means and energy to help those in need. However, after 12 years, Oprah is closing it as soon as the remaining funds have been spent. Her two major charities—the Oprah Winfrey Foundation and the Oprah Winfrey Leadership Academy Foundation—are not affected. Much of what motivates Oprah is her desire to do good and, like the missionary she once dreamed of becoming, to bring a message of goodness to others. But one person alone, even one very wealthy person, cannot help multitudes in material ways. Thus, the impulse behind the formation of the Angel Network was to inspire the fortunate to return something to society through good deeds and/or money. From the beginning, participants in the Angel Network, with another famous

charitable group, Habitat for Humanity, have provided homes to thousands of families and have funded college scholarships that allow needy
and meritorious students to seek higher education. The network has
given extremely large awards to people whose lives have been used in
the service of others. The two earliest Angel programs are well known:
the Build an Oprah House, a joint effort with the Habitat for Humanity construction group, and The World's Largest Piggy Bank, an appeal
to collect money for underprivileged children. When Oprah has a sale
of items in her Chicago shop, money from Oprah's Closet has been donated to her Angel network.

In 1999, Oprah undertook still another business venture; as a cofounder with Geraldine Laybourne and Marcy Carsey, she bought 8 percent of a new cable company called Oxygen Media. One reason for the
purchase, she said, is always to have a voice—that is, a vehicle to express herself in a way that is different from network programming. It
was oriented toward women and topics that concern them, though on
occasion the program subject matter had been directed to a wider audience. Despite 24/7 programming, the network did not achieve the
hoped-for success. No matter that it added a new chat program called
Oprah After the Show with working women in mind, the cable channel
was faltering, in part because it was available only to a limited number
of people, fewer than half of the homes in the United States. Also, poll-
sters have said that the majority of women viewers preferred to watch
the Lifetime channel, known as the "Television for Women" channel.
Oprah has now changed the focus of her broadcasting and gone in another direction.

Nevertheless, Oprah could be a poster figure for the advertisement
"You've come a long way, baby." No matter the barricades and hardships along the way, even as a very young child of four or five in the segregated state of Mississippi, where her grandparents had almost nothing,
she had a sense that her life would be different even though she could
not articulate her feelings. Four decades later, a middle-aged Oprah,
remembering those childhood days and longings, talked to the spring
1997 graduating Wellesley College senior class about the journey they
would take into the future. Telling the young women about herself, she
reminded them that life itself is a journey, and she listed a series of
things that have been important to her. As she spoke of what she'd

learned from her own pilgrimage, she exhorted the graduates to follow certain guidelines that have served her well along the way. She had to discover who she was and who she was not, and she reminded each of them of the need to gain that kind of knowledge from their own experiences.

It took Oprah a long time and many lessons to discover we can only be ourselves, not somebody else, no matter how admirable that somebody might be. When reminiscing about her beginnings, she made fun of her own early pretenses, her attempts to emulate celebrities she admires. To pretend to be someone other than who we are leads to disaster, she has told numerous young people. Crediting Maya Angelou for helping her understand the principle of leading from truth, she urged a young Wellesley audience and others to do the same from the beginning, not after multiple disappointments. Living that way, Oprah maintains, is central to one's survival. So, too, is acceptance of our mistakes, but not acceptance alone; it is using all experiences to become wise, to grow beyond failures and move ahead.

In rereading the same journal she has kept for decades, she told her Wellesley listeners she is able to trace her own personal growth from the days of adolescent silliness and immaturity to adult understanding of how to live each moment. She importunes the Wellesley graduating class, as she has exhorted viewers of her television show and readers of her magazines, to emulate her experience of keeping a journal, but not just an ordinary journal. It should be "a grateful journal," the kind of record that matters, because that type of narrative leads to focusing on plenitude rather than on lack. The grateful journal enriches life. Belief in possibility, in the abundance of the universe, becomes belief in what our individual lives can be.

Several years later, Oprah agreed to be the speaker at the Duke University commencement of her godson, Will Bumpus. Will is the son of Gayle King, Oprah's closest friend. A year earlier, she had done the same for his sister, Kirby Bumpus, at Stanford. In an interview, goddaughter Kirby told a student writer for the *Duke Chronicle*, "Oprah doesn't really do commencements" unless she has a special connection to the person who asks her. Obviously, students at Duke benefited from the Oprah connection; the majority at Duke, when the news was announced, appeared to be struck by Winfrey's star power. That star power was evident as she returned to Duke to fulfill her promise; she arrived to cheers and cries of love from the students. After asking the mothers in the audience to rise and congratulate her godson, she joked about her relationship to William, who is reticent about knowing her. In the serious part of her speech, she returned to one of her most important messages: enhancing one's own life by enhancing the lives of others; and she mentioned some of the people who had inspired her to do good.

Duke administrators noted their delight in Oprah's acceptance of the invitation, following it up via e-mail with the notice that Oprah will receive "an honorary doctor of humane letters degree" at the ceremony. The degree, as described in the e-mail, is in recognition of Oprah's use of her celebrity to further education and literacy and other "important causes." Because Oprah usually declines such awards, the vice president for public affairs and government relations (without mentioning Oprah's "special connection") considers her acceptance as "a testament to [her] great esteem and respect" for Duke. However, another student writing for the paper a few days later expressed a different take on the entire event. He begins his column with a variation of lines of an early poem: "I sing of thee, Oprah Winfrey. You are a shining beacon of daytime television and a selfless philanthropist—you gave Dr. Phil his own show." Mocking the enterprise, he asks, "Could it be that Duke University had actually secured a speaker with an IQ score higher than 12?"

An unfortunate incident later marred the impression of Oprah's relationship with her godchildren, but briefly. Protective as she is of them, she could not keep newspapers from reporting in October 2009 that Kirby played a role in the firing of two members of the staff of Oprah's private plane. The accusation was that they had sexual encounters while aboard the plane; thus the firing. But the accused man brought suit against Oprah, and various stories then surfaced, only to disappear from the papers shortly afterward, as do many cases in which Oprah is involved.

From the time Oprah realized she'd been given a second chance in life by her father, she has worked unceasingly not only on her career but also to build an image outside the world of entertainment. Among the many important roles she has played, one of the most meaningful took place after the catastrophic events of September 2001, when, as master of ceremonies, Oprah led an interfaith ceremony at Yankee Stadium in New York. Through talks, music, and writing, Oprah has addressed the specificity of loss and despair as well as other wrenching issues of life, probing the dark places and the light of possibility. In her magazine, in column after column titled "What I Know for Sure," she writes of sadness and joy, of deprivation and fulfillment, of ordinariness and miracles, of soup and sunsets. All of these, she declares, are part of life's journey, and surely of hers. But every life creates its own path, although everything along the way happens for a reason and can add up to wholeness if we will it. Oprah's counsel about following our individual path tells us we are responsible for our own happiness: we must give love first to ourselves and then to others.

Still, as she points to her own life as an example of possibility, she knows, even as she gives her inspirational talks, that few people will ever come near the eminence she has reached.

NOTES

1. Roger Friedman on Fox News, as reported by columnist Liz Smith in the *Baltimore Sun* in July 2008.

2. MKE online, 19 May 2005.

3. Richard Rodriguez, *Hunger of Memory: The Education of Richard Rodriguez* (Boston, 1982).

4. Richard Corliss, review of *The Color Purple*, *Time*, 20 Apr. 2009.

5. Ben Brantley, review of *The Color Purple*, *New York Times*, 2 Dec. 2005.

6. Dorothy Gilliam, "Black Men Ill-Served by Brewster Place," *Washington Post*, 23 Mar. 1989.

7. Gregory Kane, "Black Male Bashing Industry Grows," *Sun Sentinel*, 12 Jan. 1996.

8. Barbara Grizzutti Harrison, "The Importance of Being Oprah," *New York Times Magazine*, 11 June 1989.

9. "'It Is Constant Work': Oprah on Staying Centered, Ambition, Letting Go—and Pajamas," interview by Lynette Clemetson, *Newsweek*, 8 Jan. 2001.

10. Jennifer Lee, "The Last Pullman Porters Are Sought for a Tribute," *New York Times*, 3, 4, and 17 Apr. 2009.

11. Martin Luther King, Jr., *Stride Toward Freedom: The Montgomery Story* (1958; New York: Harper Collins, 1987).

12. Jesse Jackson quoted in E.R. Shipp, "Rosa Parks, 92, Founding Symbol of Civil Rights Movement Dies," *New York Times*, 25 Oct. 2005.

13. Charles Johnson, "The End of the Black American Narrative," *American Scholar* 77, no. 3 (Summer 2008): 84.

Chapter 3

MEDIA MOGUL

Several years ago, when *Washington Post* columnist Howard Kurtz wrote the book *Hot Air, All the Time*, he listed names of performers he labeled as "high priests of talk." Who could foresee that one of them would become, as another writer described, "America's motivation Queen"? All of the performers are familiar to any television or radio listener and even to people who are neither but know the names from general conversations held over the years. Of the seven Kurtz chose from both daytime and nighttime talk shows, Oprah was the only woman. Although today there are several women daytime competitors, her fans continue to make up one of the largest audiences of daytime television watchers. Journalists designated Oprah the "queen of daytime television" because of the large number of women who opted to watch her programs rather than other offerings, day or night. Polls reveal that more women viewers prefer the lighter fare of daytime talk over the subject matter of evening talk shows, which are more news oriented or erudite in contrast to what many critics call the sensational, sentimental, hokey, and true confessional topics of daytime programs. Women watch daytime shows in larger numbers than men. The subject matter of both daytime and evening programs may be the same—that is, serious and important—but the presentations have been worlds apart. However, more changes have occurred in evening presentations than in daytime, inevitably as audience numbers have declined and networks attempt to find ways to keep or improve ratings.

Another columnist, Judith Timson, wrote in the *Globe and Mail*, "I'm trying to remember what our world was like before Oprah remade it." Through her show and magazine, which reveal Oprah as a salesperson of sentiment, good feeling, and self-improvement, Timson writes, "We have been given a transformative way to view our lives." So significant is *The Oprah Winfrey Show* that toward the end of 2008 it was added to the Spanish-language offerings for secondary schools in six major Hispanic television markets: Chicago, Los Angeles, New York, Houston, Miami, and Dallas.

Perhaps the most basic reason for Oprah's ongoing popularity is the one given by an Internet entertainment writer, who saw her as "a best girl friend to women." But Timson's view of Oprah's persona is that she makes herself "indispensable." In this new era of blogging, the same description seems to apply, despite the hostile statements that appear when some viewers decry some of her actions. Unlike letters to the editor, many of the blogs appear unedited, using language that would be bleeped from television and radio and kept out of newspapers. Blogs about controversial subjects concerning Oprah may cover 20 or 30 pages at a time. Numerous pages of angry blogs appeared on the Internet when Oprah refused to have Republican vice presidential candidate Sarah Palin on her show prior to the 2008 election. When Oprah did invite Sarah Palin to appear on her show after the election, the former candidate turned her down. However, once Palin had resigned her position as Alaska's governor and had a book to market, she changed her mind and appeared on Oprah's show in November 2009, a year after the election.

Television critics and comedians were not kind to either the guest or the host, although Palin's appearance provided a much-needed boost to the show's ratings. Fairly or not, after much hype before Palin's visit, the actual show was uninformative. Oprah's role the critics found either sycophantic or supportive. Aside from the barbs Palin sent the way of Senator McCain's staff, television newscaster Katie Couric, Levi Johnston (the father of Palin's grandson), and the staff of *Newsweek* magazine that had printed on its cover her photo as a hockey player, she had little to add to anything she had said previously or elsewhere—except for labeling Johnston's upcoming photos in *Playgirl* as "porn." However, a writer for the *Los Angeles Times* found Johnston preferable to interviewers (without actually naming Palin, Oprah, Walters, and King), because he was "at least" able to keep audiences awake.

A few months after Palin's appearance on Oprah's show, her daughter Bristol was the guest. As might have been anticipated, newspaper reports about the show emphasized Bristol's anger at her son's father and her plan to remain celibate until she marries. That situation went back and forth several years later, providing much publicity for both Bristol and Levi.

Inspired perhaps by Palin's mention of porn, the following day, Oprah returned to the type of discussion she had eschewed for awhile. As Michael Langston wrote in the *Examiner*, "Oprah . . . jumped full feet into the tawdry topic" with her guest, former porn star Jenna Jameson. Jameson talked about the large numbers of women who are interested in pornography and about the memoir she'd written in 2004, *How to Make Love Like a Porn Star: A Cautionary Tale*.

Television talk shows are as old as broadcasting, but they came into their own sphere in the 1960s. On occasion, writers have compared daytime talk shows to soap opera because of the similarity of content, so it is not just happenstance that talk shows have replaced a number of soaps, although a few soaps have been able to keep going for decades, as have Oprah-type talk shows. Scholars of popular culture have linked the roots of such shows to 19th-century life, with its particular form of tattletale tabloids, theatrical melodramas, carnival acts, and advice columns for women in daily newspapers that became the forerunners of the late "Dear Abby" and more recent, generally less friendly, modern guides to living. Additionally, the pre–television-era true confession magazines, once the favored reading material in hairdressing salons, are considered precursors of talk shows. Covers from *True Story* and other confessional magazines predating World War II framed and hung in chain restaurants are intended to capture a sense of a less sophisticated era long since passed. A *True Story* cover hanging in a Cracker Barrel restaurant along Interstate 95 obviously captivated its readers with the top headline: "Truth Is Stranger than Fiction." That and the title of the lead story, "My Own Love Trap," could easily be today's program on television, not excluding Oprah's show (though the details of the story would surely have been far less explicit in the past). Love lost, found, betrayed, and betraying are frequent topics, although the formats differ. The links between such older forms of popular culture and today's talk shows reveal a comparable selection of subjects considered appealing to women. Nothing is random in the choice of subjects chosen by producers, who not only are aware of women's interests but also watch rival programs, observe figures in the world of entertainment, and keep up to date with tabloid and gossip publications such as the *National Enquirer*, *Star*, *Globe*, and *People*. Oprah's life is a favorite subject for these publications. Until recently, assertions that all talk shows, daytime and evening, had some of the same characteristics are now only partly accurate. Since the 1990s, the focus of some day and evening programming has been altered, leading writers to note that even serious news programs have become more entertainment oriented, while some daytime programs have offered more consequential discussions. Holding the interest and attention of a changing population is a constant and major concern of networks. In that sense, networks and newspapers have similar problems; moreover, the public has been warned about the possibility that newspapers may disappear, to be replaced by the Internet, and network revenues are down.

News reports are shorter. Lighter subject matter often is introduced, and opinions of news people rather than objective factors are voiced more and more frequently—most often on cable shows. Perhaps the impetus to lighten evening talk came from the appearance on playful late-night comedy shows such as *Saturday Night Live* of former president Clinton, former vice president Gore, former president George W. Bush, and President Obama, who all took the opportunity to reveal themselves as regular guys. Reporters have called attention to their frequent appearances on television—although less so for Bush. First Lady Michelle Obama became the first person to share the cover of Oprah's magazine since it was introduced. Interviews with presidential wives, not only on television but also in the magazine, have added to Oprah's cachet.

The popularity of such appearances and increased numbers of viewers led to more spoofs during the 2008 campaigns. Favorites among them were satires of vice presidential candidate Sarah Palin. That show garnered the largest audiences in the history of *Saturday Night Live* and was repeated several times. Palin also was a guest for one episode of the show. Even a stand-in Oprah appeared on one of the programs. Satire, surprisingly, does not appear to disconcert or discourage most viewers, regardless of their political affiliation. Oprah seemed not to object to the comedy show during the run-up to the election. And Palin sold a record-breaking number of her memoir books a year after the 2008 election.

At the opposite end of the spectrum, producers have attempted to increase the shrinking numbers of viewers of their regular evening talk programs by inviting reputable and prominent journalists as guests. (Some of the newer cable programs appear to thrive on combative speakers.) Members of every recent administration also have become frequent guests on nighttime shows as well as Saturday and Sunday daytime talk programs. The popularity of the numerous weekend talk shows has networks vying for the same participants, who frequently go from one program to another. All sides gain mileage from such events: politicians presenting their views in what appears to be a less partisan environment and hosts in raising the bar on topics and issues.

Over a period of about two decades, weekend and many daytime talk shows (particularly the frivolous ones) have been at their height, leading journalist Peter Carlson to label them "America's great growth industry." Daily talk shows have proliferated, and only some of the more offensive programs were discontinued even though many became more and more sensational when no topic was taboo. Participants willingly shared personal and private elements of their lives with viewers. Despite doctors' reports that patients generally are reluctant to discuss sexual matters with them, it seems those very people are ready to go on television and tell all. Many of Oprah's shows have supported such discussions of intimate matters. Sometimes the comments by Oprah or visiting experts have been used to emphasize the uninhibited nature of the show or guests. And, although there are fewer sensational presentations than before, they still occur with some regularity.

Interspersed with prosaic or meaningful topics have been some unusual confessions. In addition to programs about homosexuality, Oprah raised the subject of husbands who have had sex changes. She pushed the boundaries of transgender by having as a guest the "pregnant" Thomas Beatie, a transsexual who was on the show more than once and is a man who has twice given birth. Six months pregnant when he first appeared with his wife on Oprah's show in the spring of 2008, Beatie had been a beauty queen in his younger days but later underwent a sex change. Although legally he became a man, he did not have the female organs removed, with the result that he was able to become pregnant when his wife of five years, Nancy, was unable to do so, even though she had two daughters from an earlier marriage. Although he and Nancy wanted a child, numerous doctors refused to treat his pregnancy, and some people, including members of his own family, regarded the situation as an abomination. Not long after his appearance on Oprah's show, Beatie gave birth to a daughter, and subsequently had another child. Not only did his presence draw many viewers to the shows, but also several newspapers reported the experiences. In the days before television, the circus might have been the forum for such entertainment.

Programs on sexual matters display many characteristics of Oprah's presentations, not only those dealing with intimate matters that account for her large numbers of fans: before-and-after photos of guests, intimate relations, emotion, and humor. Still, there have been angry reactions to the more graphic shows, even though warnings are issued in advance about the suitability of the material. Sex therapist Laura Berman was the guest expert on a show discussing the topic "Behind Closed Doors: Sex Therapy." Writing for the *Sun-Times* before the show aired, Berman answered typical questions posed by people concerned with the material and issues in sex therapy. In a reassuring article, Berman sought to allay worries people have in their sexual relationships; on the show, her discussion was both more open and intimate than that in the written piece. Berman will continue to appear on future programs when Oprah moves to OWN.

Because of public interest—or prurient interest—in the matter of sex changes, the following year, staff from Harpo notified an Edmonton, Alberta, Canada, woman of the plan for Oprah Winfrey's show to have a program on sex-change surgery. The unnamed woman was seeking a sex change in Canada. Although there was no immediate date for Oprah's show, the studios were considering the subject of transsexuals. In the past, there had been funding for sex-change surgery in Alberta's budget, but that had been eliminated in 2009, because various individuals and groups organized to defeat the plan. It was suggested, however, that sex change might become a topic for a future program.

Although there are serious presentations about sexual matters, there are also lighthearted ones as well, as with a guest appearance by Steve Harvey, popular talk show host and author of *Act Like a Lady, Think Like a Man*. With a live audience apparently consisting entirely of women, as well as preselected women on Skype (the Internet calling system) from various cities who asked questions that seemed previewed, Harvey's appearance on Oprah's show was a combination of fact and humor about the war between men and women. As they were being beamed in via television, the remarks and questions of those outside the studio focused on sex, sexual relationships, and activities.

Oprah had featured an entire episode introducing Skype to her viewers. Through the use of Skype, Oprah has been able to hold talks with anyone, anywhere, at any hour. The technology, which is only a few years old, continues to expand. And Oprah, who appears always ready to try new things, uses Facebook, YouTube, and Twitter (although, reportedly, she has tired of this last one).

Everyone during Harvey's guest appearance was openly humorous about sexual parts, sex toys, heavy petting, and oral sex. In response to several questions, Harvey played two roles: the surprised man, innocent in his comments, as he comically rolled his eyes, and wise advisor to the women on how to behave with men. With a change of mood, Harvey listed five questions women need to have answered when they begin a serious relationship with a man.

For her part, Oprah laughed along with the audience as Harvey joked about the surprisingly frank queries and revelations. Only when the issue became one of honesty and fidelity between a couple did his tone change. So too did Oprah's. Although she was uncharacteristically reserved about such matters, her body language clearly revealed her own strong feelings. Her O magazine, like many (or most) women's magazines, frequently publishes articles by therapists about fidelity and related matters.

When Oprah started in Chicago in 1984, nobody anticipated the effect her program would have. Having replaced the irreplaceable Phil

Donahue, she always credits him for his pioneering work on television in creating the one topic format that she emulated. She insists that his dissenting voice has been important for the health of television. Donahue's show had established the pattern not only for Oprah but for all the other daytime talk shows. However, Donahue also had multiple detractors, as has Oprah, even though the type of criticism differs.

Donahue has turned away from talk shows to concentrate on serious documentaries. In much the same way, Oprah has become more involved in other types of programs. Nevertheless, some of the criticism of Oprah by media critics still is valid. With discussions described as "sensational," such topics continue to be explored on her show. Writers have noted occasions when Oprah became uncomfortable with the subjects on her program; though she appears to be less so with the passage of time, it is reflective of changes in our culture. Contending she has no desire to manipulate people or take advantage of their miseries, she has said frequently that her desire in life is to do good. Looking at her contributions to national and international betterment, who can question her assertions? Most critics, despite their cynicism and a certain mockery of the breadth of her statements, acknowledge the truths of her intentions.

Television ratings are always dependent on audience interest. To keep people tuning in, it's necessary to provide variety in shows, and some topics have been extremely provocative. From the beginning, talk shows have run the gamut from sleazy to serious. In that lineup, Oprah's programs have generally been ranked at the classy end in both style and execution, leading to her top ratings and many Emmy Awards, including a Lifetime Achievement Award. Individual honors continue to come in, such as those for her philanthropic activities, which include her Angel Network and many other causes all over the globe—all of which have helped raise awareness and money.

Substantive alterations took place in Oprah's telecasts once she decided to raise the level of her programs. During the years that competition increased among daytime talk shows and subject matter became more repugnant, The Oprah Winfrey Show made important strides toward abandoning the tawdry factor. While competitors seemed to compete for the title of most revolting and shocking, she frequently enhanced the quality of her shows.

Nevertheless, she has not always escaped the minefield; even when experts are featured in discussions about anything of a sexual nature, numerous critics attack the programs. Currently, bloggers—many of whom are anonymous—are the most hostile. Ironically, they seem to be among the audience for her shows.

Meanwhile, other talk show hosts sometimes presented such offensive programs that one writer labeled them "the swamp." Of course, not all audiences appreciated Oprah's efforts to offer more quality programs. At times, viewers have been fickle, preferring to tune out Oprah and tune in other hosts or soap operas or game shows. Popularity polls taken periodically reveal a seesawing between hosts. But even critics, who usually find daytime shows worthless, trashy, and objectionable, approved of some changes in Oprah's programs. That doesn't mean all journalists have credited her efforts to improve the caliber of talk shows; some writers, whose field is television culture, continue to fault her programs. The anti-Oprah critics voice dismay at the role she plays in U.S. cultural life, seeing her as pandering to and supporting mediocrity. Yet when she became a spokesperson for the Obama presidential campaign, there were those who also criticized her for that.

She has been faulted for being anti-male, perhaps because her audiences are mostly women. Black journalists, in particular, have expressed intense anger about what they see as her unfriendly attitude toward black men. Sensitivity to that subject has not changed over the years, so that Oprah's involvement with the movie *Precious* brought about more attacks on her judgment and supposed animosity. The fact that Tyler Perry also was a coproducer of the film seemed not to lessen the anger of some newspaper writers, nor did the presence of Oprah and Gabourey Sidibe (who played Precious) at the 2010 Oscar event, where Oprah spoke of the young star's achievement as a "classic Cinderella story."

Despite widespread praise for the film and its stars, a similar reaction to that of the past was heard: that the film demeaned African Americans. The writer Ishmael Reed voiced the same type of comments that had been made years earlier with the film *The Color Purple* and other films that focus on the lives of African Americans. Ironically, after many years, the book *The Color Purple*, which was published in 1982 and won a Pulitzer Prize, is still discussed and admired by many critics.

Classes in literature often study the book, and the movie was Oprah's introduction as an actress; the show also was a hit on Broadway and elsewhere, with the current producer being Oprah Winfrey.

Another novel, *Push*, might have been overlooked had it not been made into a film, particularly under the auspices of Oprah. As critic Ishmael Reed describes it, the subject is the "merciless abuse, grossly incestuous abhorrent degradation of a young girl." The subject is one that Oprah has been interested in for years, primarily because of her own painful history as an abused, neglected child, raped by a family member and her mother's boyfriend. Although the film did not win an Academy Award, it did win at Sundance and abroad, in Cannes and Toronto. Perhaps some of the writers and readers who turned away from the film did so because, as one wrote, life has enough pain and anguish without seeing it in the movies.

There will be many more films on Oprah's new network. Although the book club may be a thing of the past, a new club is being formed, the Documentary Film Club, whose first offering, *A Family Affair*, was scheduled to be shown on OWN in 2011. The documentaries planned for the new club will focus on "emerging creative voices." No doubt the lives of women will continue to be a major theme and interest in Oprah's future work, just as her television programs have been.

Divorce has been a topic shown from several perspectives on Oprah's program. On one show, Haley, a sophomore in college, and her mother, Michelle, were the guests for an episode titled "Women Leaving Men for Other Women." In a frank discussion, both mother and daughter described their experiences after Michelle and Haley's father divorced after a 24-year marriage. Although the husband/father and his family considered the situation (that is, Michelle's homosexuality) abhorrent and against their religion, Haley protested their views, stating it was the divorce that made her unhappy, not her mother's homosexuality. Jesus never said a word in the Bible about sex, she said, and her mother's sexual orientation has nothing to do with her goodness as a person or as a Christian. God, alone, can judge, Haley stated, and she herself has no right to do so.

The subject of divorce is addressed from differing perspectives on different shows. On another Oprah program, the issue of loyalty and disloyalty was explored, with guests consisting of a father and his two children, Daisy and Chris, as well as a divorce counselor. In a previously made film, two other children talked about their mother and her boyfriend, while Chris wept as the children described their sadness. When Oprah speaks of the rage that children can develop, the guest counselor explains that children must express their feelings; however, it must be the parent who approaches the child for such a discussion in order to take the pressure off. Often, children blame themselves for the breakup of their parents' marriage. Even though the counselor reassured Daisy and Chris of their innocence in the matter, they spoke of things they did to try to bring about their mother's return. But the sad truth, according to the expert, is that they didn't cause her to leave, nor can they make her return. He advises, as a rule, both parents together should tell their children the truth. They need to tell children about their own sadness, that they are going to live separately, and stress that the children are not to blame. Further, he says, parents should practice in advance what they need to say, knowing that the children will cry, but they must also listen to their children.

After Oprah asserted it is never too late to heal damage, another film was shown on the program, featuring the same counselor and a 16-year-old girl, Ebony, who felt guilty about telling her father years earlier she had seen her mother embracing another man. After her parents were divorced, for seven years she carried the burden of believing that she had caused the divorce. She turned her sense of responsibility against herself and became sexually promiscuous with as many as 22 partners. She also took drugs and became pregnant but lost the baby. Her parents knew nothing about her activities, and she feared telling them. But, on the show, the counselor had her confess to both parents through a film that was shown. Although the father assured Ebony he will always accept her, the mother does not. Counselor Neuman wanted the mother to differentiate between the girl and her behavior, and the mother admitted she had not handled the situation well.

Oprah takes the opportunity to express a point of view she holds strongly: it is necessary for parents to talk to their children in situations of this nature. Oprah bluntly asks the mother whether she was aware that Ebony had seen her embracing another man. When the mother denies it, she also confesses she'd moved away before telling her child about the upcoming divorce.

Both Oprah and Neuman are in agreement that children need adults
to talk to about important personal matters, and if they can't discuss
such things with their parents, there must be adult friends to whom the
children can turn. People familiar with Oprah's history understand the
impetus behind her views.

Varieties of sexual themes appear frequently on the show, with the
discussions having become more open over the decades. In advance notices of upcoming shows on sex, viewers are warned that such programs
are meant only for mature audiences. Accordingly, Hal Boedeke, also
known as "the TV Guy," writing a blog for the *Orlando Sentinel*, humorously states, "Lady O wants to make sure adults are getting the Big O."
Nevertheless, although some viewers may protest about the presentations, the numbers of viewers have not diminished. Apparently, the
popularity of such discussions as marriage, divorce, and sex increases
viewer interest. In support of such findings, on one Oprah program,
Oprah's guest, a professor from the University of Utah, discussed her
13-year study about women's sexuality, which resulted in the book *Sexual
Fluidity*. Among the findings was women's attraction to other women,
and some people expressed surprise that the writer was able to work on
such a controversial a topic in Utah. Her response to such questions was
to point out that the University of Utah is a great place and no different from any other academic institution.

Years ago, when Oprah decided to improve the nature of her program, more professional guests were added, so that a number of the issues discussed have had serious and thoughtful analysis. On days when
the country has been eager for solace as well as information about
significant current events such as the wars in Iraq and Afghanistan,
the economy, or careful consideration of other major happenings, *The
Oprah Winfrey Show* attained stature commensurate with some of the
best television offerings. At such times, her broadcasts have focused on
the problems confronting the nation, and she has brought in experts to
explain and air multiple points of view. Frequently, issues of concern to
all Americans are on the agenda.

It seems prescient of Oprah and her staff to have had a show in
September 2009 about health care in the United States; soon the subject became a linchpin in the new president's program following his
election—but it became a topic that led to much controversy among

the electorate and, according to a number of election analysts, was a major factor in the loss of many Democratic governors and many Democratic seats in Congress. Michael Moore, maker of the film *Sicko*, was a guest on Oprah's September 2009 show, "Sick in America." Moore's premise, supported by Oprah, is that the system has failed large numbers of Americans. In preparation for the show, one of Oprah's employees called several insurance companies about three different cases that needed health insurance, and in each instance the company representatives found reasons to deny coverage to the individuals. Several of the insurers were among the largest in the United States: Blue Shield, Blue Cross, and Aetna. Moore, Oprah, and a Princeton University health care economist argued that all Americans have a fundamental right to health care, whereas a guest from the insurance side countered with the statement (one frequently repeated by insurance company spokespeople) that Americans have better health care than people in foreign countries. Although the insurance industry representative pressed for a balance between private and public care payment, the problem of health care in the United States remains contentious.

When Oprah has experienced certain health issues herself, the entire world learns about her physical ailments while she shares personal information. Her rejection and later acceptance of the idea of menopause gave rise to a publicizing of what one writer calls "the new attention-grabbing younger sister of menopause, called 'perimenopause.'"[1] Many doctors approved the publicity given the problem, although other physicians and scientists objected to the commercial exploitation of the subject by various sellers of medicines, books, and supplements. Nevertheless, when the hour devoted to perimenopause on Oprah's program came to an end, the e-mail response was so overwhelming that it caused Oprah's site to crash, as has happened after other programs viewers cared strongly about.

Several years ago, an Oprah program about postpartum depression explored the grim subject of mothers who injured or killed their children. It followed the structure of most Oprah shows, with different stories, taped segments, testimony by some of those affected, an expert advisor—usually a doctor—and research data. The program provided much information and was different from the carnival setting and atmosphere that often has surrounded other media presentations of the subject. Some talk shows and newscasts turn painful or tragic events into entertainment. Despite the important educational value of a program, some talk shows use sentimental techniques to arouse the audience to great emotional heights, with excess sometimes taking over to the detriment of the somber warnings.

Emotion on Oprah's show is not always focused on the sorrowful. Every show has an advertising component, and Oprah mentions the names of the gift-giving companies several times throughout the hour. The variety of subjects and guests obviously account in part for the popularity and durability. Still, some topics resurface frequently, and some are highly charged.

Oprah periodically has taken to the road with a "Live Your Best Life" tour. When she first began her biennial project in 2001, a "personal crusade," she said she plans to continue it in the future. The idea behind Live Your Best Life may be used in a different format or venue, and the plan may involve a complete change from the past. It is not known whether Oprah will take it out on the road again.

A typical tour took place in Philadelphia several years ago. Calling her "the Amazon queen of touchy-feely," David Hiltbrand, a reporter for the *Philadelphia Inquirer*, describes the crowd as "screaming" upon her arrival in a limousine and "practically levitating" when she took the stage. Although the cost of tickets was high, most of the crowd seemed to think it worth the price. What they did get, writes Hiltbrand, was a "cross between a revival meeting and a self-help (one day) seminar." Oprah often refers to her work as a mission, and, according to the statistics of *Fortune* magazine, these self-affirmation tours, which inspire the thousands of women ticketholders, bring in more than $1.5 million. The rules for the events were similar to the regulations of her television show; attendees didn't know the subject matter or format in advance; they were not allowed to have a photo taken with the star; nor were they permitted to seize the microphone during the afternoon session, when members of the audience participated.

During a two-hour morning program, Oprah spoke about her childhood on her grandmother's farm in Mississippi, and she spoke about her trip to Africa during the Christmas season. Typically, the message of her talk was of the need to find "the seed of grace" in the unhappy episodes of existence (as in her own bad experiences). "She recounted

Perhaps it is the nature of such programs that may leave viewers dissatisfied. A one-hour show that includes numerous advertisements surely cannot begin to solve a lifelong, deep-seated illness. Thus, critics may be justified when they speak or write about the shallow nature of such a presentation. However, purveyors of a program that earns $6 million per week, $300 million per year, and $75,000 for a 30-second advertisement, seem not to worry about gripes from critics.

Much ink has been spent on Oprah's style, which is always touted as refreshingly extemporaneous; that is, she doesn't like prepared scripts for herself, preferring a looser, more folksy approach. This same technique lost her a news announcer's job in Baltimore, yet led to her prodigious success as a talk show host in Chicago. Although numerous articles speak of the spontaneity of the star—that is, her impulsiveness, even toward self-confession—various reporters have called her shows scripted and managed action used to create a sense of authenticity. However, others, including journalist Marcia Ann Gillespie, have defended her, saying that Oprah doesn't always speak pleasantries. Neither does she provide meaningless talk. Still, even when she appears to be asking and commenting instinctively, it usually results from careful advance preparation. Another critic disputes Oprah's authenticity, labeling her a con artist. Another voice in the conversation, well-known authority on male and female speech patterns Deborah Tannen, has spoken of Oprah's natural ability with rapport talk, which is typical of women's conversational patterns. Nevertheless, in actuality, talk shows have very little spontaneity, although audiences have been led to believe that most talk shows are a type of shoot-from-the-hip production.

Such behavior is attractive to the audience, and being seemingly unscripted allows Oprah to use her special type of humor that her audience delights in. On a show dealing with marital issues, Oprah injects humor that lightens the tension: you have great sex; you're rolling around in bed, having a great time, and then the next morning find he's still an idiot. The humor is not always so blatant; sometimes it is only suggestive. Scripted? Perhaps, but probably not. Her often risqué humor leads comedians to engage in some of their own, with imitations. A memorable example occurred on *Saturday Night Live,* when the actor satirized both Oprah and the title of a play with a portrayal of her interviewing first ladies in a session called "The Vagina Monologues." Oprah seems to find laughter in much that others would not. She engages the audience in the fun not only verbally but through body language—a raised eyebrow, exaggerated eye movements, and other facial expressions and gestures. And when she is really amused, she brings a deep, long, throaty laugh into the mix. Further, she has coined a humorous vocabulary for body parts, such as vajajay for female sex organs, that a friendly audience finds both funny and acceptable.

When the program is given over to fashion, in which the theme may be a new look for the season, Oprah's humor punctuates everything: minidresses, denim, sweaters. Sometimes she will speak mockingly of her own body, and, as she looks at one of the sleek models, Oprah clowns; commenting on the wide separation between the breasts of the model, she asks with pseudo innocence, "how do they do that?" But she does love clothes, as is evidenced in the hundreds of glamorous photos taken of her over the years. On occasion, the entire hour on the show features high-end designers whose pricey clothing might not fit into the range of most Oprah watchers, but even if the audience doesn't buy the products, they enjoy the display. Oprah so enjoys shopping, not only for herself but for many other people, that her enthusiasm becomes infectious.

A serious subject that Oprah returns to periodically is bullying. One of her most memorable instances occurred when two young women authors were guests on the show early in the 2000s. Both women, who are friends, had written books about bullying among girls. Rachel Simmons wrote *Odd Girl Out: The Hidden Culture and Aggression in Girls* and Rosalind Wiseman wrote *Queen Bees and Wanabees: Helping Your Daughter Survive Cliques, Gossip, Boyfriends and Other Realities of Adolescence*, which became the source for the movie *Mean Girls*.

Therapists frequently connect brutality to women as an act of bullying, and physical attacks on women as an extreme form of bullying. Abduction of girls is a more alarming part of that pattern, a topic that Oprah has been determined to bring before the public. Among the large number of girls who have been violently seized, most have also been raped and murdered. Survival is rare, but even more rare is long-term survival as a captive of the rapist/captor. In attempting to keep the different types of violence an ongoing subject for her audience, Oprah wanted to interview Jaycee Dugard, a young woman who had been kidnapped 18 years before being found alive. During the years of her captivity, she had been forced to live in a hut adjacent to the home of the captor and his wife and had given birth to two children. Although Oprah had made her first ever attempt to tell a producer she wanted to interview the young woman, the family refused.

Oprah, always determined to explore the hidden and secret elements of bullying that becomes violent, chose to bring the subject of domestic violence to her show in a program called "The Rihannas of the World." Oprah used as prime examples two famous stars of the music world, Rihanna Fenty and her boyfriend, Chris Brown. During an argument between the two, Brown had beaten Rihanna brutally until someone called the police. Yet Rihanna was reluctant to press charges against Brown, despite Oprah's warning that a man who hits once will hit again. Chris Brown angrily defended himself on other talk shows, pointing to the help he had given Oprah in entertaining students in Africa. Because of that, he thought Oprah should have been more helpful to him. Oprah's response was to advise Brown to seek counseling, which he clearly needed.

A reporter following the Rihanna episode on the show tracked down the ex-wife of a famous gospel star, BeBe Winans, who had been on Oprah's show a number of times. His wife was also the victim of domestic violence, and newspapers had reported the story in a way that could not be ignored. Yet, despite the ongoing court case, Oprah continued to promote the gospel singer's albums, according to his ex-wife, Debra. Finally, the message reached Oprah, who then barred the singer from her show. In talking emotionally to her audience about violence, Oprah offered a grim statistic: one in four women and girls or more suffer from a form of domestic violence. Nevertheless, Oprah's work, Anna Quindlen's best-selling novel *Black and Blue*, other books—both fiction and nonfiction—essays, and seminars about violence do not appear to have altered the numbers.

Not long after the airing of the show with Rihanna, Oprah had as her guest Connie Culp, a woman whose husband had shot her in the face with a shotgun several years earlier. The severe damage to her face led to the first facial transplant in the United States, but 80 percent of Culp's face was destroyed, as was its sensation and her senses of taste and smell, and today she is legally blind. The transplant saved her, although her photographs reveal a woman whose face can never be considered normal. Thomas, the husband, was sentenced to a seven-year prison term despite his attempt to commit suicide—which he botched.

When Culp told Oprah she had considered taking Thomas back after completion of his prison term, Oprah asked her for reasons, which seemed inexplicable to both Oprah and her audience. Today, Culp is still thinking about divorce.

During the period that Oprah's show was focusing on the topic of abused women, a domestic violence shelter called New House was given a $10,000 grant by Oprah's Angel Network in October 2009; the money is to be used for ongoing activities in the program, which provides safe shelter, education about violence, and services to abused women and children.

Not long after Oprah's shows focused on the issue of violence, leading newspapers featured reviews of a book written by President Obama's half-brother. Titled *Nairobi to Shenzhen*, it is semi-autobiographical and includes details about his father's violent treatment of his mother, an American woman who married his Kenyan father after he was divorced from the future president's mother.

Another horrifying incident of violence was the topic on Oprah's show in November 2009; but that time it was violence by an animal, a chimpanzee, on a helpless woman who lost her eyes, entire face, nose, lips, and hands. The chimp was owned by the woman's employer, who had brought him up as a pet. Although the woman survived, she is to-tally blind, has no mouth with which to eat, and only one thumb that surgeons had attached to a hand. Her dependency on others is total. Although the victim wears a hat and veil to hide her face from viewers who would be shocked and horrified by her appearance, she agreed to remove those coverings briefly at Oprah's request. Unlike programs on the show of human violence against other humans, the reaction of the audience had to be entirely different, leaving them to wonder how such an event could have taken place and what possible remedy there can be. Human attacks are generally unpredictable, but that is far less true of animals. Almost a year after the victim's appearance on Oprah's and other programs, a news report stated that she was denied further treat-ment for her injuries because of the "complexity" of her case.

Bullying as a form of violence isn't confined to one gender. Suicide is not rare in both sexes who have been bullied. A case of bullying led to the death of a young teenage girl on whom a devastating hoax was played. Through the Internet, the mother of a rival girl was able to create a fictional young man who purportedly was interested in the vulnerable girl. After leading the child to believe she had an admirer, the woman began to destroy the girl's confidence and self-esteem to the point where the girl committed suicide by hanging herself. Although the perpetrator of the lie was arrested and brought to trial, nobody can predict the ultimate effect the publicity will have on other young people.

Some psychologists believe that sexual bullying of boys is the most harmful of all forms, because it is attached to the sense of masculinity. In May 2009, Oprah's show focused on the deaths of two 11-year-old boys, one from the island of Saint Croix and one from Georgia. The mothers of the boys were guests on the program, in addition to a psychologist who talked about the warning signs behind suicide. He warned parents to be more conscious of a child's depression as well as changes in ordinary daily habits. Parents often are unaware of events that lead to depression, and schools usually ignore such things, Oprah's guest stated. Vulnerability in children is a topic Oprah has returned to again and again. Vulnerability is not new, but opportunities for harm have expanded in this electronic age, along with schools, blurbs, and gangs.

Still another Oprah program, as well as one on the *Ellen DeGeneres Show*, featured the bereaved mother of an 11-year-old boy who had committed suicide. The mother, Sirdeaner Walker, became an advocate for safety in schools, appearing before Congress to urge support of a bill requiring schools receiving federal grants to provide bullying prevention programs. Her story about her son's despair is used to highlight the inadequacy of schools to handle the problem of bullying. Although Walker had apprised members of the staff at the school about the situation, the school took matters into its own hands without bringing in trained professionals and worsened the situation that led to the death of the child.

An Oregon author and founder of the faith-based group, The Protectors, started a letter-writing campaign to have people send to Oprah stories of bullying of their children. Calling it another type of civil rights movement, Paul Coughlin, founder of the group, believes that "bullycide" is driven by despair and that other reactions to bullying are problems in public education, psychological issues, and even mental disorders leading to school shootings.

Bullying may lead to not only suicide but also murder. Further, it is not limited to girls or boys, straights or gays, or members of any one ethnic group. In the late 1990s, the United States and other countries were horrified to learn of the murder of a young university student in Laramie, Wyoming. Twenty-one-year-old Matthew Shepard was targeted by two young men who deliberately set out to rob a gay man. Not only did they rob Shepard, beat him, and smash his skull, they also tied him to a fence with a rope and left him to die. At the murder trial, a girlfriend of one of the murderers stated that they wanted to teach Shepard a lesson: not to come on to straight people.

Following Shepard's death, several attempts were made to pass a federal bill against hate crimes, but all of them failed. Today there is hope that such a bill may pass in some form. There have been songs, films, documentaries, and a play about the Shepard incident to bring attention to such crimes. Matthew's mother, Judy, also wrote a book about her son's murder. Grief counselors have become part of American psychology, and Oprah has also had them on her program.

During the period that Oprah was focusing on violence and bullying, the question of hate crimes arose once again with the shooting and deaths of large numbers of soldiers at Fort Hood, Texas, in the fall of 2009. The assailant was a military psychiatrist, an American Muslim who did not want to be deployed to a country populated by other Muslims. In the aftermath of the event, many discussions about hate crimes took place, when various people classified the incident as such. Although it was not possible for Oprah to be present in the hospital where the wounded were recovering, she interviewed one of the wounded soldiers, a woman, who was said to have fired at the assailant as he shot her three times. The assailant's fate has not yet been determined.

Violence as a social issue in the United States has long been an important subject for Oprah. Almost two decades ago, in recognition of Martin Luther King, Jr.'s, birthday, Oprah announced that she would undertake the topics of racism and the judicial system and race relations. The series covered many topics related to violence: from racism and interracial hatred (including Japanese Americans and Native

Americans) to fear and hate crimes. So much has been written about
the effect of television on U.S. culture and daily existence that many
of the reviews, articles, and books begin to sound the same. Television
plays a central role as image maker and in terms of its impact on attitudes, behavior, philosophy, politics, and spending patterns on people
around the world. Most journalists agree that endorsements on television by high-profile celebrities of anything from merchandise to child
rearing have more commercial worth than anything other individuals
might provide. On all Oprah programs, advertising, which occurs every
few minutes, consumes huge amounts of time. During one show, the
advertisements shown ran the gamut from large to small items and from
personal to impersonal: cars, weight loss, animal food, bug spray, fast
food, dishwashers, cheese, and syrup. Stars are part of the sales package
of programs, issues, and merchandise. On the other hand, those programs (and magazines) also gain substantially through identification
with various commodities. There are many women who not only look
at merchandise on television but purchase articles Oprah recommends.
On one program after Oprah called attention to a medicinal com-
pound that supposedly enhances a woman's sex drive, she brought on
a flurry of phone calls to a small Maryland pharmacy making the custom
mixture.

No matter the product, many affected companies have remarked on
Oprah's extraordinary influence on sales. Because of the confidence she
has instilled in audiences, they will follow her recommendations, says
the president of a branch of a publishing company, so that Oprah "creates markets all the time." When a show provided a demonstration by
Art Smith, author of *Back to the Table* and Oprah's former chef, the
presentation gave Oprah another opportunity to clown and do a bit of
sashaying around as she proclaimed her love of potatoes. The subject of
food and the ways it is served provides the advertising opportunity to
push the products of various chains. But as Oprah gives prices, she soft-
ens the fact that she is advertising, humorously noting that she wants
the discount being offered.

There is, however, a small group that questions the honesty of her
recommendations. Finding almost everything Oprah does to be manipulative, commercial, and self-serving, one disgruntled former employee
of Harpo published a screed about the star on the Internet. Claiming
that Oprah has business ties or a quid pro quo arrangement with many

corporations, networks, and publishing houses, the writer calls her a world-class phony who is able to deliver audiences because her name sells everything, and companies are not interested in how she does that. (Nobody would contest the first claim, but the second one is unknowable.) The author, Elizabeth Coady, who had been a senior associate producer for *The Oprah Winfrey Show*, wrote the piece as a form of protest against the confidentiality contract that restricts people for life for writing or talking about Oprah. Coady claims she wants to write a book about Oprah's operations, but the courts have upheld the agreements.

Although the millions of admirers far outnumber the critics, there are other dissenting voices besides Coady's. A book called *Everybody Loves Oprah* quotes and names some hostile journalists. One such journalist is P.J. Bednarski of the *Chicago Sun-Times*, who wrote 20 years ago that Oprah was amoral about sexual matters and uninvolved with important moral and social issues. In the two decades that have passed since Bednarski criticized Oprah, many of her activities, as well as the praise she has earned for them, contradict Bednarski's statement. The first thing most people say about the star is how much good she does. Other negative remarks by Bill Zehmer of the now-defunct *Spy* magazine, voiced dislike of her speech, her use of famous names, and her flippancy, and he finds the people who work with her sycophantic. He even derides her appearance, as did many journalists in earlier years when they discovered her Achilles heel—her weight. Because Oprah herself often voices her unhappiness when she gains weight, it became an important issue. However, Oprah's appearance over the years—her hairdos, makeup, jewelry, and clothing—reveal her as savvy about her looks. And now that she has reached her mid-50s, she seems reconciled to not being svelte.

The frequency of exposure on television is also a major factor in selling a product or, as Oprah's boyfriend Stedman Graham labels everything, a brand: books, movies, political positions, and even the politicians who espouse the positions. This fact explains the constant polling by companies employed to track the effect of products that cannot be measured through sales figures. It is no surprise that the benefits behind sales or image go in two directions—to the talk show and to the purveyor of a brand or product.

Almost every study of popular culture finds that television blurs the diversity of U.S. life and culture. No matter the topic or guests, the underlying structure and values are those of middle-class America. An Indian writer, Shraddha Jahagirdar-Saxena, however, points to Oprah's ability to reach out to everyone—that is, "the common man"—with issues that affect many, such as weight, abuse, and discrimination. The audience must be comfortable. Therefore, solutions to problems must conform to those particular values, which writer Barbara Ehrenreich describes as the middle-class virtues of responsibility, reason, and self-control. Ehrenreich, an essayist, professor, prolific nonfiction writer, and social commentator, is interested primarily in the lives and status of women. Her most attention-getting book is *Nickel and Dimed: On (Not) Getting by in America*, but she has also written analytically about the entertainment business, describing Oprah's shows as a type of lesson delivered in the guise of entertainment.

Although not all talk shows nor their audiences are the same, Oprah's live audience generally is 80 percent white, middle class, and female, and they want to hear about the problems of other women, even though the guests may very well conform to a different social, cultural, or economic group than the viewers. Researchers inform us that viewers find it satisfying to hear people speak of their problems, regardless of whether they identify with the problem. There also is a type of catharsis in the very expression of what the audience regards as forbidden or sinful. Ratings rise when the topics are sex, drugs, and incest. Such was the case with the story actress Mackenzie Phillips told on Oprah's show in September 2009, when she talked about her book and the "consensual relationship" she had with her father. The following February, on a different show, Phillips retracted the word *consensual*, saying she had learned that incest is never consensual with a child. In a sense, the appeal of taboo subjects is similar to that of certain types of mystery and crime novels for large numbers of readers. The most horrific plot and episodes are acceptable, even pleasing, to the least bloodthirsty individuals, because, as psychologists inform us, these individuals can have the experience without participation or any of the danger or consequences. Soap operas have had similar appeal, but those facets of popular culture, somewhat like the "true story" of women's magazines, have disappeared or taken a different tack.

The harshest media critics find two opposing characteristics in day-time television: one is as amplifier and manipulator of the conventional, the ordinary, and the bland, which projects accepted stereotypes rather than exploring the wide differences in human behavior. Its opposite is a type of reductive tabloidization that sensationalizes, simplifies, and exploits individual narratives with a style that flattens everything into sound bites. Complex issues are watered down to suggest instant solutions and results. In the brevity of television time, drug or sexual abuse, poverty, violence, and other major social problems are shaped into manageable stories, the equivalent of three-act plays with introduction, development, and resolution. The most extreme conduct is turned into theater, and reality is replaced by that theater. In the course of an hour minus the time devoted to commercials, problems are presented, dramatized, discussed, and solutions appealing to audiences are found.

Daytime television is aimed at a mass audience, as are most movies, and it employs many of the same techniques that are based on alterations of time. Inasmuch as the events narrated on the program took place previously, unlike real-life situations, they can be speeded up or slowed down; scenes are instantaneously cut from one to another; experiences and episodes, which in actuality may be unrelated, are collected and made to seem part of a story; most techniques of filmmaking are brought to bear through use of multiple cameras, zoom lenses, foregrounding or distancing of images, lighting and use of scenery, sound effects, and music. Background scenes from other sources clearly have been filmed in advance. Take the example on Oprah's programs addressing the issue of cross-dressing and gender change: a guest's lifetime struggle; relationships with parents and siblings, wife, children, and the outside world; decisions; and results are all explored within the limitations of a television hour. It is a pattern that is used over and over. Because of varying types of viewers, daytime and evening television have some important differences. Although both use celebrities and/or experts, the numbers are not the same; daytime shows by and large, except for their hosts, are usually not dependent on such outside stars or pundits.

Although *The Oprah Winfrey Show* brings in outside stars, often from the entertainment world, daytime programming seems to prefer everyday, average guests, whereas evening programs seek professionals. Most nighttime talk shows, with the exception of those hosted by comedians, focus on news or politics. Even though producers of both day and evening programs seek spirited participants who are not opposed to verbal conflict, the types of program participants are not alike. Daytime shows privilege ordinary people over experts, because their stories and exchanges are more personal and emotional, which is what their audiences expect and tune in for.

Hosts are seldom associated with a program's initiation, although the producer must always put the host in the forefront. The producer, who is usually a woman, must also find a new take on stories to make them interesting. In fact, as Ehrenreich claims, "the plot is always the same." Thus, to capture the attention of the audience, producers constantly seek guests who are picked not only because of their stories but also for their personalities and looks; the producer seeks and deliberately fosters impassioned revelations from guests. Although the seeming simplicity of the presentation is actually artifice, as writer Jean Shattuc points out, very few viewers realize that the participant—that is, the nonexpert guest—has had what amounts to brief lessons in acting before the show; the producer and aides have coached the guests in what might be called show-and-tell methods. Like the director of a movie, the producer seeks to bring out the strongest kind of emotional presentation but also wants to keep it at a controlled pitch. Opposite the cool of professionals and experts, the nonprofessional guest with a narrative to tell is encouraged to reveal every feeling, orally and physically, so that both the studio audience and the home viewer are caught up in the story. To avoid the occasional mistake, the producer thoroughly checks the backgrounds of guests in advance, from letters attesting to the truths of their stories to supporting statements, tapes, and pictures, and perhaps information from physicians. The producer must approve and even improve the nonprofessional participants' appearance, clothing, hair, and makeup prior to the program so that they are appealing to the audience.

Many people disagree about the significance of talk shows. The devoted followers who faithfully watch the programs claim that the shows add meaning and understanding to their lives. Almost without exception, viewers speak affectionately and admiringly of Oprah. Some, who follow every story about her, talk as if a close relationship exists between them and the star. Former Harpo producer Coady describes reactions of audiences at shows: they cry when Oprah enters her television studio, gush when she speaks to them directly, and long to be touched. Journalists write of occasions when Oprah has left the stage to hug a member of the audience who has revealed a traumatic experience. All daytime hosts—unlike those on evening and weekend programs—present an aura of warmth, intimacy, and friendliness. Everyone is on a first-name basis, and most hosts, including Oprah, use personal pronouns as often as possible to create an informal atmosphere. Where some hosts hold a microphone while walking around, Oprah will sometimes sit in the audience and, on occasion speak with a few people during the break. This may appear to be a spontaneous act, but the producers have selected those people before the show. The conversation may then serve as friendly transitions between the segments of the show that have been broken into frequently by advertisements. In a one-hour program, the actual time given to the subject may be less than that devoted to the advertisers.

Some writers—popular culture scholars for the most part—find talk shows shameful, not necessarily because of the subject matter but because they believe the guests are exploited. Journalist Barbara Ehrenreich, describing the participants, sees them as so bereft of love, respect, and hope that they are willing, even eager, to reveal the most intimate aspects of their lives. Their homes, she claims, are often "trailer parks and tenements." Many live in poverty; they may be on welfare or unable to pay their bills, or they may work two jobs to survive. No matter their situation, they are turned into exhibits for the purpose of entertainment. The guests often allow themselves to be humiliated while the audience goes "slumming," says another writer. Some journalists have disparaged the shows; Janet Maslin called them "muck marathons," whereas Anna Quindlen described such programs as an airing of dirty laundry and the revelations as "the dark night of split levels."

Television, after all, is a business, and the entire venture is based on a syndicate's vision of viewers as a commodity that must be sold to advertisers who have a product to market. However, it falls to the producers to keep a show looking fresh and different from its competition. Generally with only a week to prepare each show, the producer is much like a newsperson working in a noisy office filled with every imaginable type of research file and publication. The subject matter, though, is social problems, not news, with emphasis on personal or domestic content. Although frequently shows move beyond the experiences or considerations of the typical viewer, the attraction is many sided, with a fascination similar to that of human interest stories generally found in the C or D sections of newspapers, which are geared toward women (although a recent newspaper poll has found those sections popular with men as well). Yet, almost always underlying the content of the talk shows are views that are conservative, conformist, and moralistic. All of this is true of *The Oprah Winfrey Show*.

The audience at an Oprah show only appears to be selected at random. Tickets are difficult to obtain and must be sent for far in advance, perhaps months before the program. Although millions of people watch the show, only 325 get in for each taping, according to Harpo Productions. Tickets are not available at the door. Because certain colors do not photograph well on television, the studio audience is asked to avoid wearing beige or white and is expected to play an active role in the show, having usually been selected by a coordinator who wants the group to seem diverse. Writing for the south Florida *Sun Sentinel*, Kathryn Whitbourne recounted the details of her visit to the show. Security, on entry at the Harpo complex, included searches of handbags and removal of cameras, cell phones, and beepers, even taking away the writer's copy of O magazine.

While guests wait until their names are called for admission to the studio, they are free to visit a gift shop that surprisingly (at least during Whitbourne's visit) sells almost no Oprah memorabilia. When gift giving is a major part of the show, the items are impressive and worthy of mention in the next day's newspapers. The topic of the never-to-be-forgotten gift of cars several years ago has become part of television lore. Those particular gifts received much attention in the press once the public learned the gift recipients had to pay taxes for the cars, which had not been purchased by Oprah but were an advertising gimmick of one car dealer (and the occasion for snide remarks about the fact that Oprah and company were not the actual givers). One excited guest sold her Pontiac in order to open a business, Big Girl Cosmetics, which was called a "beauty empire" five years later. Cars are but one of the items audiences have been gifted with. Over the years, Oprah has given away UGG boots to her staff as presents and also made them a must-have item for many others; Apple iPods; books galore; and shopping carts filled with products from sponsors. One report on such gifts mentioned the delivery of uniforms from Chicago for staff to wear when delivering "special gifts" to people in the audience. (The uniforms are also said to have "special significance" to fans of the show.)

Gifts vary in cost and value, but one of Oprah's "favorite things" to give away was a refrigerator that had a built-in television set and radio. That gift provoked great excitement—more than was visible when she had distributed debit cards sponsored by Bank of America (when it was more affluent) to a surprised studio audience who learned that the money had to be given away to individuals in need or to charities. Oprah wanted the audience to experience the feeling she has—that gift giving is a source of happiness. However, she gave an additional gift of DVD recorders—a keeper—to the more than 300 people in the audience. Rumor has it that when Oprah moves to her own network, the "favorite things" part of her shows will be abandoned.

Surprisingly, considering Oprah's reputation for generosity, there were no giveaways for the general audience at the show attended by Whitbourne. That appears to be typical, unless giveaways are central to a particular show; only a box of tissues may be found under the seat, for what Whitbourne refers to as "those touching moments." Before the program, some members of the audience, in addition to the guests, also have had coaching, and during the show, the camera will focus on them. The lighting is directed toward those particular people, though the entire audience is expected to get involved, if only to applaud, ask questions, or show emotion. A warm-up precedes the program, and then the host appears.

Viewers who have watched talk shows are probably aware of the structure followed by all of them, but writer Jean Shattuc has formally broken that down into seven parts describing a model, even to the number of minutes generally spent on each segment.

The first section is the longest, and the last section is the shortest. Part one, introduction of the topic and guests by the host, consumes between 13 and 17 minutes, during which the host plays the perfect listener. The problem or challenge is explored in part two, in 6 to 9 minutes, by various people—the host and members of the audience, who ask questions and may contribute information about similar experiences. Part three is even shorter, 4 to 6 minutes, time partially expended by divergent points of view; at that point, if an expert is brought in, that person adds another tier of information to the matter. The audience is then given 3 to 6 minutes in segment four to question the expert. Other guests may be involved, or perhaps the host will abandon the role of listener and become a participant who tells her or his story. Once the issue has been developed and explored, the time has come to find resolutions, and 2 to 5 minutes are given over in part five to various possibilities; by then, host and expert are on the same side, although the audience may not agree. Another 2 to 5 minutes, in part six, are spent in exploring possible answers and validation. The final segment, part seven, has almost no time to wrap things up, between 30 seconds and 2 minutes. The concluding statement, by expert, guest, or audience participant, is invariably hopeful and positive.

Oprah's show is usually taped several weeks in advance of its airing, providing the producers the opportunity to edit it and exercise some control over what is shown. The exceptions to the advance taping are those that cover breaking news and depend on immediacy for their impact. Even though the audience is aware of most of the preparation and earlier planning, few people resent it. Critics may question Oprah's sincerity and view her as a skilled actress, but viewers see her as natural; they approve, laugh, and applaud her outspokenness; so implicit is their trust in Oprah, they do not seem to know or care that everything on the program is managed and not spontaneous.

Many writers—journalists and scholars alike—have emphasized the fact that Oprah is a highly visible black entertainer, but her audiences are predominantly white. Although on her program she frequently deals with racial matters and furthers activities of blacks in art and education and now politics, her race is apparently unimportant to her white viewers, central to her black viewers, and analysts regard her as "a comforting non-threatening bridge between black and white cultures." African Americans, until recently, have not been very visible, although the change of administration with a mixed-race president has altered the dynamic. Some of these perceptions result from Oprah's earlier remoteness from both political activism and the civil rights movement.

However, it has also been pointed out that the commercial aspect of her show—that is, the advertising—requires maintenance of a neutral stance on race. And, although her active role in the campaign, nomination, and election of Barack Obama was a meaningful departure from her previous position, she did not follow the suggestions of some of her supporters to accept a job with the new administration.

In her series on racism, however, Oprah did not remain neutral. Although a variety of opinions were expressed, all the speakers agreed that racism is undesirable. Oprah's perspective agreed that racism is undesirable, and her view on racism is described as "therapeutic," because she has said that "the lack of self esteem" brings about "all the problems in the world." Numerous scholars fault that approach, which they name as "identity politics." Oprah insists that racists are ignorant and afraid. They must change their attitudes, and, unless they do, generation after generation will perpetuate the same biases. Language itself, even unknowingly, can be racist, and Oprah herself confesses to having used racist expressions. Because anger solves nothing, she and the 1992 series facilitators said, and continue to say, it must be supplanted by forgiveness. People must change their attitudes, beginning in their hearts. Some scholars—among them Janice Peck—have criticized these views, however, as too subjective and too utopian for very complex issues.

One black member of Oprah's audience in 1992 challenged the views expressed, telling her: "Listen Oprah, when you leave your show, you go to a lavish home. Lots of us don't go home to lavish things. We go home to empty refrigerators, you know, crying kids, no diapers, no jobs. Everybody ain't got it like everybody got it." Oprah has been faulted for failing to pursue the matter of inequality in politics and economics. Yet little has actually changed economically for the underclass of blacks in the United States in the early part of the 21st century, and, although more and more people of color have moved up economically, television programs do not necessarily reflect the changes that have taken place in the culture.

According to the lengthy article by Janice Peck in *Cultural Critique*, when views of this sort were expressed on the show, the star would go to another speaker or a commercial.[2] Thus, according to some analysts, the emphasis was on "individual transformation, which both Oprah and her predominantly white, female constituency" favor over societal change. Similar to the framing of the race series, a number of Oprah Winfrey program subjects are topical matters that have been discussed in other media. Individual transformation is a staple, a building block in Oprah's philosophy, something she returns to again and again on the air and in person.

There is no reason to believe her core message will change in the future, even after her move from network daytime television to cable. After leaks and ongoing speculation among television speakers and watchers, Oprah tearfully announced she was going to bring her network talk show to an end early in 2011. At that point, she had been on the show for 25 years, and she "[felt] in her bones" it was time to change course and do other things. There was almost a Wordsworthian melancholy in her statement—no grieving for the past but rather gaining strength from it.

Whereas the majority of her faithful audience seemed devastated by the upcoming change, critics for the most part agreed with her decision, and many believed the change would be refreshing and exciting. They pointed to Oprah's savvy and almost unerring choices in her work of the last 25 years.

The Harpo organization, her spokespeople said, would remain in Chicago, the home city, but many questioned what would happen once the show came to an end. The new show is not be produced in Chicago. The change brings a loss for Chicago, as well as a number of television stations, no matter what the speculation is about the future. Columnists talk of the financial loss that will be sustained by networks—not only to affiliates carrying the show but also to programs that followed it. Chicago writer Mark Brown for the *Chicago Sun-Times* mentioned rumors that Jerry Roper, president and CEO of the Chicagoland Chamber of Commerce, said that Oprah has been more than "a local icon." Another called her "an economic engine" who might move her organization to Los Angeles.

A number of names have surfaced as possible replacements for Oprah's show—more and more of them as the date draws closer for Oprah's departure. However, another talk show and magazine entrepreneur, Martha Stewart, has apparently been influenced by Oprah's decision to change to cable. Shortly after Oprah made her announcement, Stewart also made hers. Two well-known people whose positions on almost everything are at the opposite end of the spectrum from Oprah have been mentioned as possible replacements for Oprah. Both are or have been employed by the Fox Network: Glen Beck and Sarah Palin. When the question was raised with Palin shortly after she joined Fox, she announced that she wanted to keep her options open. Palin has numerous admirers, but she has not had a television show; Beck not only has had his own show, but also was said to bring in more viewers of other talk shows among longtime Fox performers. In a Gallup Poll, according to the *Salt Lake Tribune*, Beck's U.S. admirers outnumber those of the Pope. The same paper and others consider him "a brilliant entertainer" but also a right-winger without a conscience who provides on a daily basis a "stew of venom and fabrication." Though it now appears unlikely, if Beck does replace *The Oprah Winfrey Show*, he would provide the television critics and audience with much material to discuss.

As for Oprah, says her closest friend, Gayle King, there should not be, nor will there be, a "pity party." After all, Oprah is leaving the program by choice and nothing else. A poll taken by the *Chicago Sun-Times* found, after Oprah's announcement of future change, that she remains America's favorite TV personality.

NOTES

1. Alex Kucznski, "Menopause Forever," *New York Times*, 22 June 2002.

2. Janice Peck, "Talk about Racism: Framing a Popular Discourse of Race on *Oprah Winfrey*," *Cultural Critique* (Spring 1994).

Chapter 4

AMERICA READS

Always looking for ways to maintain the attention and involvement of her audience, and with an eye on ratings, Oprah and company introduced what was, at the time, a novel idea: a monthly television book club. (Other shows and television channels briefly adopted the idea.) Oprah would chose a book she'd read and enjoyed, then announce the title on the air; a program with the author's appearance would follow; and, finally, a group of diverse, carefully picked, packaged, and screened readers would discuss the book. At the beginning, every month, (except in summer) a book title would be announced, although there would be no regular day that the club would be on the program. A decade later, there were no definite schedules. Between 2000 and 2009, 36 books were assigned for club readers, but each year had a different number of books. In the first year of the club, there were nine readings, but, by 2009, only one book was on the list: *Say You're One of Them*, a prize-winning collection of African short stories by a Nigerian priest, Uwem Akpan, who studied writing in the United States.

Before the choices were to be named on the air, sealed boxes of books were sent to public libraries with the labels "Do Not Open Until————." With the usual declarations, hype, and advertising, the club was born in televisionland, in 1996, when the first book discussion took place, about Jacquelyn Mitchard's *The Deep End of the Ocean.*

From the beginning, every book chosen by Oprah became a best-seller and an exceptional boon to the publishing industry. A June 5, 2009, article in the *New York Times* (with no attribution to a particular author) examines both Janice Peck's *The Age of Oprah* and Oprah's influence on her book club members. Quoting Peck, the reviewer writes that the club has elevated Oprah "to the status of cultural icon," an expert who "tells people what to read," the "lessons" to be learned, and the "questions to ask." Furthermore, says the reviewer, Oprah's chosen commentators are expected to "agree with her . . . reading of the book." Everything appears to be about self-help—the same theme of her television show. Although the reviewer finds both the show and Oprah's approach to books "sentimental, shallow and manipulative," the effect on the audience is powerful; it places Oprah "as the savior of women from themselves," and, incidentally, makes Oprah and the publishing industry large amounts of money. Peck has pointed to a notable difference between the lessons Oprah imparts and those of classrooms: Oprah is concerned with self-discovery and wants the focus to be on lessons learned about oneself, whereas university classroom instruction tends to focus on separating the self from the work and therefore maintaining objectivity.

Linton Weeks, in the *Washington Post,* called Oprah's choice of books the equivalent of hitting the lottery for writers, but that same description has obviously held true for publishers.[1] Throughout the country, bookstores large and small, knowing the effect of Oprah's pronouncements, immediately stocked numerous copies of the recommended book. Even a writer's first novel could sell as many as a million copies, and, as an editorial in the *San Francisco Chronicle* noted, "even classics that were getting little traffic on library shelves" were being sold in the millions. *Publishers Weekly* backed up the data of Oprah's influence with the claim that hardcover and paperback books could not get onto best-seller lists unless readers knew the author's previous work or were an Oprah pick.[2]

Oprah's choices are always available in paperback and thus available to a larger number of readers. Once her book club became a reality, a browser or reader going into any bookstore and numerous coffee shops could not fail to see a special display, shelf, or bookcase, given over to "An Oprah Selection." Her chosen books even had an imprint to that effect. Only a year after the introduction of the book club, *Newsweek*, along with other magazines, labeled her the most significant person in the modern book world, and one *Newsweek* writer, in reviewing a thriller, had words of advice for publishers about turning their books into best-sellers: "pray for an act of God. . . . or Oprah." Inspirational books, even if not chosen for Oprah's club, became very popular as a result of exposure on her show, particularly after the events of 9/11. One was a book of poetry, *Heartsongs*, whose success was fueled by a visit of the 11-year-old author, Mattie, who later died of a severe form of muscular dystrophy. Not only did his first book become a best-seller, but after his appearance on Oprah's show, the child signed a five-book contract. Oprah called him inspirational, a "friend," and "an angel on earth." When a Maryland park and statue were dedicated to the boy's memory, Oprah was in the group of celebrants.

Not everyone had liked Oprah's pushing the young poet's work. Journalist Robert Elder, a reporter for the *Chicago Tribune*, commented: "Sentimental? Yes. But publishers have found that sentimentality sells." Elder, publishers, and Oprah are not the only people involved with books who have discovered the value of sentimentality: author Tom Clancy earlier gained considerable publicity for several years when he wrote and talked about his deep affection for the afflicted child and had dedicated a novel to him.[3]

Writer David Streitfeld (then on staff at the *Washington Post*) was one of the few writers who found Oprah's efforts commendable in urging people to read and compared her effectiveness in getting people interested in books to that of 19th-century tycoon and philanthropist Andrew Carnegie, who, among his other deeds, endowed 2,500 libraries. But a *Washington Post* colleague of Streitfeld's, Amy Schwartz, was not as fulsome with her praise, raising the possibility that Oprah was simply harvesting the returns of a recent national revival of reading.[4] Nonetheless, so influential was Oprah considered in her effect on national reading habits that, in 1999, the National Book Foundation, at an elegant black-tie affair hosted by actor Steve Martin, presented Oprah with its 50th anniversary gold medal. Even a decade later, Oprah's influence on reading has remained significant. Hers has been the largest book club in the world—ever. It is important to note, as *New York Times* reviewer David Carr did, that she is open with her audience and "never has a piece of what she is pushing . . . she is not for sale."[5] However, the books are for sale, and most importantly the booksellers order whatever Oprah recommends, knowing that there will be a huge readership for the product.

Accepting the medal from the foundation, Oprah spoke of the paramount role books had played in her life. She said that books have always been its most pleasurable part. They've also helped her to learn about herself and the world. Singling out Maya Angelou's autobiographical work *I Know Why the Caged Bird Sings*, she has talked of it as a work of validation for her as an illegitimate, poor, black Southern-born teenager who had suffered many hurts. For the first time, she understood that it was possible to move beyond her misery to a better life. At that point, she began to understand the force of writers and their books.

Yet, despite her passion for the written word and after several years of praise for her effect on the publishing industry and the reading public's increased interest in books, Oprah, who had been nicknamed the "queen bee of book clubs," suddenly decided to abandon the club as part of her television program. On a Friday show (often a day when announcements are made that don't make the news), she informed the audience that the novel *Sula* would be the last book chosen for the club. She announced, in a statement that would provoke criticism, that she no longer could find interesting books to read, introduce, and discuss on her program. Although Oprah did not tell the audience of other factors in her decision, there was more to the matter than lack of worthy books.

Regardless of the huge number of books sold, from 600,000 to a million new copies per book, a market survey revealed only a limited viewing audience for the television discussion of books, considerably less than those who watch Oprah's regular daily programs. The shows about books became less frequent over the years. Experiments with the format had been tried to maintain interest—informal dinners and conversations with authors, films of dramatic scenes from books, even discussions with women whose life experiences were like those of the book characters—but the numbers of viewers still dropped. Also, reportedly, sales of books were beginning to flatten (though Oprah's picks continued to sell more than other works). Meanwhile, an "inside source" leaked the somewhat curious disclosure that the task of screening one book per month was exhausting for Oprah and her staff, "the single hardest thing that had to be done for the television program." If so, it is surprising that Oprah continuously refers to books she is reading or has read. Friends claim that she prefers reading to television, and an issue of her now-defunct magazine *O At Home* contains a lengthy article with photos about her books and library in her California house.

Some of the publishing companies sturdily supported Oprah's decision publicly—after all, how could they do otherwise, given the important financial boost she'd made to the industry? Random House put a full-page "Thank you, Oprah" in the April 12, 2002, edition of the *New York Times*. The company expressed gratitude for the years of work she'd devoted to "books, authors, and readers." Nevertheless, it was a serious and unexpected blow to the publishing industry, and several spokespeople felt her statement was an unjust disparagement of U.S. publishing. Although the demise of the club unquestionably was a great disappointment to many writers who wanted to be chosen, it meant much more to the publishers who had made many millions from the sales.

Reviewers also were skeptical about the reason given for disbanding the club. As Carlin Romano of the *Philadelphia Inquirer* pointed out, the final book Oprah picked, *Sula*, had been written 28 years earlier by Toni Morrison, one of four Morrison novels Oprah had chosen. Romano questioned why "out of decades of published fiction in English" she was unable to recommend a single novel each month for the club. Romano's piece turned more derisive with the comment that anyone as rich as Oprah could certainly give up the arduous task of a monthly book selection and take an easier road for her program "like talking between commercials or serving in the *Israeli Defense Forces*."[6] Critics also pointed out that more variety might prove more palatable to readers as well as reviewers, some of whom found the Oprah selections excessively restrictive—that is, with a sameness from one work to another.

Although fans continued to associate Oprah with books, a number of negative statements were made about her choices. Critic Carol Muller listed a series of "Oprah topics" that she found in books she was reviewing. Those topics were listed without comment as possible themes for Oprah's programs and for articles in Oprah's magazine: lesbianism, abuse, osteoporosis, devotion, retardation, and a crisis of faith. Such adverse judgments about Oprah's subject matter are related to various earlier deprecatory reviews by others, criticizing many of Oprah's choices as focusing on dysfunctional people. For instance, *Wall Street Journal* writer Cynthia Crossen might have been speaking for various reviewers in stating that the reach of Oprah's book selections went from "A (abused) to B (battered)." Such descriptions are frequently applied pejoratively (mainly by men) to books—and movies—favored by women. Another reviewer, Robert Clark, suggested that the term "woman's novel" should be dropped for her choices, and "the Oprah novel" should be substituted because her selections have the same formula.

The excuse given for *The Oprah Winfrey Show*'s abandonment of the book club had numerous people wondering about Oprah's judgment. There was a loud, sometimes angry, outcry and not a little scorn from readers, comedians, and even comic strip artists. There was humor as well: columnist Ben Crandell, writing in one of his "South Beach" reports in the *Sun Sentinel* in April 2002, headlined it as "Oprah's Shelved, So Others Must Pass on the Good Word." With strong, tongue-in-cheek language, he called Oprah's dismissal of the club "Betrayal. Intrigue. Ruthlessness . . . heartless . . . shocking . . . callous." (Other book clubs have since been launched; one in particular in Britain, seeking what is known as "the Oprah effect," has been touted as bringing in a "whole new generation of literary superstars.")

Another farcical illustration of the mileage gained from the clumsiness of Oprah's action appeared in a mocking comic strip drawn by Matt Janz. Titled "Out of the Gene Pool," the strip had Oprah speaking of the boredom she had felt in reading while she ate her lunch; no longer interested in the book, she put a carrot in her nose; that experience, which she describes as "spiritual," provides "rebirth."

The cartoonist, making fun not only of Oprah's loss of interest in books but also of her television persona, satirizes both the star and the audience. An easy target for ridicule, in her pronouncement about the disappearance of worthwhile books and her public personalizing of all her experiences, she became a satirist's dream. Janz mocks her television persona, her interest in things spiritual, and her unsuspected but apparent belief in the phoenix myth—regeneration from ashes. Characteristically, she reveals everything to her audience because she wants to include them in her awakening, the great phenomenon of renewal. But what an awakening she has had, she tells the audience, the abandonment of books for carrots. Examining a centuries-old debate about mind and body, the cartoonist skillfully and humorously conflates body—that is, the carrot—with spirit. Oprah's renewal comes from a vegetable, not from some clever or brilliant thesis or work of art.

A further spoof refers to the huge headlines and lengthy stories that supposedly appear in the next day's newspapers. Newspaper reports tell of many thousands of women who also want to thrust carrots up their noses and experience what Oprah did, so that they overrun grocery stores and hospitals and bring about a surge in the stock market.

Six years after the first of the books was introduced, in the summer of 2002, Oprah's Book Club was put to rest. Was it predictable? Did the majority of readers like her choice of books? Apparently so, considering the vast numbers of sales. Oprah's good friend, writer Maya Angelou, weighed in, stating that she didn't agree with all the choices, but reading is what matters. If, indeed, lack of audience interest was the problem—rather than the lack of good, readable books—could the cancellation of that feature in the show have been premature? Considering the vast amount of publicity given to the dustup Oprah and company had with one of the novelists, Jonathan Franzen, shortly before the decision to give up the book segment of the program, interest in the book selections (among readers, nonreaders, and, in fact, general interest throughout the country) was aroused to a pitch not enjoyed before and could only have served to swell the numbers of the show's audience. In what may be an exaggeration of the entire affair, the cultural critic of the *Chicago Tribune*, Julia Keller, has written that "it was the Franzen episode [that] put [the book club] on the map." Keller considers Franzen's *The Corrections* so important in transforming "literary culture in 2000–2009," because it "made her book club controversial" and U.S. readers like controversy. Keller is not alone in her view that the book club has been an "astonishing cultural force."

The Corrections, like all of Oprah's choices, became a best-seller from the moment it was selected for the book club. Because of a public brouhaha with Oprah, Franzen became the most-written-about writer of that year. Without the Oprah association, *Washington Post* book reviewer Jonathan Yardley asserted that Franzen would not have achieved much commercial success. An Oprah choice for the book club was a guarantee of a vast readership. In several columns, Yardley reaffirms his belief that Oprah genuinely champions books, but he also hastens to inform readers of his thorough dislike of her television program. The one time Yardley watched it, he "nearly gagged on all the treacle and psychobabble."

Book critics have noted that all books anointed by Oprah become best-sellers, bringing in millions of dollars to the author and, of course, the publishing industry. For many writers, that recognition has opened the doors to further opportunities. Franzen, for example, whose name became known everywhere with the reading public, has become a regular contributor to prestigious magazines, even though in the eyes of many, he had committed the unpardonable sin of ingratitude as one of the chosen. Despite the renown and money gained, Franzen objected to being placed in a class that included "schmalzy one-dimensional" books. His own book, said Franzen, is in the high art tradition, and he didn't want to be known as an Oprah Book Club choice.

Sides in the conflict were chosen, but far more were and are on Oprah's team. In addition to her loyal audience and readers, those who expressed their opinions in print, among them people in *New York* magazine, *Newsweek*, the *Boston Globe*, and the *Chicago Tribune*, called Franzen stinging names that he duly records in an essay. To one he was a "mother----er," to another a "pompous prick," an "ego-blinded snob" to a third, and to a fourth, a "spoiled, whiny little brat."

It is surprising that the Oprah producers in their background checks of participants in their programs overlooked Franzen's essays and his hostile statements about the shamelessness of television. He proclaimed his longing to return to a time when the public and private worlds were separate. How could anyone, including Franzen, have thought he could be a candidate for any television program that thrives on the personal and intimate? When, in 2010, Franzen published another novel, *Freedom*, which achieved notoriety almost before publication, Oprah and Franzen reconciled. All apparently was forgiven on both sides, and the "new" Franzen is now described as "mellow."

Not many authors are reluctant to become known to the public, particularly when their books, no matter how well written, significant, or appealing, more often than not have a limited audience. Given the thousands of books published each year, wide readership is like a game of chance. Furthermore, even with strong reviews, many books fail to attract attention. Works of nonfiction, apart from politics or history, have more of an uphill fight to reach large audiences.

Not all of the books Oprah periodically singled out are novels, nor have they been works to be discussed by the club. For a number of years, Oprah also selected nonfiction publications for themes on her program. Her mostly female studio audience may consist of mothers and daughters, some young, depending on the topic, or older women, and few or no men or fathers. The fact is that Oprah's viewers and readers, in and outside of the studio, have been primarily women.

One tenet of many of these programs, and stressed also through the club—is an Oprah mantra: everyone, male and female, young and old, has to learn for herself or himself that our lives are in our own hands. We cannot bypass either hurtful situations or the person who causes suffering; the person who has given us pain or made us angry, according to Oprah, must be made aware of the issue. It is essential to assess our own feelings and, if necessary, get help from those around us whom we like and trust so that we are enabled to speak out. When we allow fear of loss to prevent us from being open and honest, we can only lose more. The subject, as in the lessons of the books, is one that resonates in many, many speeches and interviews that Oprah gives, reflecting her own learning curve over the years.

By urging girls and women to refrain from expressing anger or aggressiveness, Oprah, in her choice of books, and the numerous pundits on her show point out that our culture has always taught dishonesty; it is behavior that must change. If, for some, openness in relationships means being cast out by friends or groups, the experience may be good fortune that leads to a more centered existence. There will be other people who feel as they do, and, when they discover those people, life will get easier.

Whatever led to the demise of the book club, less than 10 months after her decision to abandon the entire concept, Oprah surprised viewers, the publishing industry, writers, and the book-reading public at the end of February 2003, with an announcement reminiscent of the late comedienne Gilda Radner's famous line, "Never Mind." Oprah was reviving her book club. Like almost every act of Oprah's, it made newspaper headlines in both the hard news sections and in the style and entertainment segments of many papers. But lest she would have to proclaim that she'd found current books alright, worthy of reading and discussing, she was going to rediscover (or perhaps discover) the classics. Although it is unclear what subjects she studied in college, like literature majors everywhere, she began reading the great writers of the past: Shakespeare, Faulkner, and Hemingway, among others. While being honored with a standing ovation for all she had previously done to inspire an interest in current books, she told the Association of American Publishers she would be returning to the recommendation of books, "but with a difference." There was speculation about whether her decision would bring the same kind of joy as her announcement several years ago of the formation of the original book club. The incorrect prediction and consensus was "not likely." Publishing, like other industries, thrives on sales, and the question was how many publishing companies had the sales rights to the old classics. Would people simply dust off old copies of some of the required books of their youth, and libraries go to their warehouses to retrieve multiple copies? How many readers would want to enter the classroom for the either first or second time? Would only English majors apply? Would the new book club take the place of the classroom and, if so, how? Would the return to classics—in the way that Oprah's other programs have stimulated viewers—lead to a renewal of interest in literature and literary degrees in colleges and universities?

The announcement of the revitalization of the club certainly brought joy to the hearts and pens of readers but also to comedians and cartoonists. Multiple writers, including the caustic British critic Christopher Hitchens, couldn't resist giving advice to Oprah. When he told a group of high school students that she should consider a discussion of Tolstoy's *Anna Karenina*, he playfully put forth the idea that it could provide material for a long, long time for Oprah and her friend, psychologist Dr. Phil McGraw. Hitchens also recommended George Eliot's novel *Middlemarch* as particularly appropriate for Oprah's show. The novel, which tells of the sexual and intellectual frustrations of an unhappily married Victorian woman, is one that, he believes, offers endless possibilities for Oprah's program. Putting aside Hitchens's humor, the choices in more recent fiction also offer the reader stories of sexual and intellectual frustration, subjects not limited to the 19th century. And Oprah has chosen a number of them. Further suggestive humor was invoked by a Chicago columnist who wrote, "She's just about the only one making our country read things that aren't printed on the sides of cereal boxes."

The club was resurrected a short time after the opening of the Oprah Leadership Academy, when Sidney Poitier's memoir *The Measure of a Man* was chosen as the first book in the new club and the 56th choice for the club overall. Oprah described the book as "a spiritual autobiography," an apt term for a work that reports on faith, race, and the influence of great leaders such as Mandela and Gandhi. In talking on her show about the actor, Oprah called Poitier "one of the greatest men . . . on the planet." In the history of films, the actor stands as the first black performer to win an Oscar for best actor. The year was 1964, and the film was *Lilies of the Field*.

It seemed for a time the classics would later have a revived chance for sales with Oprah's new club undertaking, even if the authors are dead. In recent years, it has become more difficult for current writers either to get published or to make any money from their writing, at least in the United States if they are not selected for special programs such as Oprah's. Also in modern times, large corporations control most of the book industry so that publication now has less to do with quality than marketability. A world-famous star with Oprah's international following can have a major impact on the rejuvenation of reading. When Oprah made the promised announcement of a newly revived book club, stores immediately were deluged by sales. And for several years, their faith and hopes were rewarded, no matter what the choices were.

Oprah soon gave up on the classics and returned to more contemporary books, which appear to have little or no relationship to each other. Like the selections for the first club, the works are mostly those of women writers, and the majority of choices are American. Rarely does she depart from fiction, and it seems as though they are much like the picks that one might make in wandering through a bookstore or library. Whether Oprah herself chooses the books or members of her staff do so is not made public. Some novelists appear to be favorites; for example, Faulkner's books have been chosen three times (a somewhat surprising choice given that college students—even literature majors—are known to need assistance with his works). However, it isn't surprising that Oprah favors novels of the South. After all, she comes from that region. In the mix of choices are some philosophic/ religious/spiritual works that surely would not have become best-sellers without the Winfrey imprimatur.

When Oprah resumed the program with her book club, publishers continued to be thrilled with its enormous impact on her following, knowing they—the publishers—had the equivalent of the baseball field story: "If you build it, they will come."

But with Oprah's announcement a few years later that she would be giving up her daily show on network television, gloom reigns today in the publishing industry. Although there has been much wavering about the matter, it appears that there will be no book club in the world of OWN. Several newspapers have stated openly that Oprah's "big switch" will not only change afternoon television but also that book publishers are facing "doom." The few details about plans for the future focus on movies—mainly documentaries—rather than books. Stock advisors speak of the loss of income for networks, perhaps for the city of Chicago, and for earlier authors as well as newer ones, whereas the new OWN channel is predicted to become a great moneymaker.

Keeping track of Oprah's wishes about her book club can be dizzying for her reading followers. After stating she was giving it up, she announced she was adding Franzen's newest work, *Freedom*, to her list. Perhaps it was the large number of positive, even glowing, reviews that led to her decision, and it was a good time to make amends with the writer. Franzen himself has reported, "All fences have been mended," leading reviewer Edel Coffey (the *Irish Independent*) to remind one how "amazing [it is] what a little success can do."[7]

A complete list of the 36 newer choices on Oprah's soon-to-be-extinct book club books might be compared to an electrocardiogram, as the lines go up and down. Some years have many selections, but the first year had the most: nine. Some years had only a single book. Before Oprah's announcement of the coming change, she had announced a type of appendage to the club, but this was another format, a children's book club known as the Kids' Reading List. A team was chosen to put together the names of books appropriate for little ones aged 2 to 12 and beyond. Oprah's favorites were included, as were recommendations from experts in the field of children's literature. Although the list is on record, little has been done with it.

One writer, unaffiliated with any of Oprah's undertakings, decided that Oprah herself would make a good subject for a children's book. Called *Oprah: The Little Speaker*, by Carole Boston Weatherford, the trade journal *Publishers Weekly* listed it along with reviews of other children's books. In Weatherford's book, the reviewer writes—in words suggesting less than a strong recommendation—there are "frequent references to God's presence . . . to almost beatific effect . . . The inspirational message comes through clearly . . ." And the work "closes on an oddly smug note . . ."[8]

As in the past, some Oprah book choices have made it to the big screen, and Oprah intends to continue that practice. Even while readying herself for the major change to cable television, she and Tom Hanks announced plans to coproduce a movie based on an Oprah book pick, *The Story of Edgar Sawtelle*. It is unclear whether all her movie productions will be on her channel. Because there are other works being considered, it may be that various types of movies will replace the book club. Even though Oprah will be giving up the book club when she leaves her show, her publication, *O, The Oprah Magazine*, which has been an outstanding success, will continue.

Three publications, called "vanity magazines" by *Washington Post* food writer Candy Saigon, dominated the women's market for several years: those of Martha Stewart (*Martha Stewart Living*), Oprah Winfrey (*O, The Oprah Magazine*), and Rosie O'Donnell (*Rosie*). Although everyone eagerly awaited the first of these, Martha Stewart's *Living*, Oprah's magazine has been more popular from the beginning. The three of them, but particularly Stewart and Winfrey, demonstrated strong qualities in all their undertakings, so that from the beginning, the magazines were expected to do well. Yet other women celebrities who also launched magazines during the same period failed in their attempts after a short period of time: Ivana Trump (whose magazine *Ivana* went under almost immediately) and Tina Brown (who left her much-praised and prominent editorship at *The New Yorker* to start *Talk*, had poor notices from the onset, despite an inordinate amount of puffery from the publishing company). The failure rate for start-ups in magazines is extremely high; even Oprah's second venture into magazine publishing, *Oprah At Home*, also came to an end.

Like Oprah, O'Donnell began as a television star. However, after six years, O'Donnell left the world of television in May 2002 (although briefly she appeared on other shows including *The View*). She also departed from magazine publishing in September 2002. Rumors had been circulating, from early on, about problems between her and the publisher of her magazine. Her exit from the magazine world, though, was stormy and nothing like the earlier move from television. In contrast to the fiasco that marked the end of O'Donnell's involvement with the magazine, her talk show was so popular she was known as "the Queen of Nice," although not everyone agreed with that description. One writer at *Forbes* called her opinionated, and only a month after O'Donnell's brief retirement from television, she proved herself to be not only opinionated but also determined to wipe the slate clean—or break it—as she scorned both the title and image that she'd previously enjoyed. Claiming "the bitch ain't so nice anymore," she began to take on other roles, including that of stand-up comic, returning, in part, to the type of comedy work she had done at the beginning of her career, except that her early comedy routines were much more wholesome than the later ones. It is apparent, however, that there will always be a place on television for O'Donnell, who is said to be returning to daytime television soon, with a talk show on Oprah's new network.

The magazine *Rosie*, inaugurated in April 2001, a year after the appearance of *O*, was a replacement for 125-year-old *McCall's*, which had been losing millions. The original 19th-century *McCall's* focused on selling dress patterns of James McCall, a tailor, but it underwent multiple reincarnations over the years, and the last one bore no resemblance to earlier issues. When the publishing company, Gruner and Jahr—a division of Bertlesmann, an enormous German multimedia group—and its staff closed down the old publication, name and all, they searched for a viable new magazine to take its place. Obviously seeking to emulate the success of the other two publications, *O*, and *Martha Stewart Living* (labeled "the mother ship of them all" by writer Candy Saigon), they focused on Rosie O'Donnell as someone who would be strong competition to both. She was famous, funny, and popular, and she showed some of the same personality traits of both Oprah and Stewart: strength and determination and staying power with audiences. Gruner and Jahr knew, as Hearst did with Oprah, it would have a ready group of subscribers from the television audience.

For a short period of time, the two stars, O'Donnell and Oprah, seemed to be almost in lockstep: television, magazines, and even books for readers. O'Donnell, though, limited her picks to children's books and even announced it before her decision to leave her long-running show. Nothing came of O'Donnell's plans for a book club, however.

When it first began publication, the new magazine, *Rosie*, seemed to fulfill the publisher's hopes, with strong sales and increasingly lucrative numbers of advertisements. Its format was standard: crafts, health, food, causes (not quite so standard, because of their controversial elements politically and socially, but they were and are O'Donnell's favorites). There was one particular topic that O'Donnell and the magazine skirted: the gay life that O'Donnell was leading quietly. Although it was not a secret, most of her audience and readership apparently were unaware of it. After all, in the main, O'Donnell projected something of a 1950s image of family life as the (adoptive) mother of several children. Then, after years of being circumspect about her private affairs, O'Donnell went public with her autobiography, *Find Me*, a book that opened the closet door. Since then, O'Donnell has made no attempt to hide the facts of her sexual preferences. She is certainly not the first or only entertainer to make such an announcement, but there may have been fallout in ratings for what was considered a family show. Her tell-all book had preceded by a month her exiting her television show. Soon after publication of her book, sales of the magazine began to fall precipitously. Few critics specifically ascribe the drop in newsstand purchases to O'Donnell's outing but rather to her social and political views. Yet these are views she has always held, and they did not appear to offend the readership previously. Soon, stories of wars between O'Donnell and her staff were being told, and then information about the hostile relationships of O'Donnell and the publishers surfaced.

Although O'Donnell had declared that she had wanted to be a cooperative member of the magazine group, she later said that had not worked, and she did not want to be a control [expletive] "like

Oprah and Martha," but she would become one. She would be as uncompromising as they are, she avowed. However, control belonged to the publishers, and O'Donnell resigned after firing off salvos against their actions. The publishers then retaliated publicly in stronger language, blaming her for destroying the magazine and violating her contract. By the end of 2002, *Rosie* was still on the newsstands, but the December issue was its last. Described by *Washington Post* writer Peter Carlson as an "awful" magazine, it is clearly finished, having lost more millions of dollars, and nothing has taken its place.

Over a period of years, Rosie has drawn comments and impersonations. Not as successful as Oprah, O'Donnell's show was never a rival to Oprah's—they were in different time slots and on different channels—nor was her decision to retire from *The Rosie O'Donnell Show* the result of competition. Neither was her resignation from the magazine bearing her name.

An element of commonality in the early backgrounds of O'Donnell, Stewart, and Winfrey seems to have driven the three of them to legendary heights. However, unlike O'Donnell and Oprah, Stewart came from a two-parent family who lived to see her phenomenal success. But Stewart's fall from grace came with the allegation that she had violated the rules of insider stock trading. The stock in question was one issued on the premise that a cancer drug being developed was going to be a new miracle drug. When early reports turned out to be unfavorable, those with inside information decided to unload the stock. Stewart allegedly heard about the upcoming announcement of the Food and Drug Administration (FDA) from her broker, and, before the news broke, Stewart had her broker sell her stock. Some financial writers pointed out that Stewart was a very small player in all of this, and some protested her trial in the media. Her defense was that her broker had been instructed to sell the stock at any time it fell below a certain price, and the sale had nothing to do with inside information. In an ironic twist of fate, after her broker's indictment and the investigation of Stewart, the FDA approved the cancer drug.

Numerous speculative stories about Stewart were printed, because television commentators and comedians found her situation too interesting to ignore. Before all this happened, Stewart headed a huge company built on revenues from a television show, magazines, and her own line produced for Kmart stores—all activities she resumed after being released from prison. A federal grand jury had indicted Stewart, charging she'd lied and misled investigators about her role in the stock sale; although there was much disagreement among prosecutors and other experts, journalists, and members of the public, the Securities and Exchange Commission brought a five-part civil complaint against her for insider trading; it was not a criminal charge, but she was found guilty. Not surprisingly, the public disagreed. Thus, when CNN took a poll, 68 percent of the responses were pro-Stewart.

Some Stewart champions, mostly women, believe the attacks on her have a distinctly antiwoman tinge, a hostility directed toward a strong, aggressive and successful woman; the accusations, her supporters say, would never be leveled against a man in the same situation.

When the indictment was announced, Stewart stepped down as chairman and chief executive officer of her company. No matter that Stewart denied all the allegations of insider trading, her company's stock fell abruptly to a small percentage of its value. The popularity of her magazines also went into a spin, and, for the first time since its inception, the media and retailing company showed losses of several million dollars. Although government lawyers were banging the drums for jail time, few independent lawyers expected Stewart to go to prison, but many expected her to pay a significant fine. That expectation was borne out. Furthermore, Stewart went to jail.

Yet her products continued to be marketed, particularly in Kmart, where the sales of her products had remained high. Today, she is shown frequently in television ads touting them, and she seems more popular than ever. As a gesture of support for Stewart, Kmart would not allow the sale of the May 21, 2001, issue of the *Globe* because the tabloid featured a story based on an unfriendly book about her. The front-page headline of the paper stated, "Mean Martha Exposed." For a time, commentators focused on the Stewart story. One instance was in fashion columnist Robin Givhan's November 22, 2009, lengthy article—with pictures—about Stewart's style of dress (dowdy and dull) Givhan's criticism of Stewart's clothing elicited protests from readers of the *Washington Post*, who questioned and made fun of Givhan's high fashion values for Stewart, a middle-aged woman in years and build, one who makes products for the lower end of the market.

Famous names are expected to sell products and magazines. Apparently, most buyers are able to separate the product and magazine from a blemished name and personal life of many well-known entrepreneurs. That has surely been the case with entertainers in other fields. Perhaps, though, it is the very taint of scandal that catches the public and the shoppers' eyes. Business assessors opine that media chiefs will continue to search for more stars who will attract purchasers, so that famous names are floated periodically in the news.

Although circulation fell for Stewart's magazine, it may or may not be attributable to the publicity about her stock trading. Significantly, despite the fact that advertising is up, news reports have also pointed to somewhat poorer circulation for Oprah's magazine, which has never been touched by scandals of any sort. Neither Stewart's nor O'Donnell's magazines, however, seem to have offered much of a challenge to Oprah's, even though there was no apparent difference to be found on the magazine racks in stores, inasmuch as some of the largest grocery chains stocked both Stewart's and O'Donnell's magazines, sometimes one or the other, but, inexplicably, not Oprah's for a long time. Although there may be some arcane reason for the choices, food stores seem to benefit from the sales of all women-centered magazines.

Oprah has been a huge factor in the sale of books, a boon to writers, publishers, and bookstores, and even to discount and department stores such as Costco, Sam's Club, and Target, all better known for food items and other merchandise. A large number of book stores carry her magazine, but most discount stores do not. Even though some stores did not publicize Oprah's book choices by distinguishing them from other books, most book stores contained separate racks of Oprah's book selections. Her logo on books reportedly increased sales tenfold, according to a report by Time Warner.[9] Although those early books are no longer featured, the ones that remained in print still carried the sticker announcing them as an Oprah choice, and once Oprah came back to the business of touting books, no matter the subject, logos and sales went up. In fact, her first book choice when renewing the club in the summer of 2003, John Steinbeck's *East of Eden*, quickly rose to the top of the paperback best-seller list.

Oprah's Book Club choices varied in number, theme, period, author's roots, and their relationship to Oprah's other picks. Furthermore, there were usually significant differences between the books chosen for the club, some of which were the work of authors who appeared on Oprah's show. One of the exceptions to these is the real life of a woman named Jaycee Lee Dugard, who'd been a child kidnap victim for 18 years without trying to escape from the man who fathered her two children. There was also the similarity between Duggard's experiences and the psychological conditions faced by an actress, Mackenzie Phillips, author of *High on Arrival*. For more than 10 years, Phillips had an incestuous relationship with her father without ending it or seeking help.

Like her television programs and her book clubs—with their enormous effect on sales—Oprah's magazine has been described by writer Patricia Sellers of *Fortune* as "the most successful magazine launch ever."[10] Although it first appeared on U.S. newsstands in July 2000, it was expanded within the year to an international edition. The international edition is as glossy as the U.S. one and almost as huge. However, the subject matter is not entirely the same. A significant percentage is devoted to South African matters and people, with both black and white women as the readership. The magazine grew in the United States to a readership of two and a half million within a short period of time. With an annual revenue topping $140 million, it is a considerable part of the Harpo empire, surprisingly profitable in an industry in which most magazines rarely make a profit in the first years after their establishment. At a time when other longtime popular women's magazines have failed, *O, The Oprah Magazine* continues to attract a significantly large number of new readers. The items advertised, photographed, and recommended to readers are geared toward the purchaser at the high middle income level: Tommy Hilfiger clothing for members of the family; Calvin Klein and Estée Lauder perfumes. The majority of items for the home—crystal and elegant table settings—would not be found in low-end or discount shops.

Success of a high-powered publication does not come without dedication and tussles. According to Gayle King, editor-at-large of the magazine, Oprah is obsessive about O, overseeing everything, even "commas" and "exclamation points," and numerous people have told of the amount of time and work she puts into it. But there also have been reports, though carefully squelched, of tension and problems in the staff. Given the tight control of all Oprah operations, the likelihood is that further information will not be provided. Only the positive stories are publicized, such as the gifts and trips she gives to staff.

From its inception, like many other magazines directed toward women, O has followed a pattern of topics known to appeal to a specific group of women, those said to be more financially upscale than Oprah's daily television watchers. O, however, includes some regular features of its own, with something for everyone, from cosmetics to books. Clearly, it is Oprah's magazine, and at times she seems ubiquitous. Following Oprah's opening essay, "Here We Go," is an attractive calendar for the month, with photographs appropriate to the season. Thus, one year, the offerings for the month of November feature knitting yarns in richly colored yarns of red and burnt orange, a teakettle and cups of hot tea, and an autumnal sunset scene; an August calendar pictures a mother and her two children bathing in the ocean. A featured statement by a recognizably famous person—such as Gandhi or James Baldwin—heads up the calendar, with aphorisms for most of the days. Every issue of the magazine has a different subject announced on the cover. Some that have appeared over a two-year period are Friendship, Success, Creativity, Family, Intimacy, Fun, Confession, Adventure, Love Your Body, Stress Relief, You're Invited, Home, To Your Health, Love, Sex, and Dating, Communicate, Balance, Energy, Truth, Freedom, Couples, Strength, and Weight. Many seem to relate to topics that are dealt with on the television show. Various illnesses, including bipolar disorder, depression, alcoholism, psychosis, and suicide, are featured, although the different venues have different tones.

Each issue of the magazine offers advice of many kinds, much of it in Oprah's pieces, as well as in the regular monthly columns, and in articles by specialists on a particular subject. Like the comments made about Oprah being the national therapist, the magazine seems to fulfill the same role. The style of O is personal, often confessional. Most of the problems of life find their way eventually onto the beautiful glossy spread, which features a photo of Oprah on the cover as well as an impressive number inside. Sometimes the cover photo is duplicated in greater detail within the magazine. And, when a particularly beautiful picture of Oprah appears in newspapers and other magazines, it also is printed in O. Over a period of several years, through photos alone, a reader may gain insight about the star's preferences in clothing, from

Oprah Winfrey stands in front of the cover of the premiere issue of O, The Oprah Magazine, *at a press breakfast in New York, April 17, 2000. With a newsstand distribution of 1 million,* O *debuted nationwide on April 19, 2000. (AP Photo/Ed Bailey)*

casual shirts and pants to elegant hostess apparel. The same may be said about her hairdos: long, short (relatively), curly, straight, flipped, upturned. All are eye catching. The covers also reveal her fluctuation in weight.

When Oprah was asked why only her picture appears on every cover, her answer was somewhat ingenuous; it was to avoid the necessity of making choices of other people every month. Only on two occasions has someone been pictured alongside her: Ellen DeGeneres and Michelle Obama. In addition to the many pictures of Oprah inside the magazine, the photos are generally of celebrities—perhaps alongside a brief article by or about them. Background scenes of flowers, green fields, and blue water abound. And, although a great many of the articles are about serious matters, there are occasional ones about pleasure, with descriptions and photos of parties Oprah has given. The settings are usually a tribute to the elegant life of the rich and famous. Against a backdrop of colors, flowers, and greenery are gorgeous shots of food— hors d'oeuvres, salad, a chicken main dish, drinks, and desserts. The table settings and linens may be like the products that the star recommends in every issue with its soft selling style in the magazine and on television. All of those displays are big business, but not the usual fare of most of her readers.

Among the monthly articles, Oprah's "Here We Go" column introduces the theme treated in the majority of articles, most written by women and for women. However, three men writers have been regulars: Dr. Phil (McGraw), Dr. (Mehmet) Oz, and Nate Berkus. The view held by readers of Oprah as a woman not only of wisdom but also tenderheartedness underlies advertisements as well as articles.

Every issue features an interview in which Oprah talks to someone famous or important to her, people she knows well or only through reputation, but generally those she admires. Some of the interviews have special interest for women, such as the one Oprah had at the home of Elizabeth Edwards when she had just written a book and appeared on the television program but before all the unsavory facts came out about her husband. On occasion, the interviews provide insight into Oprah herself. Oprah always credits her friends for the help they have given her in good times and bad. However, Oprah would undoubtedly say it is almost impossible to fend off the press—both reporters and television commentators—who search out scandals. Not only did Elizabeth Edwards write a book about her life, but so too did John Edwards's former aide, Andrew Young, and Young's wife, Cheri, produce a tell-all book, *The Politician*, which purportedly outs John, Elizabeth, and "the other woman." (The Youngs were guests on Oprah's show, during which Oprah pointedly revealed distaste for the entire matter. When Edwards's mistress and mother of his child Rielle Hunter was questioned by reporters about revealing photographs and a story in a magazine—not O, *The Oprah Magazine*—she was critical of Oprah and her "belief systems about sex." In the back-and-forth stories that have been printed, it seems as though only Oprah escapes with her dignity intact.) Later, Oprah had Hunter on the show as a guest, although, to date, Hunter has not written a book.

In the constant effort to provide multiple points of view—and not just happy, positive ones—varied positions are shown whenever possible in the magazine. Thus, in the issue filled with testimonies to the value and importance of friendship, there is also a thoughtful piece on ending friendship: why and how it happens and when it should happen. Not all friendships are forever, and one must face such realities honestly. Illness and health are frequent subjects in O, and when some particular spark catches the attention of the public, Oprah interviews for the magazine unusual people whose strength and willpower in the face of a ravaging disease inspires others. (Although illness and health are not usually the focus of plots in book club choices, the books also frequently seem to have links in their subject matter; reviewers sometimes suggest that certain novels would be good choices for the club because they are depressing and/or painful.)

Every month, at least one article—and sometimes as many as four articles—about health is printed in the magazine. The matter of weight, particularly, always a staple of women's magazines, gets much attention. Inasmuch as it seems the entire world watches Oprah's weight, O provides a forum to reveal her successes and failures, just as she has on her shows for years. In one issue, she listed the many different diets she tried. However, as faithful readers and viewers know, one diet after another has failed, as is evident in magazine photos and her daily show. However, over time, there has been a diminishing of that discussion.

Advice of all kinds is given in every issue, such as the understanding of and information about money in Suze Orman's column "Financial Freedom." Hers is a practical guide to the management of money. Orman, like several of the other contributors, answers questions of all kinds, primarily about money and investments. Occasionally, though, she moves into other areas, such as providing an executor's checklist for handling a will. Unhesitatingly, she tackles problems of modern U.S. culture and mores in discussing important and sensitive issues. A central theme is the way women control their own income. Traditionally, even when both partners in a marriage worked, they pooled their salaries, with the man taking charge. However, as the ratio of working women increased and people began to marry later, women became more independent and accustomed to handling their own finances. Orman looks at the situation from many perspectives, yet advises women they do not need permission to control the money they earn. Power shouldn't be apportioned according to the size of a paycheck. (Perhaps this should be part of Oprah's admonition not to give away your power. It is central to her views.)

Beauty, health, and style articles appear in every issue, as well as a monthly self-help piece by Oprah called "Something to Think About."

This turns into a written exercise with the listing of numerous questions that need to be answered by the reader in the spaces provided. The segment becomes a kind of self-therapy as the reader follows the technique occasionally used by therapists, including Dr. Phil in his own monthly advice column "Tell it Like It Is." He answers questions that are asked by individual readers, but the advice may be applied to a much wider audience.

More and more often in recent years, Oprah has written of events from her childhood, remembering her grandmother, who, despite her harshness and rigidity, communicated unspoken affection to the little girl through small actions. Even though she was unaware then of her grandmother's love, the events she recalls from those early days have come to her slowly over time, as in the "Aha" moments others have described each month. After years of trauma in several relationships, Oprah began to recognize the gifts her grandmother gave her. Perhaps remembrance of things past serves her like the "grateful journal" of the type she has advised young women to keep. The aha moments of hers and others take on the quality of epiphanies, turning into the light of recognition.

Oprah is a sharer, which is different from relinquishing control. When we share, we help others as well as ourselves. Talk is sharing— talk is healing, she tells readers, as a strong believer in communication and intimacy. Talking isn't whining or being humbled and defeated. It is like a building block of character, and those who refuse to bow to silence and isolation elicit her admiration. Not only on television but in her magazine she often speaks of her early hard life; yet there is never self-pity, because she has learned that individuals must take charge of their lives and find their own happiness. Everyone yearns for family and affection, but such longings are not always fulfilled.

At various times, Oprah has spoken of her own traumatic introduction to sex. Although what Oprah tells the reader about her early life is no longer new, she identifies with those troubling points underlying teenage sex: the failure of parents to communicate with children, the distances between them, the need girls have for love and acceptance, and the pervasive unhappiness and self-blame resulting from sexual activities. The fact that Oprah is now middle aged and has dealt with the anguish of her experiences long ago does not alter the similarities of root causes. In every period of life, children and adults deserve love and approval, but they do not always find it. In an almost a Wordsworthian view, Oprah writes that one must not grieve for what is not given, but take another path. Whatever our achievement, success in life comes from learning to love and accept ourselves. Central messages such as these account for the affection and trust of women worldwide and undoubtedly will continue to be important in the time remaining for *The Oprah Winfrey Show*, the ongoing *O* magazine, and other Oprah undertakings.

NOTES

1. Linton Weeks formerly wrote for "Style" in the *Washington Post*.

2. "The Oprah Effect," *Publishers Weekly*, Oct. 2006.

3. Robert Elder, of the *Chicago Tribune*, didn't much care for Mattie's poems. He sees cynicism in the publishers, Tom Clancy, and Oprah, suggesting they are opportunistic in using the child's work and fatal illness for their own gain.

4. Amy Schwartz, "Will Oprah Save the Book?" Dec. 1996. Amy Schwartz is a former columnist and editorial writer for the *Washington Post*. She currently works as vice president for education and youth at the Wilson Center.

5. David Carr, "How Oprahness Trumped Truthiness," *New York Times*, 30 Jan. 2006.

6. Carlin Romano writes for several newspapers. In this piece, he takes Oprah to task humorously for her obviously manufactured excuse to cancel the Book Club. In contrast to the seriousness of most critics, Romano and Matt Janz, although writing for different papers, find much humor in Oprah's activities.

7. Edel Coffey, "Jonathan Franzen: Oprah, Obama, and My Smelly Socks," *Independent* (Ireland), 5 Oct. 2010.

8. Review of *Oprah: The Little Speaker*, by Carole Boston Weatherford, *Publishers Weekly*, 22 Feb. 2010.

9. Kate Pickert, "Oprah's Book Club," *Time*, 26 Sept. 2008.

10. Patricia Sellers, "The Business of Being Oprah: She Talked Her Way to the Top of Her Own Media Empire and Amassed a $1 Billion Fortune. Now She's Asking, 'What's Next?,'" *Fortune*, 1 Apr. 2002.

Chapter 5

SCHOOLS

Although Oprah had given money to schools over time, it was in 2002 that her dream of building schools in South Africa began to take physical form. She had promised "Madiba"—the clan name given to former South African president Nelson Mandela and the first black man to achieve that office—that she would build a school there. During an early trip to Soweto (an acronym for South West Township), Oprah was accompanied by a reporter for a brief visit to the home of some prospective students she had met previously; her visit was to acquaint herself with some sense of their lives. The two girls—cousins who would be among the chosen students—lived with five other people in a two-room shack. As is typical in many communities, word of Oprah's visit spread quickly, and outside the house women began "ululating the . . . freedom line of the 1980's," but it soon became "Viva, Oprah Winfrey."

In 2003, ground was broken in the town of Henley-on-Klip for the Oprah Winfrey Leadership Academy for Girls located south of Johannesburg, South Africa. Oprah told a reporter she hoped the school would be "a reflection" of her. It took until 2007 to get the school up and running. Comprising 52 acres on a 28-building campus of dormitories, an audiovisual center, gym, and tennis courts, it is, as one new student called it, a "fairy tale come true." The fairy tale is the result of Oprah's earlier promise to Mandela.

Oprah, as well as numerous other Americans who had given donations to the new school, made the 10,000-mile trip to South Africa for the opening event. She had spent between $40 million and $50 million to build the academy,[1] but she declared that the money was meaningless to her in light of her dream that the girls would be the future leaders of the country. As Oprah cut the ribbon, the flags of South Africa and the United States were raised simultaneously, bringing tears to her eyes. From the 3,500 applications for admission, 152 applicants had been selected. They would be the first graduating class. At a later date, the number of students would be expanded to 450. When questioned about the racial backgrounds of the girls and how they were chosen, Oprah stated that all the girls had been interviewed, and among the interviewees were black, white, Asian, Hindu, Muslim, and Christian girls. Although she did not tell the reporter who among them had been chosen, she emphasized that the school was open to any qualified girl who had good grades, showed leadership skills, and came from an underprivileged home. Some pictures of a few girls were made public.

All the girls selected personally by Oprah came from poverty but were A students. One example given of the type of families the girls come from is of a mother who is also a grandmother; she supports her own family as well as several orphans from her income of $50 per week from a fruit and vegetable stand and monthly food baskets from charity. The maximum family income for any of the chosen girls must be under $700 per month, a great contrast to that of Oprah—also a child of poverty, who is now said to be the richest African American of the century. The chosen girls are given everything needed without any payment. Although they have known nothing but poverty, at the academy, they are exposed to all the classes—and more—that elite schools provide for their students. Drawn from various parts of South Africa, the students are housed in a $40 million school, each girl living in a two-bedroom suite. Dormitories have wood-burning fireplaces in the lounges; there is a health center, a science center, computer labs, and a library. One reporter compared the facility to a luxury hotel. Among the students

U.S. talk show host Oprah Winfrey, center front, applauds with schoolgirls in Johannesburg, on August 20, 2006, during her visit to South Africa to interview prospective pupils for the Oprah Winfrey Leadership Academy for Girls. (AP Photo/Benny Gool)

are many who have lived their lives without running water and had to carry buckets of water on their heads for all necessities.

Very much aware of the conditions of the state-funded schools in South Africa that were established during the years of apartheid, Oprah has sought to overcome, for at least some girls, the crowded, poorly equipped, and even dangerous schools. The children have had to struggle against gangs, the temptation of drugs, and the sexual environment that leads to teenage pregnancy. Their South African teachers and administrators were said to be chosen from among the most outstanding in the country, with the hope that within a few years of studying at the academy, the girls could "live the dream . . . of Harvard and winning a Nobel Peace Prize."

Oprah is one of the most generous philanthropists on the globe, and the recipients of that generosity are the children of the world. Oprah has said, several times, she never had children, and now she can bring up the children of others.

The greatest problem Oprah expected for the students was in the African perception and treatment of women in a culture that does not value them, and Oprah finds it vital that those girls, as well as other females, become conscious of "their own power and possibility."[2] Winfrey frequently says "she wants to nurture kids." Everything in the girls' lives seems to concern her. She even took an HIV test in Capetown, South Africa, to encourage her students and their families to do the same, because of the pandemic that is sweeping Africa; almost 1,000 people die each day from the disease, and a larger number become infected. A bleak future faces the young, with an estimate that only about half of them will survive to the age of 60 unless the disease can be eliminated.

Oprah wants the girls to have the happy childhood she never had, with education as the way forward. Perhaps her example will make a difference—with CNN and *Time's* description of her as "the world's most powerful woman" and *The American Spectator's* view that she is the most influential woman in the world. President Obama has a more regional—and perhaps more realistic—perspective of the possibilities; he acknowledges her power and influence within the United States.

Donors for the academy have come from many different areas. One unexpected name is that of Dallas billionaire Harold Simmons, who in 2006 gave $1 million to the academy as part of a $5 million pledge. A few years earlier, Simmons had contributed $3 million to the committee the American Issues Project for ads linking the prospective president, Barack Obama, to former activists in the Weather Underground, a group associated with illegal activities decades earlier. Apparently, Oprah's support of candidate Obama did not interfere with Simmons's gift to her academy.

Oprah established three charities with gifts estimated to surpass $200 million in 2007, and this amount undoubtedly grows larger each year. The three charities are run separately and differently, but her personal foundation, the Oprah Winfrey Foundation, helps support multiple groups in education, medicine, and the arts and has the largest amount of money dedicated to her charities.

Some of the groups are entirely dependent on the foundation for support. However, Oprah's major philanthropic interest is said to be Africa, where Oprah and her Angel Network have contributed a large amount of money to 40 or more organizations, many of them in Africa, though not nearly the amount given through her personal foundation. Much of the money for the network has been raised through contributions from people who want to help worthwhile causes, such as the catastrophic Hurricane Katrina in the United States and the 2004 tsunami in the Indian Ocean. Soon after Oprah's decision, however, to move to her own television network, she announced that the Angel Network would be disbanded, even though the statistics about its work are outstanding: 150,000 donors brought in more than $60 million. Two hundred grants were given to the United States and more than 30 abroad. The money was used to build 55 schools in 12 countries, as well as to provide school uniforms and supplies.

Dave Hoekstra, a writer for the *Chicago Sun-Times*, called Oprah "America's guardian angel," as he tells the story of a donation she made to the Angel Museum in Beloit, Wisconsin.[3] When Oprah had Cher on her program several years ago, the conversation turned to angels, at which point Oprah wondered whether there were any black angels, because she had never seen any. The overwhelming answer came from many places in the world: 700 black angels, a varied group of pieces ranging from an expensive Armani to folk art, which Oprah donated to the museum. All of these have become part of The Oprah Collection in which the only work without wings is a figure of Rosa Parks, whom Oprah calls "her personal angel."

The Oprah Winfrey Operating Foundation is the organization that is responsible for her Leadership Academy in Gauteng, South Africa. To people who question why Oprah built her academy in South Africa, her response is that she felt it was insufficient to always give money to charities. A number of bloggers were critical of her choices, complaining that Oprah was seeking glory for herself with her efforts in Africa. However, Oprah's response to such remarks was that she wanted something more tangible than writing "check after check." The impressive, even lavish, buildings of the academy also led to criticism that such edifices did not belong in an impoverished country. But Oprah defended her decisions, reminding magazine writers who interviewed her about the school that the girls in the new academy had "never been treated with kindness," had never been "surrounded by beauty," never were "told they are pretty." She wants them to have and to hear what she did not when she was a child.

Furthermore, domestically, Oprah continues to give funds to some of her U.S. favorites: Mississippi State University, Morehouse College, and a well-known finishing school in Farmington, Connecticut, called Miss Porter's, to which she sent her nieces, although the school is best known for its rich, ultra-white student body and exclusivity.

Among former students at Miss Porter's school were Dorothy Bush, mother of George H. W. Bush; Jacqueline Kennedy; actress Dina Merrill; and socialite Barbara Hutton. It has been written that Oprah's leadership academy was modeled after Miss Porter's school. Although the girls come from a world of poverty, at the academy they are exposed to all the classes and amenities that elite schools provide for their students. The many donors to Oprah's academy support the idea that Africa needs educated young people to become the leaders of the future.

When, three years after the opening of the academy at Henley-on-Klip, the girls put on a weeklong arts festival, it was attended by their benefactor as well as friends and contributors to their studies; featured were dance, acting, art, design, photography, cooking, and storytelling. An emotional Oprah talked of the experiences the children had before they came to the school, and the girls themselves told stories of their lives of deprivation. Yet within three years of starting at the academy, they could fulfill the dream of education and a meaningful future.

The $40 million school now houses about 300 girls from various parts of South Africa. Even though the school has outstanding facilities and provides the girls with every opportunity to learn about music and the arts, Oprah has tried to enlarge their experiences in a world unfamiliar to them. Because they were studying acting at the academy, Oprah wanted them to attend an actual theater. No girl at the school had ever been to see a play before Oprah took them to see *The Lion King*, written by an American but set in Africa and later made into a Hollywood movie.

Like Oprah, the entertainer Madonna also has spent much time in Africa, but in the East African country of Malawi. It is located east of Zambia and became an independent country in 1964. There are significant differences, though, between the activities of the two women. Although Oprah refers to the girls at her academy as her daughters, Madonna clearly wanted a more personal relationship with the children, and she made news with her adoption of a baby boy from Malawi.

The child was living in an orphanage, even though his father is alive. At first the father gave permission for the adoption, but Madonna encountered difficulties immediately, not understanding laws about adoption in Malawi and not heeding warnings by a social worker about the problems that would ensue. Some people, including Madonna, have proceeded with their plans for Malawi and its inhabitants. Human rights groups in that country went to court to prevent the adoption; and in the United States, as well as Britain, adoption agencies suggested that people focus on the needs of thousands of children in their own countries. Madonna, in defending her actions, talked of the dire straits many children face in Africa because of disease, poverty, and lack of care and hygiene. Madonna finally succeeded in her adoption of the boy, David Banda, as well as that of another child, a girl, a few years later.

Madonna's squabbles with people in Malawi, however, continued when she announced she wanted to build a school for girls in that country. The quarrel was over a land dispute near the capital city of Lilongwe. Although Madonna paid the villagers $115,000 for the property, the 200 villagers living on the land refused to move. The government took Madonna's side in the argument, stating that the land did not belong to the villagers, who had been given the right to live there only on a temporary basis. As of 2010, the issue had not been resolved. Reportedly, the school will cost $15 million to build. And still another entertainer, Ricki Lake was also involved in opening a new school for AIDS orphans founded by her friend, Malawian and former nanny Marieda Silva, in 2008 in that country.

Yet another celebrity built more schools in another African country. In West Kenya, the tennis star, Serena Williams, opened two secondary schools, each of which will hold 250 to 300 students ranging in ages from 15 to 18. Although she has had no teaching experience, Williams has been teaching in the second school, an activity that differentiates her even more from Oprah and Madonna, and her schools have been built with help from the Build Africa Organization.

Philanthropic efforts such as school building by stars such as Oprah and Madonna cost enormous amounts of money initially, and sustaining them financially is an ongoing expense. Madonna's initial plan was to spend $15 million, even before ground was broken. Oprah's outlay was $40 million before her academy opened in 2007. Charitable gifts and events will always be required to keep such schools operational, inasmuch as there can never be tuition fees to sustain them. Typical of that money-raising activity was an auction of 150 pieces of Oprah's clothing in early 2010. With a staff member of her magazine, Adam Glassman, Oprah selected 150 items from her wardrobe to sell on the online eBay. The clothing may be called "castoffs," but many of the items were intended to be gifts Oprah bought or was given. The money raised will go to her academy. If a less famous person than Oprah were selling clothing on eBay, it would not be news covered by journalists, but the elegance of the clothing, as columnist Amanda Pendolino wrote, was the typical "classy and gorgeous" Oprah style: a Carolina Herrera dress of purple; two evening bags—one a Bottega Veneta and one a quilted Chanel; a pair of red suede open-toe heels by Prada; satin pumps by Jimmy Choo; a pair of pointed-toe Prada boots; and on and on. Even the journalists longed to own something from the collection.

Oprah has been inspired by many people, but one of her favorite memories is of a Christmas when her mother warned the children to expect nothing, yet three nuns arrived with food for the family and toys for the children, including a doll for Oprah. Such memories undoubtedly have influenced her decisions in her philanthropic activities.

Oprah's life is so busy, and not everything is reported, even though it often seems that the press follows her every move. When Americans criticize Oprah for her largess to African schools, it may be that the press is less aware or less interested in her charitable work at home. Local rather than national papers are usually the source of information about such activities. For example, a local paper in Newark, New Jersey, the *Star-Ledger*, reported a $500,000 gift that Oprah made in 2009 to St. Benedict's Prep school, as part of $1.5 million given to five nonprofit schools and organizations in Newark. Mayor of Newark, Cory Booker, has been praised for interesting Oprah and other philanthropists in helping not only St. Benedict's but also a charter school, a drug rehabilitation facility, Integrity House, and a shelter called Apostle House for women and children. The mayor, who is credited for his vision and constant efforts in the city of Newark and who founded the organization Newark Now, met Oprah through Gayle King. In thanking Oprah in a public statement, Booker spoke of the large numbers—

hundreds and hundreds—of families in his city who are being helped because of Oprah's commitment to serving others.

In 2007, another dimension had been added to Oprah's philanthropy: a new program called Oprah's Ambassadors, which was a combination partnership between the Angel Network and Free the Children. The network has brought a pairing of North American schools with five areas of developing nations. An example of the way the network operates may be seen in a community in southwest Florida. At the Immokalee Middle school, an after-school program has been started that teaches the children about Third World countries, and they learn about ways they can help. That particular school, regarded as a significantly impoverished school itself, began holding fund-raising activities to help other children in Africa get classroom supplies. The lessons learned are twofold: about the life of the African countries to which the materials are sent and the knowledge that there are people in the world who have less than the students in Immokalee.

Edgewood High School in New Jersey was chosen as an Oprah Ambassador School for 2008–2009. Like all the ambassador schools, it was given both a curriculum and finances to start a student organization that would raise money for projects. Students are chosen on the basis of interest; at Edgewood, they would work daily for a half hour after school on a project they selected; in this particular school, they decided to focus on global matters and the attempt to collect funds toward building a school in Kenya. Multiple activities were begun with the hope to achieve the projected goal.

Newark, New Jersey, is a large city that has a well-known mayor, but other U.S. cities have benefitted as well, even though there is not the same cachet attached to their names as Oprah's Leadership Academy. An organization called the U.S. Dream Academy established learning centers in 10 U.S. cities: one each in Baltimore; Philadelphia; East Orange, New Jersey; Houston; Indianapolis; Los Angeles; Memphis; Orlando; and Salt Lake City and two in the District of Columbia. It also has been the recipient of million-dollar gifts from Oprah's foundations. The learning centers are after-school programs rather than a full-time curriculum, with a mission to provide mentoring for at-risk children who are in danger of incarceration. Through academic and social values training, the plan is to break that cycle. Money is raised not only by donations from individuals and corporations but also fund-raising entertainment.

Oprah's engagement with the various leadership schools has many facets, including activities to further the training of members of the staffs. Opportunities to gain scholarships of various kinds for African girls have also been made available. A Cape Town young woman who had graduated with a degree in psychology became the single candidate from the continent to be given an Oprah scholarship to New York University, where she would study for a master's degree. Originally from the impoverished community of Uitsig, Ravensmead, and later from Belhar, the young woman spoke proudly of her grandfather and teachers, who always encouraged her. Among others to get higher-level training were some of the teachers from the leadership academy who'd been chosen to come to the United States for a course offered by a California technology organization. With increased sales to developing countries that seek to improve both their economy and scientific literacy, U.S. companies want to train teachers in the use of new technology, training that will benefit all African countries, not only South Africa.

Yet the country of South Africa, according to some of its critics, has failed to fulfill the promise of its earlier years of the Mandela era. When a columnist for the *New York Times* interviewed the Anglican South African archbishop, Desmond Tutu, in 2010, about current problems of his country, Tutu was pessimistic. He spoke of the apparent failure of the dreams that had existed during the Mandela era, describing South Africa as having the "most unequal society in the world. The poverty in which [his] compatriots live," Bishop Tutu said, is "debilitating, inhumane, and unacceptable."[4]

Of course, the future of all the African countries concerns many people around the globe. Even though Oprah is often called the most influential person—or one of the most influential people—in the world, not everything becomes wine and roses. Failures large and small make the future seem as unhappy or even more so than the past. Although Oprah is commended by millions of admirers, others take note of her failures. When the leadership academy first opened, a U.S. woman, Joan Countryman, served as the interim head for only eight months. She'd been chosen for her experience as an administrator of an American Friends school in Pennsylvania. After she left, a few other women served briefly, before a permanent headmistress filled the post. Then, ironically, after working just nine months at the academy, that head-mistress/principal of the academy, Nomovuyo Mzamane, was dismissed in the aftermath of a sex scandal involving one of the dormitory ma-trons. (The principal had no role in the scandal but was considered at fault for not preventing it.)

Late in 2008, Mzamane brought a defamation lawsuit against Oprah, with the claim that Oprah had made damaging remarks against her in the case against the dormitory matron, Virginia Makopo, by charging the headmistress Mzamane with failure to deal with the scandal of sexual molestation in the school. Because Mzamane's former employer had been the Germantown Friends School in Philadelphia, it was the venue she knew; thus she filed suit in that city. When she failed to find work in Philadelphia after she'd lost her position in Africa, she claimed that the scandal and Oprah's remarks about her were the source of her problem. Mzamane had been the third headmistress/principal to leave the school since its opening. Further allegations of sexual abuse followed, not by Mzamane, but of six girls at the academy, and part of the aftermath included expulsion of four girls and the suspension of three. Seeking damages in the range of $250,000, Mzamane defended herself against Oprah's statements, claiming she was "demoralized" as the result of her "public lynching."

Oprah's lawyers asked for dismissal of the case on two grounds: first, that Oprah had not said anything libelous; and second, that federal court in Philadelphia was the incorrect jurisdiction for a hearing, inas-much as Oprah does not live in Philadelphia, nor does she have busi-ness there. Additionally, Mzamane's employment contract of $150,000 per year included a clause requiring that arbitration be the route to fol-low in any employment disagreement. A judge in Philadelphia, how-ever, agreed to hear the case on the grounds that Oprah's remarks had been inflammatory, and he ruled that the case should go before a jury. The newspapers were enjoying the notoriety that Oprah would bring to the city; the *New York Post* stated, it would resemble "a visit from royalty" because of the expected crowds. In addition to the courtroom in which the case was to be heard, two adjacent courtrooms were to be set aside. However, after all the hullabaloo, the case came to an abrupt end once Oprah settled the suit when—according to the news reports—the two women "met . . . face to face to end the saga," and no lawyers were present during their meeting.

As usual, bloggers wrote pro and con remarks about the event, but, typically, Oprah's staff released no further information about the matter, and that was the end. But bloggers, who are often venomous in their anonymous comments, accused Oprah of lying and several called her "Doperah."

Although the case in Africa against the dormitory matron, Tiny Virginia Makopo, was filed in 2007, it did not come to court until July 2008. The accusations of abuse of the teenage students over a period of four months had led to Makopo's arrest. In October of that year, the trial took place. Fourteen charges were brought, each of which was denied by Makopo: indecent assault, common assault, soliciting a minor to perform indecent acts, and verbal abuse. Details of each count were listed by the South African prosecutor, Etienne Venter; the defendant, Makopo, denied all 14 charges, which also included assault against a woman colleague. Needless to say, the case received wide publicity because of Oprah's fame. Among the many newspaper reports, those by the Sowetan press were most prominently quoted abroad. They described the plaintiff, Makopo, before the hearing as attempting to hide in a "female lavatory." She was unsuccessful, inasmuch as the papers were able to see that "she was dressed in a blue skirt and a yellow Mamelodi Sundowns football club jersey, and big dark sunglasses."

A few months before the trial took place, a police officer had been honored with an award for his investigation of the child molestation case. He came from a special unit in Vereenig that examines situations of family violence, child protection, and sexual offenses. The reports in newspapers stated that the unit had considered "three serious cases of indecent assault."

Oprah herself did not attend the African trial and would not discuss it in specifics, although she had sent a U.S. lawyer as an observer. Those comments Oprah did make were about reaction to the events that disrupted life at the school. What she learned throughout the process shook her to the point she called the entire experience "the most devastating of my life."[5] She also took the blame for hiring employees in an inadequate screening process. Oprah apologized to the parents of the girls, speaking not only of her feelings but also her concern that she had disappointed them.

The six girls, aged 13 to 15, were allowed to testify for the court on closed-circuit television, and all proceedings were closed to the public. Because of the ages of the girls, they could not be identified, but as each charge was listed in detail, the 28-year-old Makopo denied them, speaking in her native language of Sotho. The hearing was held in April 2008 in Seblokeng Magistrates Court, outside the city of Johannesburg, over a period of several days.[6] Before the surfacing of these serious problems, there had been various complaints from parents, but they were of minor import. Some compared the school to prison, where there were restrictions on visits, phone calls, and e-mail. Others protested that their girls were not allowed "junk food," and the parents did not like the fact that they themselves had to go through a security gate in order to visit the school.

One parent stated he had allowed his daughter to withdraw from the academy because she had not been treated well by the headmistress when she was ill. The child received no support or counseling from "the very people who were supposed to be looking after her," he said. Although Oprah asked the girl to return, also meeting for two hours with the family to discuss the situation, the girl preferred to return to her former school. The father expressed gratitude for the opportunity Oprah had given his child, but the girl did not return to the academy. At the end of that school year, Oprah gave what she called a celebration dinner; others called it a "post-scandal celebration"; some named it an "end of the year party"; and still others said it was a "holiday celebration." Oprah, in a traditional African dress, was greeted warmly by the children. Surprisingly, present at the party were the student and her father who had first called attention to what became the sex scandal. However, despite their presence and Oprah's public praise of the girl, the girl continued to refuse to return to the academy.

Oprah's unhappiness about the situation was clear in the few public statements she made. Before learning of the abuse, she had called herself the protector and "mamma bear" to the girls, whom she considered her daughters, and she felt she had failed the children.

One problem after another has surfaced at the academy. In April 2009, newspapers reported another sex scandal during which seven students were suspended, although only one of them received notice that she'd been found guilty of sexual contact with another student;

of harassment; of bullying; and dishonesty in denying the truth when questioned by investigators. The incident and suspension of the girls were confirmed by one of Oprah's representatives, but no further details were given because everything about the matter was confidential, in keeping with the school's policy.

In 2008, Oprah cautiously began the search for a new headmistress for the academy, choosing the managing director of the organization Search Associates to head the recruitment for someone with international experience. Oprah, who likes to be in control of most of her projects, showed a strong interest in finding an Australian teacher. Although advertisements for the position were printed in a number of newspapers, she had the director for recruitment, John Magana, sign contracts that would limit the amount of information revealed in the search.

Perhaps her interest in Australia had been sparked by an invitation Oprah received to visit an Aboriginal community in Australia where a festival was to be held. The area, described as the "spectacular Malkgulumbu Falls," is in the Northern Territory, the town of Beswick, 250 miles from Darwin. Even though Oprah could not attend the central Arnhem Land arts festival, she did invite a Cape York Aborigine, Tania Major, to be a keynote speaker at the academy. Major had been chosen as the 2007 Australian Youth of the Year; undoubtedly, Oprah's interest in indigenous people and culture had been a factor in the invitation.

Darwin, the capital city of the Northern Territory, Australia, is both the most populated city in the territory and the least populated capital city of Australia. The original inhabitants are the Larrakia people, who are also known as the Aboriginal people. Although the population is comprised of people from different backgrounds, it has the largest number of Aboriginals of any Australian capital. Its proximity to Asia made it a target for Japanese war planes in World War II, and more bombs were dropped on it than on Pearl Harbor, Hawaii, by the same Japanese fleet. Darwin is a getaway to Asia and is closer to the capitals of five other countries than to the Australian capital. A department of education oversees all activities for students but is said to focus on indigenous students and in the last few years has restructured the schools. The choice of an Aborigine girl to speak at the academy opens many possibilities not only for her future but for other Aborigine girls as well.

When Oprah was interviewed by the *Cape Argus* newspaper in Africa, she spoke of mistakes she'd made at the academy, in being too protective of the girls and of appearing to keep them isolated. (These were criticisms made by parents and others with a greater knowledge of South Africa.) Perhaps, she said, the school should have had a more mixed group academically, rather than choosing only the most gifted, but she also spoke of her hopes for the girls; they are thriving and have exceeded her expectations, "fulfilling [her] dream and vision." Through the girls, she finds inspiration to keep going.

Periodically papers report on another lawsuit filed against Oprah or Harpo Productions, and sometimes reports appear about Oprah and Harpo filing suit against someone. The company has to keep a team of lawyers occupied frequently. Although Oprah has used the phrase "Aha moment" in her magazine for several years without any problem, in 2009 the well-known insurance company, Mutual of Omaha, filed for a trademark called "Official sponsors of the aha moment." Harpo sued, but the insurance company did not retreat easily. With some movement back and forth between two parties that did not want to surrender, but with neither anxious to have more publicity, Harpo and Mutual of Omaha settled quietly.

Washington Post columnist Eugene Robinson wrote two columns critical of Oprah's involvement in building schools in Africa instead of in the United States. Robinson believes that the primary obligations for Americans are for America. He points out that many U.S. schools are "failing [and] dysfunctional," yet "in the inner-city schools [he] visited, most students desperately want to learn." He makes several points about contradictions in Oprah's statements about teenagers in the United States and Africa, but his emphasis is on the needs of poor school-age children in the United States.[7] In a *Post* column written 10 months later, Robinson scolds Oprah: "This Isn't About Oprah." He is annoyed by her remarks about the school scandal, because, he asserts, she seems to make everything "about her, not the alleged victims." At the end of his column, however, he offers an olive branch, saying Oprah does know the most "sacred trust" is in "caring for other people's children."[8]

A blogger, who gave his name and spoke of his country as South Africa, pointed out that he was not being unpatriotic when he was critical of Oprah's undertaking. His statements about his concern could well have been enlightening for U.S. readers, when he objected to the selection of only poor girls for the academy. Why should there not be a mixture of rich, black girls, coloreds, and Indians (Asians), he asked. After all, they are the mixture of people in South Africa, and the academy should reflect that.

The academy court case remains a topic of interest for many people in Africa and the United States. Soon after the scandal erupted about the academy, a former Peace Corps volunteer wrote an article for the *Providence Journal* titled "Gift to Africa Teaches Oprah Painful Peace Corps Lesson." Denis Farrell, the volunteer, had been in Zambia when Oprah first began the work of building the academy, and, although he left Africa in 2002, before the school opened, he continued to follow the development of her project. What he writes is both a caution to those who would naively offer help to Africa without knowing the difficulties and praise of Oprah for her efforts.

Farrell sees irony between expectations of success and the realities that follow. People are "charmed" by the children, and impressed by the adults "who have big plans" but no money, and so the philanthropists build "school[s] . . . clinic[s] . . . librar[ies]." Through such actions, the giver "feel[s] like a hero." But actually it is all like gossamer because things fall apart.[9] The writer compares himself in his first days in Zambia to what Oprah felt when she went to South Africa: "Pure joy and compassion." However, he questions anyone's desire to provide "a Western solution to an African problem" and, in particular, Oprah's plans to give the girls all kinds of luxuries they have never known but which will make "leaders" of them. When he writes "hmm" to her naïveté, the reader recognizes the questions he poses. Can Oprah succeed where others have failed? Did anyone warn Oprah about "Ukwa" (jealousy in the Senga language) . . . or about "corruption . . . deep poverty . . . rampant disease," or changing social attitudes and behavior?

There are so many failures and disappointments that follow from the actions of well-meaning people, and the dire consequences are much greater than those that westerners can understand. Farrell recommends that it would be wiser to scale back in every way, in ambition and spending, to get to know village people and to explore examples of smaller, less ambitious projects.

Some Africans have nothing but praise for Oprah's undertakings and urge her to continue them in the hopes that the children's lives will be better and that the children will be the leaders and educators of the future. They don't question the possibilities. In the academy there is on display a painting of Oprah carrying a child. It had been given to her by a woman in Texas who wanted to bring Oprah's attention to those who struggle with terrible diseases. However, the painting suggests for the viewer a more far-reaching meaning: to do good for a child; to reach her when she is only at the beginning of her life; and to educate her so that she, like Oprah, will bring hope and meaning to those who follow.

In every issue of O, *The Oprah Magazine*, Oprah ends with a signature column, "What I Know for Sure." The January 2008 piece describes her experiences in the nightmarish aftermath of the sex scandal at the academy. She remembers Betty Rollin's book, *First You Cry*, and she did just that. But then she moved on. With the founder of the Houston, Texas, Child Trauma Academy, they put together a plan that she followed, first during the difficult weeks in Chicago, and later after her arrival back in South Africa. Using what she had learned from Eckhart Tolle's book, *The Power of Now*, Oprah decided she would deal with the situations as they arise. She founded three teams: an investigative team first, a psychological team, and, for a new beginning at the academy, a fresh educational team.

Along the way, friends wrote letters of encouragement. One reminded her of the reality, in effect, "what is, is," and such things "come with the territory." Another said, "Every time a heart breaks . . . somewhere something beautiful is being born." A determined Oprah was ready to start again. Yet Farrell's experiences in the Peace Corps in Africa has led him to say it isn't easy to change the world: "The real test comes when things fall apart."

NOTES

1. Roger Friedman, "Oprah's Charities Worth More Than 200 Million," Fox News, 5 Jan. 2007.

2. Oprah has said this many, many times in many places, as well as in O.

3. Dave Hoekstra, "Angel Museum a Heavenly Attraction in Wisconsin," *Chicago Sun-Times*, 11 June 2010.

4. Desmond Tutu, interview by Deborah Solomon, *New York Times*, 4 Mar. 2010.

5. Eugene Robinson, "Oprah's Learning Curve," *Washington Post*, 5 Nov. 2007.

6. Reported in *Cape Argus* (South Africa), 29 July 2008.

7. Eugene Robinson, "It's Not All about iPods," *Washington Post*, 9 Jan. 2007.

8. Robinson, "Oprah's Learning Curve."

9. This is the title of a famous African book by Chinua Achebe. Achebe used a line from the poem "The Second Coming," by William Butler Yeats. Farrell's reference invokes both Yeats and the poem, but the reference by Farrell is used to invoke the problems Oprah has faced and continues to face in her African school.

Chapter 6

LIVING LIFE THE OPRAH WAY

Throughout the years, Oprah has hosted many shows on topics that also fill central roles in all magazines, not only hers: food—good and bad; weight—healthy and unhealthy; physical fitness; spiritual happiness; and emotional strength.

Oprah's focus on healthy bodies and minds helped make her a top player in television, radio, and publishing, but it has been her unplanned as well as her planned engagements that revealed the extent of her influence on consumers. Currently, it is the matter of talking on cell phones while driving; more than a decade ago, it was the meat industry, when she joined other prominent figures in discussions about beef and attacked the industry for selling unsafe products. Oprah's involvement in revealing the dangers of eating beef that could be tainted brought on a firestorm from all segments of the industry: the economy was affected, cattlemen were enraged, lobbyists were perturbed, and, in Amarillo, Texas, the industry's lawyers brought suit against Oprah. If so famous a star had not been involved, the case would not have attracted much interest, but it became a major story pushed by media attention. With an atmosphere resembling that of a circus, Amarillo and the rest of Texas were in the news as long as the case continued. Lines of people and automobiles—sporting pro and con bumper stickers—filled the streets, in addition to fans, photographers, and imported preachers.

Oprah won her case, not only initially but also on appeal, with the people closest to her giving moral support. However, the case was soon forgotten; restaurants soon took orders for beef; there have been fewer details of Oprah's eating habits; her magazine's food section is not taking a position about good and bad food; and the United States apparently is back to eating hamburgers. Although, more recently, the matter of tainted eggs has been in the headlines, Oprah did not discuss it on her show.

Oprah's current campaign is about having people pledge to refrain from using a cell phone or texting while driving. She also includes the use of hands-free auto devices in the pledge, and will not be deterred from enforcing it among her own employees. They, and others who

Oprah Winfrey reacts to a fan reaching out to her as she leaves the federal courthouse after jury selection in Amarillo, Texas, January 20, 1998. A jury of eight women and four men was selected in the multimillion-dollar defamation case pitting Texas cattlemen against the talk show queen. (AP Photo/Eric Gay)

might be affected by her influence, reportedly are fearful of resisting her decree; as "Just Plain Darren" of East Coast Radio writes, "You don't mess with Oprah." Her influence spreads far and wide. Columnist Peter Bart states, without much exaggeration, her "empire is wealthier than an emirate," and "her devotees seem to yearn to touch the hem of her garment."

As Oprah began her newest venture, much about the future was unknown, except for the news releases that came out—and most provided the same information. However, much has been also going on behind the scenes while Oprah along with her staff and colleagues determined the direction OWN would take. The news reports talked of the shows that would be starting sometime in late 2011. Although dates and information were contradictory, the show was actually launched on January 1, 2011.

With the title "Winfrey Launches Rehab Show," the announcement gives the debut date as January 11 for the eight-episode program that will focus on issues about food and eating disorders. It is a one-hour documentary series, during which the treatment center and a group of people will take part for a period of 42 days. The announcement of the program notes that it presents a "rare look inside," one in which "patients face their demons" in their attempt to discover "what's behind the food."

Anyone who has the least familiarity with Oprah's show or magazines knows about her lifelong battle with food and weight and her challenges over the years with one diet or another. As nutritionists from the University of California, Davis, Judith Stern and Alexandra Kazaks have written in their book *Obesity*, if people could control their weight through willpower, there would be no problem. Fifty short biographies appear in their book, one of which is Oprah's. Like others who have struggled with obesity, Oprah has sought the magic pill or diet. In 2008, she went on a vegan detox plan, and at the same time her Web site offered a healthy menu. Like everything else that Oprah does, it was news around the world, with enthusiastic response to the plan, at least temporarily. A Canadian reporter chided her about the "21 day cleansing diet." With her pleading words "Oprah, Oprah, Oprah," writer and comedienne Linda Cullen professes admiration but also sees "a disturbing trend" in the many diets Oprah has followed, and she lists a few, including the names of some gurus that have become "gazzillionaires" because of Oprah's imprimatur.

Other plans followed, such as the announcement of a future anniversary issue of O. Also, the magazine will continue to include recommendations about diets and related topics. Perhaps there will be future articles about Oprah's personal struggle with weight, even though she now appears to have separated herself from the subject.

More information given to the public, not about the magazine but about future career plans, was the all-encompassing new program's cable name. Known as *Oprah's Next Chapter*, it was chosen to replace the 25-year-old *Oprah Winfrey Show*. The program will be in prime time, and Oprah no longer will have a daytime offering.

When questioned by interviewers about the reasons for the dramatic changes that will be made, Oprah states: "I didn't have a life. . . . I only get to live my best life on the cover of the magazine."

OWN: The Oprah Winfrey Network that she and Discovery Networks hold jointly, once launched in 2011, according to the *Christian Science Monitor*, "is very likely the first television network based around a single person." That shouldn't surprise anyone, considering all the enterprises Oprah has been involved in over the years with the empire she built, as one report put it. Oprah consistently promotes self-improvement and celebrities. Oprah watchers know her empire is part magazine, part radio, part a channel on XM Sirius satellite radio, movies, and the Harpo production company. When she moves to her new venue, she will be hosting a show two to three times a week, unlike what she has done for 25 years. Few details have been given thus far, but it has been announced that her programs will not come from her Chicago studios. When reporters asked her about the amount of work she's putting in to get ready, she responded that, in looking at tapes, not only is she "up to [her] knees, [but] up to [her] thighs."

The self-improvement themes will continue to be a feature on the new channel. Some programs will be partly original shows, and some will focus on Oprah. Even though Oprah will not be on every program, the chairman of the new network, Mary Altaffer, has assured backers and viewers that Oprah will be in charge "behind the scenes." The new shows on OWN are expected to reach about 80 million homes. Those announced to date run the gamut of topics, including familiar names: people who have appeared on earlier Oprah programs, such as Lady Gaga; Gayle King (who will appear regularly with her own program); Shania Twain (the Canadian country singer who will host a series called *Why Not?*); Dr. Laura Berman (author of *The Book of Love*, sex therapist, and "guru," described as making the discussion of sex lively in "juicy . . . installments" as a regular on Oprah's show); and there will also be well-known people from a wide variety of activities, including theater, journalism, politics, and business. However, before those future appearances take place, Oprah is planning a program during which she will travel around the globe interviewing guests.

Some media experts are concerned that there will be saturation on the new network because of the dip in Oprah's ratings that has taken place in the past decade or so. However, the defense for that is to compare Oprah's numbers with those of other stars and to find little difference.

Meanwhile, assessments by pundits of past and future activities have been flourishing. Now that Oprah's highly successful magazine has celebrated its 10th anniversary while others have failed, nobody predicts its demise. Some reporters have counted the pluses and minuses for the magazine. One instance comes from Courtney Hazlett, who, in her MSNBC program, *The Scoop*, listed Oprah's monthly appearances on the cover of every issue in 119 different outfits, 74 different hairstyles, and with 2 convertible cars. Hazlett quotes Oprah's statement about her "all-time favorite" cover, the August 2004 issue, which showed her on a beach, where it was chilly enough for the photographer and crew to follow her with heaters—obviously it wasn't August for the shooting. Outstanding books also get a nod in the same anniversary issue, with 10 of them "that rocked Oprah's decade." Thus far, it appears there will be no continuation of any type of book discussion in the new shows, popular as they have been. Oprah has frequently changed her mind about matters concerning the book club.

Oprah inevitably is a star maker. Over the years, she nurtured many people who appeared on her show regularly until they had followings that enabled them to fly on their own. That type of move was described several years ago by Roger King, himself a star maker, as "taking some of the gamble" out of the business. There have been dieticians and cooks—among them, Rachel Ray, who has her own show, a line of kitchen products, and cookbooks. Ray has had a number of appearances on Oprah's program and the Food Network. In the line of a succession of Oprah's chefs is Art Smith, who had followed Rosie Daly. Smith and Daly each wrote a cookbook. An Oprah magazine cookbook was published in 2008 that received much praise, particularly for its stunning photographs.

Art Smith now owns several prestigious—and expensive—restaurants, is a recognized philanthropist in his own right, and is so popular as a result of exposure on Oprah's show that newspapers carried the story and pictures of his marriage to his companion of 10 years, Jesus Salguerio, an artist and cofounder of Common Threads, a national program for children. Smith's book *Back to the Table* was a best-seller as he traveled across the country giving promotional talks to groups. One media relations director described audience adoration for Smith, which is not surprising given that he tells them not only about his book and recipes, but also stories about his life and his "precious" and "slightly eccentric" mother, Addie Mae Smith, who went along with him on an African safari trip.

Others made famous through association with Oprah include Bob Greene, exercise trainer and author of books about health; Phil McGraw, the psychologist Oprah brought onto her show for numerous programs about mental health; Mehmet Oz, a practicing heart surgeon, who, like McGraw, followed the trajectory from television guest to daily host and monthly columnist as well; and Nate Berkus, a popular designer who also went from Oprah's show to one of his own, although television critics have been suggesting it may not survive in the ratings game.

Musing about his years working with Oprah, Berkus reminds people he's been on the show 66 times and has done 127 makeovers, during which he discovered large and small lessons about "our humanity." In calling his new venture—a daytime talk program—a "conversation," he credits Oprah for much he has learned. While on her show, he reported on home and fashion interests just as he did for her now-defunct magazine *O At Home*. On one of Oprah's shows featuring gays and sometimes their family members, Berkus was included. Regulars devoted to the program follow the lives of many people associated with Oprah and thus are aware of the death of Berkus's partner in the tsunami that struck Asia in 2004, when the two men were there on vacation. Berkus has been significant in O, *The Oprah Magazine,* but now that the decision has been made to shift the taping of the daily Oprah television program to New York, the future is cloudy for Chicagoans such as Berkus, even though the announcement was made that Harpo, with its many branches, will remain in the city, and Oprah has opened another shop in Chicago, indicating she is not cutting entirely her connection to Chicago.

All of these people have shared interests with Oprah—some strictly with food and diet, some with exercise, and one with mental health. A reporter for the *Washington Post* likened a "top-ranked televangelist in the Arab world" and "New Age Guru," Amr Khaled, to "tele-megastars Joel Osteen and Dr. Phil," whereas a number of critics have faulted McGraw for what they have labeled "five minute therapy," a charge, naturally, that he disputes. Whether it is his visibility in so many of Oprah's undertakings or his audacious and sometimes combative daily television show that is the source of the negative assessments, his articles fit into an established pattern of most women's magazines.

Oprah continues to control the Dr. Phil program, but a few years ago there was a dustup over his interference in the problems of the singer Britney Spears, even though, ironically, he was practicing without a license, because he'd allowed it to lapse. However, he maintains an extremely high rating on television. His show has a staff of about 300, his elder son Jay also has a television program, Dr. Phil's self-help books have sold in the millions—adding to the millions of dollars he earns from his shows—and he continues to tour in many places with the program he calls "Get Real." Rumors about the state of his marriage circulated a few years ago after some gossip was printed in the tabloid press. A number of blogs and various comments also appeared, such as the recommendation that the marriage counselor get marriage counseling, and some papers reported Oprah's displeasure about the stories. Most of the criticism of McGraw advises the public that his show is a form of the five-minute therapy he has been accused of. Solutions must be offered by the end of the one-hour program. Yet, despite negative comments from the press and the reputed anger of Oprah, McGraw's popular column is still run in her magazine. He gained some publicity during the celebration of the 10-year anniversary of the magazine when the show was being taped at Radio City Music Hall. Oprah and Dr. Oz helped him shave off the mustache, described as a "trademark soup strainer," he'd worn for more than 40 years.

Dr. Mehmet Oz has interests not only in the mental and physical elements of health, but also shares an additional passion with Oprah: spirituality. *Forbes*, describing him in a lengthy interview, reports Oz's belief "that spirituality is as important as material life."[1] In another lengthy piece about Oz titled "Dr. DOES-IT-All," Frank Bruni of the *New York Times* describes Oz glowingly not only as a host for television and radio, but also as writer of books and articles for magazines, and "one of the most accomplished cardiothoracic surgeons of this generation."[2] Oprah's label for Oz is "America's doctor." Before leaving for his own show, Oz appeared on Oprah's program 55 times. Undoubtedly her affection for him led to the celebration with champagne for the entire audience on Oz's last appearance on her program. Oprah has told him she wants the show to focus on people, and that is what he is doing.

From left, Dr. Phil McGraw, financial advisor Suze Orman, host Oprah Winfrey, Dr. Mehmet Oz, and interior designer Nate Berkus participate in The Oprah Winfrey Show *live from Radio City Music Hall in New York, May 7, 2010. (AP Photo/Evan Agostini)*

Because of his popularity, his is considered a strong lead-in for other shows and has been drawing large numbers of viewers from the beginning. Attributing much of his success to the focus on any one of the five most popular topics—sex, aging, weight, energy, and personal relationships—he notes that most people always want to understand and improve such things. Weight seems to be the leader in the number of times a subject is introduced; Oz showed a gastric bypass film on one of Oprah's programs and continues to speak of food as "a socially acceptable addiction" that must be dealt with psychologically.

Oz's books, *You* guides to health, written with another physician, Michael Roizen, chair of Cleveland Clinic's Wellness Institute, have had sales estimated to be about 9 million copies. The success of the bestseller, *You on a Diet*, was attributed "in no small part," said a reporter, to Oz's good looks and appearance in scrubs on Oprah's show.

In addition to being listed by *Time* magazine among the world's most influential people, Oz has been writing for the *Chicago Sun-Times* since 2008, and in the near future will continue to write columns for *Time* magazine. Somehow, Oz continues in his major activity, though only on Thursdays, as a heart surgeon at New York Presbyterian Hospital/ Columbia University Medical Center, and, if that were not enough, he supervises HealthCorps, which he started as a nonprofit in 2003, to place in high schools health educators who have recently graduated from college. It hardly needs saying that Oz is a firm proponent of exercise and healthful foods, often doing programs about weight and frequently appearing with Oprah to advance health causes for children. He is a man who practices what he preaches and even dances on his shows.

Of the entire group of people whom Oprah has made famous, Bob Greene may be the closest to her personally. He has mentored her for a number of years on diet and physical health but also sees the importance of spirituality for Oprah's "Best Life" theories. But no matter how wise his philosophy and training have been, and even though Greene's *The Best Life Diet* received the highest score in the 2007 *Consumer Reports* rating of diet books, without his association with Oprah his considerable successes probably would not have occurred.

Oprah met Greene briefly while living in Florida, and he later moved to Colorado. Shortly after beginning work at a spa in Telluride,

fortuitously he met Oprah, who owns a house in the area. The meeting at first was one in which there was no shared interest. Oprah, then
and for many years after, was self-conscious about her weight, and
Greene, who knew nothing about her, didn't even own a television
set. However, she became his first client at the spa, and it was not long
before Oprah followed Greene's guidance in health and fitness. His
philosophy is one that he labels "getting real," a phrase also favored
by Phil McGraw. To Greene it consists of sensible eating and exercise. He continues as her expert in many health issues, in addition
to writing about such matters in her magazine. Oprah coauthored
Greene's first book, and he later became one of the hosts on Oprah
Radio XM, which formerly had been *Oprah and Friends*. His show
airs on Saturdays, with other Oprah favorites hosting on other days:
best friend Gayle King, mentor Maya Angelou, writer Lisa Kogan,
sex therapist Dr. Laura Berman, and spiritual leader and writer
Marianne Williamson.

Even though Greene entered her life as an adviser on weight, which
in the past was a major topic on her show as well as in the magazine, she
no longer discusses the matter at length. Over the years, her weight made
her the butt of many jokes not only in the lighter sections of the newspapers, gossip columns, style sections, and humorous essays, but even in
business and financial news. From the time she first became a television
host in Chicago, the descriptions about her size were as unflattering
and cruel as reporters could make them: "hefty," "heftier," "zaftig," and
"fat city." Even on the Internet she was described as a virus that could
expand or shrink. Tabloids seemed to find more unflattering photos of
her than any other paper did, even while her own magazines showed
her as healthy, fit, and gorgeous. Her clothes are fabulous—although in
the early years they always seemed to exaggerate her flaws. Her makeup
is glowing, her hairdos ever changing and eye-catching. She no longer
seems preoccupied with weight, and for whatever reason, most of the
press no longer sees her as a target. At times she endured a formidable
program combining dieting and workouts with Greene as her personal
trainer. On television and in her magazines, a smiling, beautiful Oprah
elegantly dressed and coifed appears. Occasionally, though, she mentions
her lifetime struggle with weight and recently discussed her own story
on the program with author Geneen Roth, who wrote the diet book

Women, Food, and God. The book is Roth's seventh, and coincidentally she lists seven guidelines for better eating. (It seems to have gained a seal of approval inasmuch as it was listed on Oprah's Web site.)

As recently as 2010, when Oprah and Greene went to Orlando, papers praised their efforts to improve the lives of their followers. In the column "Oprah's Guru Brings Best Life Inspiration to Orlando," Ginger Brashinger, of *The Southwest Star*, credits Greene for providing insight about the role of food and exercise in everyone's life. Greene's focus was on "emotional eating," a subject well known to Oprah, who made it a frequent subject on her show over the years.

In photos of Oprah over the 25 years in which she has been in the public eye, she is thin, thinner, fat, fatter. Often recently, she may be seen standing behind some object or sitting down, yet the self-consciousness appears to be gone, and she can laugh about weight. She spent years in her search for the magic bullet of weight loss, carrying on an obsessive search for the holy grail of the body beautiful. Although there are still a few papers that consider her struggle a topic of humor and speculate that the rest of the world does so as well, an Australian reporter finds some shards of sympathy, saying Oprah probably "has suffered more indignity" about the matter than anyone else in the public eye.[3]

The question of racial discrimination also arises periodically, but Oprah chooses not to go down that road, and rarely does she have to confront the issue. When questioned about an unpleasant matter that happened in France—she was turned away at closing time from Hermes, an elegant shop in Paris—she spoke of feeling humiliated but not ready to give a label to the reason even though others implied it was racism.

Not all cultures obsess in the same way: white South Africa, for instance, a country in which racial issues remain a significant matter, seems more interested in her weight than in her race, which might be attributable to Oprah's former preoccupations but also to the popularity of her magazine and programs in that country. Sometimes, she confesses some small matter about her appearance, like the time she had her ears pierced at age 51, done before a live audience by a plastic surgeon on her program. Her magazine always shows gorgeous and famous people who have improved something in their lives, with fantastic results. Further, she appeared on one of her Friday programs with her hair au naturel, and everybody loved it, thinking it was a weave. Oprah's magazine does not discuss failures, although the tabloids are ferocious in their pursuit of any failure to be found in Oprah.

As for Oprah herself, perhaps now that she has passed her mid-50s, she accepts the fact that she cannot be a size eight. She has told interviewers she believes in a quote from a poster she keeps in her Chicago home; it is from the good witch Glinda in *The Wizard of Oz:* "You don't need to be helped anymore." One might argue those glad tidings seem to apply only to the star herself, for, as authors Weston Kosova and Pat Wingert point out, millions of her fans "regard her as an oracle." But Kosova and Wingert also write she has a very contradictory type of persona: on the one hand, she's a "down-to-earth-everywoman" and on the other "an unapproachable billionaire." They note that she regards herself as a teacher and a guide to better living, yet some of her advice and promotions aren't good, and "a lot" that her frequent guests provide "is just bad." Additionally, they state, Oprah doesn't seem to know the difference between "gush" or nonsense and useful, worthwhile information, seeing her guests as "prophets," with her not knowing how to differentiate.[4]

For years she has had a routine to get her through her long and arduous days—the early hours as well as early taping of her shows, supervising the running of Harpo, endless meetings, and travel, which has become more frequent in recent years. An adoring public continues to follow her every move, although there are Coleridge-like voices that predicted future doom. But Oprah has usually been surefooted in her career choices, and when things do not turn out well she rarely hesitates to cut the string. She has done that in relationships, in business activities, even in philanthropic endeavors. Not only does she have followers around the globe, but she even has those who mimic her style on foreign television. Although China is one of the few countries that does not broadcast Oprah's shows, there is a program in China whose host has been described as "China's Oprah." Chen Luyu, host of *A Date with Luyu,* explores issues that have traditionally fallen under the censorship ban in her country, sexual matters that are taboo topics—lesbianism, transsexualism, and AIDS. Yet she has not been censored.

Being on Oprah's program—as she was—would not have influenced the number of Luyu's viewers, which run into the millions, but for other people in the entertainment business, an invitation to appear on The

Oprah Winfrey Show is a commercial goldmine for individuals, products, and, as all publishers know, books (a fact that everyone associated with writing, publishing, and selling books is deeply concerned about, now that Oprah is moving on to other things.) However, she will continue to be a drawing card for advertisers, as is anyone close to her. *Advertising Age* made the point that Oprah's friend Gayle King (who also is editor-at-large for O, *The Oprah Magazine*) was given Dove's first Real Beauty Award.

Oprah's Harpo Productions attempts to hold tight control on all things. In 2005 reporter Alessandra Stanley labeled Oprah "a self-help evangelist," . . . "someone with a messianic sense of purpose."[5] That description seems to apply even more so today, as one follows what Oprah has called her "big life." Talking to another writer who queried her about future shows, Oprah revealed no specifics about her involvement, but the messianic sense Stanley sees permeates all such discussions. Oprah wants to continue meaningful programming that will inspire people and lead them to think differently about their lives. In the past few years, her growing interest in religion and spirituality has taken many turns.

She doesn't believe in organized religion. God, she has said, is "the life force" or "nature" or "Allah." In her philosophy, church is in oneself. Anything is attainable if a person finds the connection to a higher power. Some years ago, she attended, for a short time, Trinity United Church of Christ, a South Side church in Chicago, the same one President Obama and his family went to before he was elected. However, in the year before the election, the pastor, Reverend Jeremiah Wright, with "inflammatory rhetoric," created a major storm among the press, the public, and politicians. With his words, "God damn America," Wright alienated many followers, including the future president and Oprah, whom one Canadian reporter, Ed Morrissey, called "the patron saint of suburban families."[6] At the time, Morrissey believed both Obama and Oprah would be damaged by their association with Wright, but he suggested that Oprah would be the bigger loser because of the appeal she has had for the public.

His prediction, however, proved incorrect for both. The new president dissociated himself from Wright. Oprah stopped attending traditional churches and wanted to separate herself from the angry messages of preachers such as Wright. Soon she began to follow a new type of

Christian spirituality, leading an anonymous friend to tell a *Newsweek* reporter, "There is the church of Oprah now," and Oprah "has her own following." It came at about the same time as the deluge of stories telling of abuse in the Catholic Church. Among columnists admiring of Oprah, Stanley Crouch wrote on November 12, 2007, "Oprah could teach the Catholic Church about taking responsibility." Prompted by the way Oprah took the blame for the problems at her academy in South Africa, Crouch berates the Catholic clerics—"those irresponsible men at the top of the Catholic Church who almost brought down the institution here in America." Oprah, said Crouch, is "the Mother Courage of talk television . . . a woman who uses her bully pulpit . . . in her efforts to right wrongs." Adding the greatest praise, Crouch compares her efforts to those of "the battered and bleeding civil rights workers."

Influenced or at least "popularized by celebrities like Oprah," public interest in self-help spirituality has taken hold in numerous places across the country. According to some, at issue is the word *spirituality*. According to a professor at the Southern Baptist Theological Seminary, where a new doctoral program about spirituality has been introduced, the term "can mean whatever a person wants it to mean." Alert Mohler, president of the Center for Biblical Spirituality, has stated that the term is a buzzword that can mean leaving out "God and Jesus" for the self, in a type of "cafeteria-style" religion. Spirituality differs from the experience of Christian spirituality, according to another scholar, in that the former is detached and "objective," whereas the Christian experience is focused on living within the faith. Self-help Evangelical pastors, such as Texan Joel Osteen, follow the theory of "self-betterment at home" and at work, whereas equally well-known Evangelical pastors such as Rick Warren stress that life is not about the individual but about God. And still another interpretation is given by Arthur Holder, professor and dean of the Graduate Theological Union in California; he compares modern spiritual seekers to the 19th-century transcendentalists Emerson and Thoreau.

Two newspaper writers, speaking of Oprah's "evolution," in which she changed from being the host of a talk show to becoming "Inspirer in Chief," refer to two books, one by assistant professor of religious studies at Yale University, Katherine Lofton, the other by author Marcia Nelson. Both have written, as have others, of Oprah's enormous influence on the book world, listing two books that have been the subject of her classes: Helen Schucman's *A Course of Miracles* and Eckhart Tolle's *A New Earth*. Oprah has described Tolle's book as the best book on spirituality she'd ever read. Nonetheless, some members of the religious right have attacked Oprah's programs and influence on her "students," calling her "the devil." However, there are also strong defenders who are well versed in the Bible and accuse the accusers of not knowing the Bible. If they had, say her supporters, they would know that Eckhart's books speak frequently about Jesus, as well as quote the New Testament.[7]

Columnists with more moderate views note Oprah's appeal to large numbers of women, such as those who pay large amounts of money to attend one of her Live Your Best Life tours. Eugene Robinson, of the *Washington Post*, notes that it is easy to make fun of her, as he does gently. But he also speaks of the rapport she has with women and the reasons for her appeal. Even women who have had great success in their own lives relate to Oprah because she searches "for the same things" they do. Her presentations, he writes, renew women who attend "services at the Church of Oprah, which is the church of possibility."[8]

Nevertheless, many Christian leaders call on their flock to "flee" or "just say no" to Oprah's "doctrines." Calling her a peddler of untruths, one of the best known voices to speak out against her is a guest columnist for the *Christian Post*: Chuck Colson, once a special counsel for President Richard Nixon. Colson was convicted for his role in the Watergate scandal and later converted to Evangelical Christianity. As a founder of Prison Fellowship, he has been zealous in trying to bring about prison reform, is the author of many books, and has a daily broadcast called *Breakpoint* on 1,000 stations. He disagrees with Tolle and faults Oprah for "undercutting Christianity."[9]

With all the negative publicity, Oprah became defensive about her choices of Tolle's books for her classes and the classes themselves, pointedly stating they were not about religion but rather to help people explore their consciousness. On her Web site, Oprah writes that she keeps Tolle's book next to her bed. Still, her statements have done little or nothing to deflate the attacks on her. There is often a great resemblance among them, but that seems not to matter to many of her critics. Lofton, however, tempers her remarks by first praising Oprah's philanthropy, but then finds it is linked to commercialism. (Perhaps a similar criticism could be made of Tolle, whose Inspiration Cards and CDs are sold on-line.) According to Lofton, Oprah's "imperative is not to save souls . . . [but] to [make] you want to return and consume the product." Oprah "is a corporation" using "a religious idiom to amazing effect." There is "an Oprah message," says Lofton, and, it states if you buy the recom-mended product your life will change for the better.

One might ask why, then, are people so gullible when there is so much negative material written and preached about her? A writer for *The Huffington Post* listed seven reasons for her powerful appeal: empathy; interaction; smiles; eye contact; gestures, such as expressive hands; pos-ture, including a relaxed body; and interaction, through listening and responding.[10]

Although few reporters mention it, another important factor in Oprah's evolution came from a trip to Israel and a visit to the Holocaust Memorial Museum in Washington, DC, where she stated she came to her understanding of power and what she, "a once colored girl," could achieve through television and all that she could do. The recognition of the failure of people to prevent tragedies and a belief in the necessity to stand up for what is right moved her even more in what she came to believe was her mission. What she has done since then clearly has expanded her many roles and sense of destiny.

Pastor Hooper at the Religious Science Church of the Desert Spiri-tual Center wrote that Oprah "is a mighty force . . . at times . . . as mighty as a river." That force has brought people, hundreds of thou-sands of them, to unite spiritually. The Reverend Hooper builds his lectures around themes that Oprah stresses, particularly the belief that there is no one way, "no one . . . ownership of the . . . river of life."

So many columnists and preachers have focused on Oprah's foray into religion and spirituality that, after a time, the intent, claims, sin-cerity, and purpose of the sermons, essays, blogs—or even whether the particular writer is hawking a book—becomes unclear. Are they fol-lowing some advice from the lengthy article taken from *Advertising Age* about having a brand? Or is it the advice the writers themselves volun-teer in "How to Get Your Brand on 'Oprah'"?

A month after Reverend Wright's intemperate remarks, Oprah started the Soul Series, on XM radio online. For 10 weeks, Oprah and author Eckhart Tolle taught the material from his book, *A New Earth*, the

Talk show host Oprah Winfrey speaks about her trip to the Auschwitz concentration camp and the importance of Holocaust education to help combat genocide during an address at the United States Holocaust Memorial Museum in Washington, DC, October 25, 2006. (AP Photo/Charles Rex Arbogast)

61st book featured on Oprah's Book Club as well as her choice for their summer reading. It was estimated to have drawn millions of people to the programs. Those interests have led to some television programs on which well-known religious figures have been guests. And there have been many nonguests hostile to anything and everything Oprah stands for or advocates.

Some people—professional and otherwise—proclaim doom for her now or in the future; others find reasons to hate her and proclaim that "the age of Oprah" is about to end because white women finally know she is black. Apparently, that sentiment is linked to being what some bloggers and other critics label "a New Age racist." Furthermore, in contradiction to the fact that her magazine remains a popular seller, these same critics predict its failure because of her egoism, her choices of new age books such as *The Secret* and *The New Earth*, and for committing the unforgivable sin of launching Dr. Phil. Because of her supposed multiple offenses against her fans, opponents predict that "Oprah worship" is over.[11] If so, how does one explain the crush that came about for seat tickets to the last *Oprah Winfrey Show?*

Calling Oprah "the Jezebel of Prophecy," a documentary filmmaker advertising his availability for interviews (but not interviewed by Oprah) produced a DVD, *Hebrew or the So-Called Negro,* warning of her destructive effect. Another, better known, seven-minute video, "The Church of Oprah Exposed," was produced by "Christian Groups." Shown on YouTube, thus guaranteeing a wide audience, it describes Oprah as denying major beliefs of Christianity. In her saying there are multiple ways to heaven, she is seen as a dangerous cultist. Reporting about the film, sponsored by the Baptist Press, is Mark Coppenger, who dislikes her religious views, calling them "the blind leading the blind"—that is, toxic New Age views. "If," he writes, "we give our love to rivals of God," God has every reason for "righteous indignation." Coppenger moves from God's indignation to his own, faulting Oprah for having her own agenda, which includes the unacceptable "cohabiting with Stedman Graham."

Some people who are interested in Oprah's love life report that she and Graham live together, and others claim that the two have separated. A few years ago, there was much speculation over a rumor that Oprah had removed Graham's name from her will. The story was neither confirmed nor denied, like most gossip about her private life. Oprah has refused to say what bequests are in her will or where her fortune will go after her death.

Graham, who has been Oprah's companion for more than 20 years, appears to play a limited role nowadays in Oprah's activities, even though the two are shown together occasionally in photographs, and more frequently during the period of the presidential nominations and election. Graham is known to be a staunch supporter of conservative Republicans, but he seemed to encourage Oprah's activities for the Democratic candidate and appeared with her, smiling and enthusiastic, at the Chicago victory rally for the new president. News reports tell that Oprah provides funds for charitable causes in Graham's hometown. She has donated million of dollars to Whitesboro, the small New Jersey city where Stedman grew up. However, the public are not privy to many

Stedman Graham and Oprah Winfrey walk the red carpet at the Kennedy Center Honors, in Washington, DC, on December 5, 2010. The 2010 honorees were Merle Haggard, Jerry Herman, Bill T. Jones, Paul McCartney, and Oprah Winfrey. (AP Photo/ Jacquelyn Martin)

facts of Oprah's personal life, and she requires staff to maintain her privacy. If private information is leaked, it is anonymous. Several years ago, the tabloid press was reporting on every sighting, but not so now, except for infrequent—and perhaps questionable—statements that Graham has other love interests, and so does Oprah, or that Graham has moved out of the apartment the two shared. Over the years, various books, magazines, and tabloids have attempted, sometimes successfully, to unearth information about the romances in Oprah's younger days. However, Oprah will not comment on those stories and, with only a few exceptions, rarely will any past lover do so either. Although there is much less news about the couple, when there is anything to report, it does find a way into papers. Even on a golf course, when Graham was promoting Athletes Without Drugs, a nonprofit organization he founded in 1985, he responded angrily to questions about Oprah's decision to leave Chicago. He blames the city for not giving her credit for all she has done and stated that people take her for granted. Oprah had no comment about his remarks. She is not concerned with such state-ments. She follows her own judgments. However, she often repeats the statement that those to whom much is given have the obligation to give much to others, and her intention is just that.

Some tabloids have questioned on occasion Oprah's sexual orientation and have reported that some of her biggest fans are gay men. The same press organizations also speculate frequently on Oprah's relationship to Gayle King. Their friendship has provided and seems to continue to provide fodder for some reporters. Although King shares many, many activities with Oprah and has become a prominent figure on her own in television and radio, as well as in Oprah's publications, both women scorn the implications of the press, and both have also stated there is no shame in anyone's being gay. Yet, on Howard Stern's radio program, Rosie O'Donnell once added fuel to the issue when she talked of a trip Oprah and King had taken that was "as gay as it gets."

Unquestionably, King, like others among Oprah's friends, has benefited from the connection to one of the most famous and richest women in the world; their friendship goes back to their days as relative unknowns in Baltimore. King, who has been married and divorced twice, has two grown children. Oprah, their godmother, spoke at both their college graduations. Since their early meetings, Oprah and King have prospered, following much the same path, and the gossipy media enjoy printing information about the expensive gifts of homes Oprah has given to King—one home in Connecticut for $3.6 million and an apartment in New York for $7 million. The same report in the *New York Daily News* states that Oprah has given King a large amount of money as well. But, after all, Oprah is known to be one of the most generous people on the globe.

Perhaps the only woman who is as close to Oprah as Gayle King is Maya Angelou, the person Oprah speaks of with love and admiration and the deep connection she feels to her "mentor-mother-sister-friend." With the rocky, unhappy, fractured relationship Oprah has with her birth mother, the reasons for the love and trust she holds for Angelou seem obvious. Despite the difference in their ages, much in their lives followed the same pattern: terrible childhoods, rape, separation and loss, betrayal. But both moved beyond all that might have destroyed them, with life stories that circle the globe.

Having declared again and again that she wants to give back to a world that has given her so much, Oprah's charitable work is unparalleled. But not everything she does strikes a note of rescue. Clearly, Oprah loves to have fun, give parties, and see friends, and over the years she has held a number of spectacular events for those she holds dear, King and Angelou. She has also given gifts to her staff. She has taken those close to her on trips and on sensational cruises. She loves to surprise people, as she has done many times, with exquisite gifts. The most famous party of all, her Legends Ball (celebrating among others, Maya Angelou) in 2006, was photographed by multiple newspapers and magazines—reminiscent of, and still talked about—the Black and White Ball given in the 1970s by writer Truman Capote. The "once colored girl," now the "queen of media," or "the Mama" as she calls herself to her African students, is frequently shown in exquisite gowns hosting her own affair or a party for charity, perhaps to raise money for the Metropolitan Museum of Art, as she did in the spring of 2010. Escorted by designer Oscar de la Renta, naturally she was wearing one of his gowns.

Oprah Winfrey has a hug from poet Maya Angelou during the Uncommon Height Award of the National Council of Negro Women, honoring Oprah Winfrey in Washington, DC, on June 4, 2009. (AP Photo/Jose Luis Magana)

Jennie Rothenberg Gritz, writing in *The Atlantic*, thinks men find Oprah "troublesome," because she has the "capacity to take over the world," and they object to the ways that women follow Oprah, who has "invaded their homes—from kitchen to bedroom." Apparently, or not so apparently, she tells readers, men object to the changes Oprah has wrought in marital relationships.

Rarely are the galas or pleasurable happenings the subjects of her shows. Rather, the seamier topics bring in the audience for Oprah's program. Scandalous news may lead to a program, as with a show featuring a prominent Colorado pastor whose secret life unfolded in the papers. Founder of New Life Church in Colorado Springs and famous as the president of the National Association of Evangelicals, Ted Haggard, a married man with five children, over the years had affairs with men. The ensuing scandal forced his resignation from his church, and, although Haggard no longer remains its minister, both he and his wife, Gayle, were on Oprah's show, speaking of their decision to remain together. They spoke of their participation in a Christian restoration team, their work in holding weekly prayer meetings on their property. All of this became public information because of Haggard's high standing in the religious community. It was not only the scandal and publicity that made Haggard fodder for the news industry, but also the outspoken book Gayle Haggard wrote, *Why I Stayed: The Choices I Had in My Darkest Hour*. The Haggards' joint appearance on Oprah's program took place shortly before the release of a documentary about Haggard, who now earns a living selling life insurance. Ted Haggard and his wife launched their new church in June 2010, but it did not have a meeting place, although they also held a "Resurrection" party. Apparently, they are not supported by any official group.

Politicians are more likely than ministers to make news with their infidelities, but, unlike Gayle Haggard, few political or pastoral wives write about them. Sometimes they appear to be tell-all, sometimes decorous, sometimes cautious. Political books more often are written by the husband, but both George and Laura Bush have become memoirists. Laura Bush's *Spoken from the Heart* came out in 2010, shortly before Oprah interviewed her and her two daughters at the Bush ranch.

Another political wife, Jenny Sanford, former wife of the governor of South Carolina, wrote about her marital situation in *Staying True*, but she did not appear on Oprah's show, although the press was all over the story, even reminding a fascinated public that she was an heiress and former banker, and showing photos of the former Mrs. Sanford happily escorted by another man. Without Oprah's golden touch, though, and no interview, the book sales were weak.

Another politician's wife, Elizabeth Edwards, also produced a personal story, called *Reconciliation*, which she talked about on Oprah's show. Perhaps before the series of scandals that shocked and even outraged the public, Elizabeth Edwards and her husband, North Carolina Senator John Edwards, were as well regarded and loved as the Haggards. They also tried to put a patch in their frayed marriage. Like the Haggards, they both appeared on Oprah's program in their super-size, elegant home, where John Edwards kept appearing and disappearing during the talk. Perhaps the subsequent events, after the publication of Mrs. Edwards's book and the continuing revelations about her husband's sordid actions became newspaper and magazine reports with tidbits of their private lives, caused their story to linger more salaciously than did the stories of the Haggards.

Elizabeth Edwards, whose terminal cancer was diagnosed during the time her husband was running for the presidency, became a much-admired, pitied, and sympathetic figure; and, if the numerous outcries of commentators and others are followed, many will forgive the sinner in Haggard but not in John Edwards. When Oprah announced that "the other woman," Rielle Hunter, would be on her show, bloggers, in large numbers, wrote angry letters, several of them criticizing Oprah. Writer Jeff Labrecque questioned whether people wanted to know any more of the tawdry details, to which the majority of bloggers said no. Nevertheless, some few admitted to prurient interest at the same time that they voiced pity for Mrs. Edwards and annoyance with Oprah. But the show must go on, and indeed it did. As anticipated, huge numbers of bloggers as well as news and television reports followed the appearance of Hunter on Oprah's April 30, 2010, program. Half a page of print and pictures in the *Washington Post* portray the two—Oprah and Hunter—seated across from each other in Hunter's living room in Charlotte, North Carolina, as they discuss what the *Post's* television critic, Lisa de Moraes, mockingly calls "Johnny Edwards's life of integrity." The details of the romance provided by Hunter sound much like a combination of a fairy tale and the old *True Confessions* magazine. De Moraes captures the essence of both, as she quotes some of Oprah's remarks and adds some equally droll lines of her own. Oprah: "Why did you, Miss Spirituality in Alignment With the Truth . . . go along with it?" Hunter, as she explained Edwards's situation, has him saying: "I want your help. I need your help." With a combination of humor and scorn, De Mores, throughout her column, lets readers know, "Really, you can't make this stuff up."

Even the sophisticated and cynical television newspeople could not refrain from showing clips of Oprah's interview. The generally business-like Andrea Mitchell, who normally avoids that type of news, had a segment about it on her program. The staff writers of *The Daily Buzz* described Hunter's responses to Oprah as "wacky, new-age like refer-ences," while the *New York Post* commented how "incredulous" Oprah often seemed. *Arts and Entertainment* was kinder in describing the event as one of Oprah's more "provocative" interviews. Online Time *Enter-tainment* compliments Oprah as "the perfect interrogator," noting that she is the television person with the most years of experience in 'in-terviewing crazies." With the title of the story "Oprah Grills Deluded Edwards Mistress Rielle," the writer captures what Oprah intended for all watchers to see: "skepticism in [her] eyes, as Hunter provided her and her viewers "the full tour of her scenic hometown, Delusionville."

As is characteristic of this type of scandal, a number of bloggers, before and after the Hunter interview, offered religious advice to Elizabeth Edwards; some recommended she leave her husband—a path she took eventually—and, not confining their hostility to John Edwards, some expressed contempt for all men who "are weak." Sales of two books with stories about the Edwards family were on best-seller lists for some time, and the authors also appeared on numerous talk shows. The story did not disappear for weeks after Hunter's interview with Oprah; still another one appeared in a newspaper, an interview with Hunter's sister, Roxanne Marshall, who spoke for Hunter's family, stating they were very upset by her behavior and her indifference to the effect on Elizabeth Edwards as well as the Edwards's children. Mean-while, the angry anti-Hunter and John Edwards blogs continued until replaced by another scandal about other celebrities. With the death of Elizabeth Edwards, only the news about her will (leaving nothing to her husband) was circulated.

Blogs about Oprah, her show, her activities, and certain lurid stories surrounding her or guests on her programs cover multiple pages on the Internet, whereas other stories languish. In reports of a tragic happening in 2005, newspapers referred to the man responsible, James Arthur Ray, as an "Oprah approved self-help guru." Ray, who continues to advertise as a motivational speaker, was involved in the attempt to turn a group of people into so-called spiritual warriors by placing them in a sweat lodge in Sedona, Arizona. For that privilege, individuals paid $9,000 each to Ray. The purpose was to purge their bodies of sin, but the result was the death of three people (two the first night and a third a week later); about a dozen (some reports say 18) became very ill and had to be hospitalized. After announcing that the deaths were not accidental, authorities charged Ray with negligent homicide, but little more news of the happening was circulated.

A number of bloggers, while not defending Ray, were very critical of Oprah's role in the event and of her relationship to Ray. The saying that "all publicity is good publicity" clearly did not apply to Oprah's part in the tragedy, but it quickly disappeared from the news cycle, and the reason for that remains unknown.

Oprah always has professionals—lawyers and staff—to handle anything that threatens her image, except now Kitty Kelley's unauthorized biography—over which Oprah has had limited control. Oprah, even though she dislikes publicity apart from her professional life, is often involved in suing or being sued. However, Kelley claims she has been kept from interviews on television programs because of Oprah's powerful reach. When questioned, though, about Oprah's refusal to authorize the book, Kelley states she was not interested in going that route. There is no question that authorization may mean oversight and interference. But Oprah's less scandalous involvement in spiritual studies and events during the past few years has brought about more sermons, reports, praise, and condemnation than anything else to date. It remains to be seen what the Kelley effect does to Oprah's image, and if there is damage, how long the aftershocks linger and whether there will be any tie-in to the spiritual part of the star's life.

For several years, numerous religious figures have attacked everything Oprah has said or done about religion and spirituality. At McLean Bible Church in Vienna, Virginia, two Christian evangelicals, Josh McDowell and Dave Sterrett, warned a crowd of 1,500 about Oprah's spiritual teachings. The warning is that Oprah has created "a hodge-podge of personalized faith, which is dangerous"—views they expressed in the book they wrote together, "O" God: A Dialogue on Truth and Oprah's Spirituality. In their attempt to refute her beliefs, they warn that she speaks of God in an impersonal way, telling us to look within ourselves, where we will find God. Although, they claim, Oprah uses biblical and Christian terms and references, they are used falsely when she speaks of Jesus and humans as part of "Ultimate Being" and "Universal Energy." If Jesus said "I am the way, and the truth, and the life," then "why can't I?" The danger, the two men say, is that such belief may lead people to do as they feel rather than to follow "what is absolute truth." They do not accuse Oprah of being anti-Christian but anti-Bible. McDowell states that Oprah finds meaning through the claims of people she agrees with rather than by serving "a jealous God" and that she apparently doesn't really question their statements. On the one hand, he praises her "passion and commitment," both of which are "genuine," but, on the other hand, quarrels with her choices of Eckhart Tolle and Marianne Williamson as teachers and leaders of things spiritual. Writer Michelle Bearden states in her review of McDowell and Sterrett's book that it won't "make it as selection for Oprah's book club." The authors' intention is to show that Oprah's spirituality doesn't fit their evangelical beliefs.

Everyone knows that appearing on Oprah's show carries cachet. However, not all appearances are equal. Ministers look to achieve publicity, and perhaps followers, from being on the prized Oprah show. Michael Beckwith, founder of the Agape International Spiritual Center in Culver City, California, and author of the book Spiritual Liberation (2009), appeared on the Oprah program in 2009. However, his claim in 2009 to a reporter at the Atlanta Journal Constitution that he is "Winfrey's spiritual advisor" has not been verified by Oprah, nor was it repeated in his Wikipedia biography. Beckwith is not the only person claiming to be Oprah's spiritual advisor; the list grows and grows.

Politicians, governors present and former, wanting the publicity or not, become the subject of contrast to Oprah. Sarah Palin, former governor of Alaska and prominent Republican candidate for vice president during the 2008 election, was chosen during that time as an example to hold up against Oprah because the star was campaigning for then Senator

Obama. In an article purportedly about Obama, author Robert Bowie Johnson concentrated on his beliefs about Oprah, none of them positive. On one side, he holds up Palin as a believer in the Christian faith, a person who is guided by God and the Holy Spirit. But Oprah, in contrast, he claims, "mocks" such views in favor of "self-adoration." His most damning contrast between the two women speaks of their belief in creation: Palin, "in the image of God, . . . descended from Adam and Eve," and Oprah, as evolving "by chance . . . [from] . . . primordial ooze . . . through worms, reptiles, and monkeys." To solidify his points, he then links Oprah to "her mentor, Tolle," because they view themselves "as God."[12]

If such harsh condemnation isn't sufficient to turn admirers away from Oprah, it is not for lack of critics. A Web site named Jesus-is-Savior speaks of Oprah as "the most dangerous woman in the world," and the author of a self-published book, *Don't Drink the Kool-Aid* (a title that refers to the tragic deaths in 1978 of hundreds of people who had belonged to a cult) warns readers of the "spell . . . [that] is over Oprah," suggesting they too will die because of her teachings. If the reader wonders what it is that Oprah has unleashed upon the world, her critics find endless examples. One person, Jennifer Simon, writing on a site called AlterNet, states she knows that her remarks will anger Oprah's "mob of followers." What are those remarks, "followers" might ask? The writer answers: Oprah has an "A-list of freaks"; she hasn't taught women to be happy at any weight; she pushes the notion that spending brings happiness; she has created "the monster, Dr. Phil, who legitimizes bigotry" and is "a sound bite psychologist." He is "her fault." But what appears to be an ongoing sin is having created a monthly magazine "more egotistical" than her television show.[13]

Oprah is attacked frequently for her association with Dr. Phil. They blame her for whatever they dislike about Phil McGraw. Someone who calls himself "Mild-Mannered Rambler"—in something of a misnomer—accuses her of letting loose on the world Phil, "an arrogant poor-excuse for a doctor," an "unethical" and "self-promoting punk," and the writer finally classifies McGraw as "just plain garbage." A reader might ask, legitimately, what accounts for the polls that show McGraw's huge ratings.

Various doctors object not only to the advice put forth by both McGraw and Oprah, but some go further, calling many of her claims about medicine "ludicrous." When *Newsweek* published a lengthy article berating her influence on the public,[14] several physicians wrote letters of support for that view, one saying she supports bad medicine in her role, creating the "Oprah-fication of medicine." Rather than having the necessary "critical thinking skills," she promotes her "New Age nonsense."[15]

Of course, bloggers again jumped into that fray, some in support of the magazine and some with anti-Oprah views, even calling her a "useful idiot"; but others staunchly defended her as "an amazing woman" as opposed to sexists and racists of "the privileged class." A physician who had been on her program several times in the past writes of her "as the best that humankind has to offer" and a role model for those who need to "become more civilized." While lauding Oprah, Mark Goulston excoriates Dr. Phil as an "opportunist" who has taken advantage of Oprah.

It was Oprah's strong endorsement of Helen Schucman's book, *A Course of Miracles*, as well as other books and philosophy, which turned a small fire into a conflagration. The Schucman book was presented through daily classes on XM radio, with central thoughts being "there is no sin," that one should not cling to ideas of "the old rugged cross," and that everyone should consider "alternative" views of Jesus. However, it was Eckhart Tolle's first book that captured huge numbers of devotees. *The Power of Now* was translated into 33 languages, and *The New Earth*, written after that, sold faster than any of Oprah's previous 60 book club choices. His work was taught online as free weekly 90-minute webinars to an audience of 2 million, in what one critic labeled "Oprah-Tolle Crazy"; whereas critic Roger Friedman compared Tolle to the character Chauncey Gardiner (Chance), in Jerzy Kosinski's 1971 novel and Hal Ashby's 1979 movie *Being There*. Chauncey can neither read nor write, is a man described in various ways by different critics, one viewing him as "empty and vapid," a blank character who speaks in meaningless language. (Was one or more of the critics thinking of Chauncey in referring to a report that "even Oprah" [often? sometimes?] "seems to have no idea what he [Tolle] is talking about"?) Another possible interpretation of the story is as satire about the foolishness of those public leaders stupid enough to imbue an empty shell—Chauncey—with remarkable or even godlike abilities. Whichever the interpretation, Friedman is undoubtedly contemptuous of both Oprah and Tolle.

Although it was Oprah who made Tolle famous, one might question the idea that she alone is entirely responsible for his overwhelming success. His books have remained on the best-seller lists of the *New York Times* despite the furor about him and his philosophy. Even the British have waded into both sides of the discussion. A lengthy article about Tolle in the Sunday newspaper the *Independent* skewers him with the description, "New Age mumbo jumbo; and no one is more jumbo with his mumbo." But, in fairness, the writer also reports on Tolle's popularity in addition to the views of an English professor who supports Tolle's Eastern, Buddhist approach, calling it similar to transpersonal psychology. And, despite the numerous detractors among ministers and laypeople who find his work "utter twaddle" and blame Oprah for turning another self-help book "stinker into a bestseller," there are fans for the philosopher from many areas of society, including academia and Christian circles.[16]

At times it seems that Oprah does nothing but work, travel for business, give talks, appear on shows other than her own, and on and on. Even when she talks of being overworked or having no life of her own, her friend Gayle King, who may know her better than anyone else does, tells interviewers that not only does Oprah thrive on doing good, but she also loves to work.

Does Oprah resemble the figure in Shakespeare's song "Who Is Silvia?" Or is the reviewer/novelist Louis Bayard close to the mark when he describes her as "a house divided: extroverted and narcissistic, philanthropic and close to the vest, nosily spiritual and hilariously materialistic"?[17]

Who is Silvia/ what is she,
That all our swains commend her. . . . .

Is she kind. . . . . ?
For beauty lives with kindness. . . . .

Then to Silvia let us sing,
That Silvia is excelling;
She excels each mortal thing
Upon the dull earth dwelling.

NOTES

1. Dirk Smillie, "A Headache for Dr. Oz," *Forbes*, 16 June 2009.

2. Frank Bruni, "Dr. DOES-IT-ALL," *New York Times*, 16 Apr. 2010.

3. Ros Reines, "We're All Weight Watchers," *Sunday Telegraph* (Australia), 28 Mar. 2010.

4. Weston Kosova and Pat Wingert, "People Wising Up to Oprah," *Zimbio*, June 2009.

5. Alessandra Stanley, "Oh, Oprah, 20 Years of Talk, Causes and Self-Improvement," *New York Times*, 15 Nov. 2005.

6. ABC News, 13 Mar. 2008.

7. Jeff McCord, "Is Oprah the Devil?," *Jeff McCord's Blog*, 20 Apr. 2008.

8. Eugene Robinson, "The Church of Oprah," *Washington Post*, 10 May 2005.

9. Chuck Colson, "Oprah and a New Earth," *Christian Post*, 28 Apr. 2008.

10. Jerry Weisman, "The Art and Science of Oprah Winfrey," *Huffington Post*, 29 Feb. 2009.

11. Anita Creamer, "America Finally Has an Oprah Overload," www.freepublic.com/focus.

12. Robert Bowie Johnson, "Sarah Palin's and Oprah's Spiritual Beliefs Contrast Starkly," *Christian News*, 15 Sept. 2008.

13. Jennifer Simon, "10 Good Reasons You Should Hate Oprah Winfrey," Nerve.com, Jan. 2010.

14. Weston Kosova, "Live Your Best Life Ever!," *Newsweek*, 30 May 2009.

15. The response to the *Newsweek* article was by Dr. David Garski and was originally published in *Science-Based Medicine* on June 7, 2009.

16. Ether Walker, "Eckhart Tolle: This Man Could Change Your Life," *Independent*, 21 June 2008.

17. Louis Bayard, review of *Oprah: A Biography*, by Kitty Kelley, *Washington Post*, Book World, 15 Apr. 2010.

Chapter 7

OPRAH'S YELLOW
BRICK ROAD

Years ago—at the end of filming *The Color Purple*—Quincy Jones told Oprah, "Your future is so bright that it's going to burn your eyes." For a long time, Oprah would repeat the statement, but it is now so obviously true, neither she nor others have to say it. The future has arrived with all its promise intact. One can tick off the work Oprah has done since those early days: Several decades in radio and television, from her beginnings in Tennessee as a young student, going on to Baltimore television in her 20s, and then on to stardom in Chicago with a television show that continued to draw millions of viewers until Oprah decided it was time to move on. Her new venture, the purchase of the new Oprah Winfrey Network (OWN), in partnership with what formerly was Discovery Channel, suggests it is all Oprah, all the time.

For many people, this has been a fortunate time in which to be living, surely more than the years when Oprah started out. She was illegitimate, born into poverty, in a small town, in a poor rural Southern state; parts of the United States still had its own style of apartheid life, and civil rights was yet to become a reality. How, in growing up, could she have envisioned even a small part of what lay ahead? Schools were segregated, and most women had returned to their homes to raise families after World

War II, while men went back to their jobs, went to universities, and re-
claimed their roles as heads of family. Television was in its infancy. Blacks
were called Negroes—not a demeaning word then, but it soon carried
heavy freight—and few people of color could enter the white world of
professions. Little more than a career in entertainment provided a door
as an opening, but even then there were barriers and limitations. With
all things stacked against her, Oprah found the way out of poverty and
all its heavy baggage to stardom. On one of her many visits to Africa, she
proclaimed her thanks to God for what she had lived to "see . . . touch,
hear, and feel."

Despite the difficulties she faced, it is certain that Oprah's tempera-
ment and will would have made her a leader at any time, because, from
her earliest days, she has believed in taking charge of herself and her
own life. But as she followed her chosen "yellow brick road," she decided
it was also necessary to help others along the way. For years she has
blithely moved on as if there has never been any doubt about her direction. When writing about the good fortune of U.S. women in contrast to
the millions, even billions, of women around the world, she has stressed
their right to follow the path of choice and admonished them to "use it."
Referring to a line from a favorite poet, Emily Dickinson, she speaks of
her own way now and in the future; it is to "dwell in possibility."

Believing in possibility has brought her joy and confidence. Her optimism is reminiscent of the words of entertainer Al Jolson—a white,
Jewish singer and actor in the early part of the 20th century—who also
climbed from poverty and hardship. Jolson's signature role generally was
that of a black man who would tell his audience, "You ain't seen nothing yet." (The lines became a popular song in the 1970s.)

In middle age, a grateful, happy Oprah is suggesting just that. She has
embarked on still another adventure. Although she isn't blinded any
more today than at other periods of her life from the reality of problems
that often appear insurmountable, she tells viewers of her shows, readers of her magazines, and her many audiences in the United States and
around the world that she constantly attempts to find some way to deal
with problems. For her there has always been a path through religion
and spirituality, a part through determination, and a part that appears
to be almost infallible judgment. Even though she has been harshly attacked in pulpits, books, magazines, newspapers, and blogs by numerous

members of traditional religions, she has always moved on. She has been satirized frequently in friendly skits and cruelly in cartoons and also undermined by some who have benefited from her largesse. Nevertheless, like Dorothy of *The Wizard of Oz*, who danced along the yellow brick road in her red jeweled shoes, Oprah keeps moving on and has left the old shoes behind. On December 30, 2010, Mary Altaffer of the Associated Press suggested that Oprah probably regards her move to cable television "as one more [step] on the yellow brick road of blessings."

Not everyone agrees with or approves of her decisions. But as a lover of gospel music, Oprah has a favorite song that seems to sum up her lifetime view: "Stand."

> What do you do when you've done all you can, and it seems like it's never enough?
> What do you give when you've given your all, and it seems you can't make it through?
> (Refrain) You just stand.

With the song serving metaphorically for the determination needed to overcome all kinds of adversity, like the Ancient Mariner of Coleridge's poem, she repeats her message again and again. There are those who feel she preaches rather than entertains, but if the criticism hurts, she ignores it and continues with what she considers her mission. She builds schools and supports those that need money to move ahead and even to survive. She gives scholarships to the worthy and needy. She can be counted on when dire emergencies arise, such as the 9/11 events, or Hurricane Katrina, or the oil spill in the Gulf of Mexico. Through all her venues, she brings to the attention of the country—perhaps not always altruistically—the hidden horrors of the human conditions in the United States and elsewhere. And much like the Ancient Mariner— who tells his tale when it is necessary, passing "from land to land" with a "strange power of speech," knowing that when he encounters certain people he must teach them with his tale—Oprah often seems to sense such needs.

From her teenage years on, she has found the strength to overcome whatever obstacles are in her path, each time finding the "one true thing" she knows and exhorting everyone to do the same. Several years ago, in attempting to explain her passion and dedication to making a difference, she wrote in a column the words of a song sent to her from Maya Angelou: "When you have the chance to sit it out or dance, I hope you dance." And even though she didn't set out to create what has turned into more than what she labels "this big life," she intends to meet all its challenges. In one forum or another—in speeches, writings, and programs—Oprah expresses her belief that it is the journey that matters. Despite the fact that her big life has provided almost everything anyone could want, her optimism suggests that the best is yet to come. The spiritual side of her nature informs her belief that she has a mission, a responsibility to the world, and even the planet, to use her life to do good. It is little wonder that entertainer Zach Braff was led to say in 2007, "In television, there's *Oprah*, and then there's everyone else."

BIBLIOGRAPHY

Achebe, Chinua. *Things Fall Apart*. Chicago: Random House, 1958.

Adler, Bill. *The Uncommon Wisdom of Oprah Winfrey*. Secaucus, NJ: Birch Lane Press, 1997.

Akpan, Uwem. *Say You're One of Them*. New York: Little, Brown, 2009.

Angelou, Maya. *Wouldn't Take Nothing for My Journey Now*. New York: Random House, 1993.

Banesky, Sandy. "Deep in the Heart of Texas." *Sun Sentinel*, 29 Jan. 1998: E1.

Bearden, Michelle. "Christian Apologists: Be Careful of Oprah's Spiritual Teachings." *Christian Post*, 25 Jan. 2010.

Bearden, Michelle. "'O' God Examines Oprah-Style Spirituality." *Tampa Tribune.Com*, 10 Oct. 2009.

Britt, Donna. "Breathing Easier with a Rare Film." *Washington Post*, 13 Jan. 1996: B1.

Britt, Donna. "Patrice Takes Oprah to Church." *Washington Post*, 17 Jan. 1995: B1.

Carlson, Peter. "The Heart of Talkness." *Washington Post Magazine*, 25 Apr. 1993: 19.

Clark, Robert. "Book World." *Washington Post*, 20 Aug. 2000: X3.

Copeland, Libby. "In the Church of Feel-Good Pop Psychology." *Washington Post*, 26 June 2000: C1.

"Court Upholds Winfrey." *Washington Post*, 10 Feb. 2000: A16.

Crandell, Ben. "Showtime." *South Florida Sun Sentinel*, 12 Apr. 2000: 76.

Elder, Robert K. "At 11, 'Heartsongs' Poet Turns into a Publishing Phenom." *Orlando Sentinel*, 12 Mar. 2003: E1.

Farhi, Paul. "Gala." *Washington Post*, 3 Dec. 2002: C1.

Franzen, Jonathan. *The Corrections*. New York: Farrar, Straus and Giroux, 2001.

Franzen, Jonathan. *Freedom*. New York: Farrar, Straus and Giroux 2010.

Franzen, Jonathan. *How to Be Alone*. New York: Picador, 2002.

Gaines, Patrice. "Giving a Hand to the Lefty of the Year." *Washington Post*, 30 Nov. 1988: C2.

Giles, Jeff. "A Death. A Mystery. A Secret History." *Newsweek*, 10 Mar., 1997.

Giles, Jeff. "Error and Corrections." *Newsweek*, 5 Nov. 2001: 68–69.

Gilliam, Dorothy. "Black Men Ill-Served." *Washington Post*, 23 Mar. 1989: C3.

Graham, Stedman. *You Can Make It Happen*. New York: Simon & Schuster, 1997.

Greene, Bob. *Get with the Program*. New York: Simon & Schuster, 2002.

Grindstaff, Linda. *The Money Shot: Trash, Class, and the Making of TV Talk Shows*. Chicago: University of Chicago Press, 2002.

Hale-Shelton, Debra. "Oprah's Chef Puts Family Time on Menu." *Palm Beach Post*, 7 Feb. 2002: FN.

Hanania, Ray. "Financial Profile: Oprah Winfrey: I'm Working for Charity Now." *Star Newspapers*, Apr. 1998: 1.

Harrington, Richard. "Diluted 'Native Son.'" *Washington Post*, 16 Jan. 1987: B8.

Harrison, Barbara Grizzuti. "The Importance of Being Oprah." *New York Times Magazine*, 11 June 1989: 28.

Janz, Matt. "Out of the Gene Pool." *Washington Post*, 4 Aug., 2002: SC5.

Jones, Quincy. *The Autobiography of Quincy Jones*. New York: Doubleday, 2001.

Kane, Gregory. "'Exhale' Adds to Bashing of Black Men." *Sun Sentinel*, 3 Jan. 1996: B1.

King, Norman. *Everybody Loves Oprah: Her Remarkable Life*. New York: Quill, William Morrow, 1987.

Kirkpatrick, David. "Oprah Gaffe by Franzen Draws Ire and Sales." *New York Times*, 29 Oct. 2001: E1, E3.

Kirkpatrick, David. "Oprah Puts Book Club on Shelf." *Palm Beach Post*, 6 Apr. 2002: 1A, 10 A. (Report from *New York Times*.)

Lacayo, Richard. "Total Eclipse of the Heart." *Time*, 25 Nov. 2002: 93.

Lowe, Janet. *Oprah Speaks*. New York: John Wiley, 1998.

Lyman, Howard, with Glen Merzer. *Mad Cowboy*. New York: Scribner, 1998.

Mair, George. *Oprah Winfrey: The Real Story*. Secaucus, NJ: Birch Lane Press, 1994.

McGraw, Phil. *Life Strategies*. New York: Hyperion, 1999.

Michaels, Bob, and Bob Hartlein. "Oprah: Who's My Real Father?" *Star*, 25 Mar. 2003: 14–15.

Nelson, Jim, Alan Butterfield, and Reginald Fitz. "Oprah Soars to Deadly 275 Lbs." *National Enquirer*, 10 Sept. 2002: 34–35.

"Oprah Winfrey." Interview with Larry King. CNN 4 Sept. 2001.

"Oprah Winfrey." Interview with Michael Logan. "The Power of One." *TV Guide*, 4–10 Oct. 2003: 37–40.

"Oprah Winfrey." Interview with Mike Wallace. *60 Minutes*. 14 Dec. 1986.

Peck, Janice. *The Age of Oprah*. Boulder, CO: Paradigm, 2008.

Peck, Janice. "Talk about Race: Framing a Popular Discourse on 'Oprah Winfrey.'" *Cultural Critique* (Spring) 1994: 89–126.

Peyser, Marc. "Paging Dr. Phil." *Newsweek*, 2 Sept. 2002: 50–56.

Roiphe, Katie. "The Naked and the Conflicted." *New York Times*, 3 Jan. 2010.

Romano, Carlin. "For Oprah, Rough Work of Reviews Is Over." *Philadelphia Inquirer*, 9 Apr. 2002: C1, C8.

Scheuer, Jeffrey. *The Sound Bite Society*. New York: Routledge, 2002.

Schucman, Helen. *A Course in Miracles*. ACIM Online Store. Foundation for Inner Peace. Orig. 1978. Rev. Ed. 1996.

Schwartz, Amy E. "Will Oprah Save the Book?" *Washington Post*, 15 Dec. 1996: C7.

Sellers, Patricia. "The Business of Being Oprah." *Fortune*, 1 Apr. 2002: 50–64.

Shattuc, Jean. *The Talking Cure: TV Shows and Women*. New York: Routledge, 1997.

Simmons, Rachel. *Odd Girl Out: The Hidden Culture of Aggression in Girls*. New York: Harcourt, 2002.

Smith, Art. *Back to the Table: The Reunion of Food and Family*. New York: Hyperion, 2001.

Tolle, Eckhart. *The Power of Now*. Novato, CA: New World Library, 2004.

"The Truth about Dieting." *Consumer Reports*, June 2002: 26–31.

Waldron, Robert. *Oprah!* New York: St. Martin's Press, 1987.

Weeks, Linton. "No Bestsellers Up for National Awards." *Washington Post,* 14 Oct. 1999: C2.

Weeks, Linton. "Oprah Pick Franzen Wins National Book Award." *Washington Post,* 14 Nov. 2001.

Winfrey, Oprah. "Graduation Address, Wesleyan University." May 1998. Middletown, CT.

Yardley, Jonathan. "The Story of O." *Washington Post*, 29 Oct. 2001: C2 and 5 Nov. 2001: C2.

INDEX

About the Author

HELEN S. GARSON, professor emeritus at George Mason University in Fairfax, Virginia, has written books about Truman Capote, Tom Clancy, and Oprah Winfrey (first edition). She is also the author of numerous articles about English and American literary figures as well as popular culture.

CPSIA information can be obtained at www.ICGtesting.com
Printed in the USA
BVOW03*2225051213

338208BV00004B/55/P